Political Islam in West Africa

Political Islam in West Africa

State-Society Relations Transformed

edited by
William F. S. Miles

Viva Books
New Delhi | Mumbai | Chennai | Kolkata | Bengaluru | Hyderabad | Kochi | Guwahati

First Indian Edition 2008
Reprinted 2010

VIVA BOOKS PRIVATE LIMITED

- 4737/23 Ansari Road, Daryaganj, New Delhi 110 002
  E-mail: vivadelhi@vivagroupindia.net, Tel. 42242200
- 76, Service Industries, Shirvane, Sector 1, Nerul, Navi Mumbai 400 706
  E-mail: vivamumbai@vivagroupindia.net, Tel. 27721273, 27721274
- Jamals Fazal Chambers, 26 Greams Road, Chennai 600 006
  E-mail: vivachennai@vivagroupindia.net, Tel. 28290304, 28294241
- B-103, Jindal Towers, 21/1A/3 Darga Road, Kolkata 700 017
  E-mail: vivakolkata@vivagroupindia.net, Tel. 22836381, 22816713
- 7, Sovereign Park Apartments, 56-58, K. R. Road, Basavanagudi, Bangalore 560 004
  E-mail: vivabangalore@vivagroupindia.net, Tel. 26607409, 26607410
- 101-102 Mughal Marc Apartments, 3-4-637 to 641, Narayanguda, Hyderabad 500 029
  E-mail: vivahyderabad@vivagroupindia.net, Tel. 27564481, 27564482
- Beevi Towers, First Floor, SRM Road, Kaloor, Kochi 682 018, Kerala
  E-mail: vivakochi@vivagroupindia.net, Tel: 0484-2403055, 2403056
- 232, GNB Road, Beside UCO Bank, Silpukhuri, Guwahati 781 003
  E-mail: vivaguwahati@vivagroupindia.net, Tel: 0361-2666386

www.vivagroupindia.com

Published by arrangement with

Lynne Rienner Publishers, Inc.
1800 30th Street, Suite 314
Boulder, Colorado 80301
USA

ISBN : 978-81-309-0967-7

Published by Vinod Vasishtha for Viva Books Private Limited, 4737/23, Ansari Road, Darya
New Delhi-110 002. Printed and bound by Anand Sons, Delhi - 110 092.

S0000 / S0630 / S

To my "Brown" side:
Aunt Diana and Uncle Earl,
Cuzzes Barbara and Dan,
and Martin and Rhonda

Contents

Preface

THIS VOLUME HAS EVOLVED THANKS TO THE STIMULUS, SUPPORT, AND INITIATIVE of key Africanist colleagues, many of whom I have met through the African Studies Association (ASA). It is certainly not the first book to be so inspired. Ousmane Kane's magisterial *Muslim Modernity in Postcolonial Nigeria* similarly begins by invoking an ASA encounter wherein Kane publicly defended the modernistic features of the Islamist movement Izala with an outraged fellow (but presumably Christian) Nigerian. ASA discussions on Nigeria are particularly known for their animation, whether or not the volatile subject of religion is officially on the agenda.

It was while attending a stimulating ASA panel in Washington, D.C., in 2002 that I decided to convene a special forum on Islamism in West Africa for the ensuing conference in Boston. A full year had elapsed since September 11, 2001, and the onset of the US-led campaign to rout the Taliban from Afghanistan. Personal post–September 11 experience in Africa, as well as the writings and communications of other colleagues, had convinced me that in certain circles throughout the continent Osama bin Laden had unexpectedly emerged as a kind of folk hero. Just how widely the Osama rage had taken hold—whether it was a fleeting Afro-pop phenomenon or a serious political challenge—began to loom as a pressing *affaire d'état*. Suddenly, sub-Saharan Africa was being reexamined by US intelligence and media alike through the prism of potential apologist (or worse) for "Islamic terrorism." What, I wondered, would the African Muslim landscape look like by the next African Studies Association meeting? More important, what was the true state of Islamism in sub-Saharan Africa?

My longstanding interest in Nigeria and Niger had sensitized me to the recent intensification of Islamism in West Africa prior to September 11. Between January 2000 and September 2001, one-quarter of the states in

Nigeria, Africa's most populous nation, had already adopted Islamic law as their overarching legal system. (Four more were to adopt sharia in the next two months, bringing the percentage of quranically compliant states in Nigeria to one-third.)

In nearby Niger, riots had broken out following the government's ratification of the UN convention against gender discrimination in October 1999, and also in November 2000 because of a fashion show condemned as profligate by the demonstration's religious leaders. Even as we at the ASA were deliberating in 2002, friends of Nigeria were still reeling from the more than two hundred fatalities that had just been occasioned by the holding of the Miss World pageant there.[1] By the time we assembled in November 2003, the United States and the United Kingdom had spearheaded a "coalition" leading to the invasion and occupation of Iraq. (Niger's phantom appearance as an alleged supplier of uranium to Saddam Hussein's weapons program only served to presage the vulnerability of West Africa in the unfolding drama and postoccupation era. So did US pressure and enticements to secure Guinea's favorable Security Council vote.) Ensuing protests in several capitals led to the temporary closing of some US embassies and consulates on the continent, as well as State Department advisories for US citizens. President George W. Bush's self-declared "Global War on Terrorism" was indeed global but, as gauged by reactions in Africa, global in ways that were not especially favorable to US interests and reputation. This was true despite Bush's July 2003 official visit to sub-Saharan Africa—a historic first for a Republican president—a trip that included lightning stops in Senegal and Nigeria.

The next step in this book's evolution occurred thanks to *African Studies Review* (*ASR*) editor Ralph Faulkingham, himself an old Hausa hand. Faulkingham proactively scouted for possible *ASR* theme issues. His kind invitation to be a theme editor for a volume resulted in a nucleus of articles that have been expanded and completely updated for the present book. Other chapters are entirely new.

Even as we were completing our manuscript, protest and violence triggered by the publication in Denmark of cartoons offensive to Muslims had spread to West Africa, leading to more than one hundred deaths in Nigeria alone. For better and for worse, our topic is important. Political Islam in West Africa is likely to be a subject of interest not only among Africanist scholars throughout the first decade of the twenty-first century, but also in other venues (governmental, military) for years to come.

* * *

Numerous colleagues had forewarned me about the "nightmare" of editing a scholarly collection, in contrast to solo authorship. Yet, only one of the present contributors accused me of "cracking the whip," and even he knew our friendship would survive the editorial slave-driving.

Under much more gentle prodding, research assistants Katja Schiller, Liubomir Topaloff, and Johanna Bernstein, graduate students at Northeastern University, have kept me abreast of unfolding events in West Africa as they relate to Islam and politics. Katja also shepherded the index.

Nearly two decades ago, Lynne Rienner took a chance on me by publishing my first book on Africa; I thank her again, this time for offering to publish my first edited book.

—William F. S. Miles

Note

1. The trigger for the lethal riots was an article by a Lagos-based fashion journalist who responded, in a manner ostensibly offensive to Islam, to religiously based criticisms about the pageant. (The Prophet Muhammad "would probably have chosen a wife from" among the contestants, she had written.) Although the journalist resigned following the bloodletting, on November 26, 2002, a *fatwa* calling for her death was announced and endorsed by the information minister of the first Nigerian state to have adopted sharia.

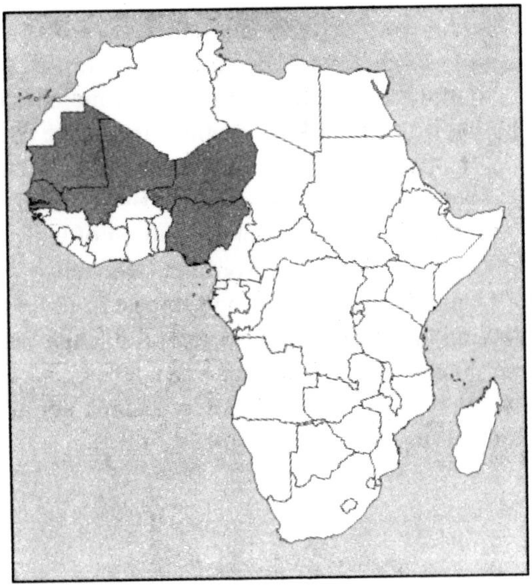

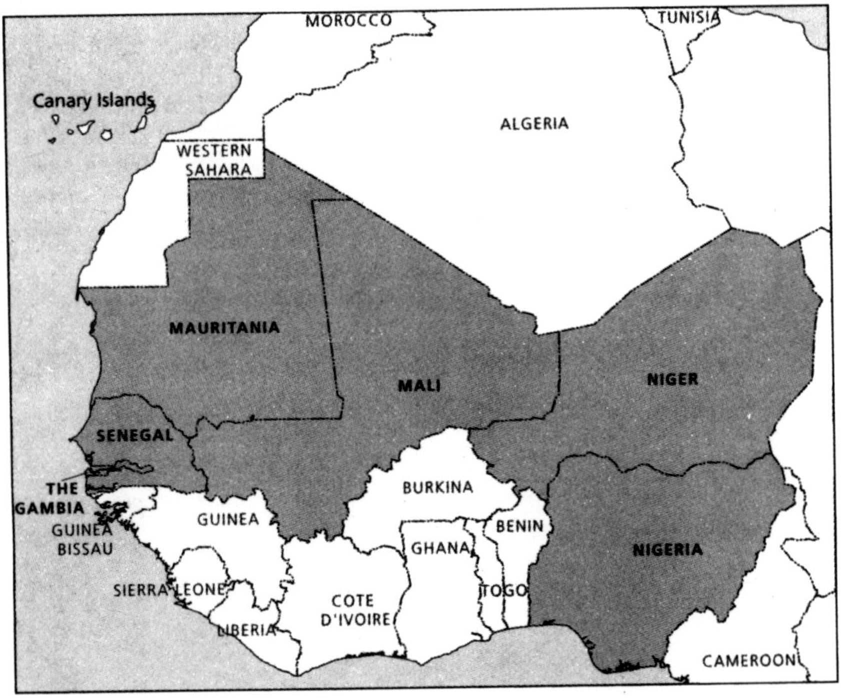

West Africa

(The countries shaded in gray are the focus of this book.)

Political Islam in West Africa

1

West African Islam: Emerging Political Dynamics

WILLIAM F. S. MILES

FOR BETTER AND FOR WORSE, INTEREST IN THE POLITICAL DIMENSIONS OF WEST African Islam has intensified significantly since the violent events of September 11, 2001. Scholars long accustomed to benign neglect in exchange for their academic labors have experienced the uncustomary sunshine of "relevance." Phenomena and developments once regarded as parochial to the region are suddenly tied to global trends, politics, and US national security. Consider these post–September 11 developments:

- The US European Command (EUCOM), based in Stuttgart, Germany, adds West Africa to its sphere of "strategic" activities. Hundreds of GIs begin to patrol regularly alongside African soldiers. NATO Commander General James Jones describes West Africa as "where the action is." General Jones also refers to the "large ungoverned spaces in Africa" as "tempting" to the terrorists.
- To train and equip Chadian, Malian, Mauritanian, and Nigérien security forces, the US State Department teams up with the Department of Defense to create the Pan Sahel Initiative (PSI). A PSI coordinator states that these forces will patrol the "ancient trade routes now used by terrorists." Green Berets are tasked to Mauritania and Mali to help "stem the movement of Muslim extremist groups, including al-Qaida cells, believed operating in the Sahara."
- In February 2004, the London-based newspaper *Al-Hayat* reports the presence of US security agents—"most likely from the Federal Bureau of Investigation"—in Timbuktu.
- In March 2004 EUCOM actively aids Chadian and Nigérien military forces in tracking to the border of Niger members of the Salafist Group for Preaching and Combat. Forty-three Salafists—

whose core includes nationals of Chad, Mali, Niger, and Nigeria—are killed.

- The next month, in a speech on US national security interests in Africa, acting assistant secretary of state for African affairs Charles Snyder singles out the Sahel and northern Nigeria as areas with pro-fundamentalist elements and therefore as possible safe havens for terrorists. Former ambassador to Nigeria Princeton Lyman descries to the Africa Subcommittee of the House of Representatives the lack of a US "presence in the Muslim-dominated north of the country: no eyes and ears . . . no capacity for measuring the trends of Islamic debate and their implications for the US." Lyman characterizes Nigeria as "a priority target" for Osama bin Laden.
- FBI agents travel to Liberia to investigate Al-Qaida profiteering from the diamond trade there, a practice that is also believed to include Sierra Leone. Burkina Faso is also implicated. Chief prosecutor David Crane of the Sierra Leonean war crimes court claims in April 2005 that former Liberian president Charles Taylor allowed Al-Qaida to "recoup, refit and refinance" in his country before and after September 11.
- In June 2005, the $6 million Pan Sahel Initiative is expanded into a $500 million Trans-Sahara Counterterrorism Initiative (TSCTI). Involved are the US departments of Justice, Treasury, and Customs, along with the Agency for International Development. Counterterrorism training, including joint military exercises, are provided to Chad, Mali, Mauritania, and Niger, along with the heavily Muslim West African nations of Senegal and Nigeria. That same month, Al-Qaida–linked irregulars kill at least fifteen Mauritanian soldiers in a military base attack.

It is perhaps gratifying to find one's region and subject—here, the Muslim nations of West Africa—suddenly à la mode. Yet spasms of general interest also carry a risk.

The danger is reductio ad Al-Qaidum. Islamic fundamentalism, the resurgence of Islam, political Islam, Islamism: however one wishes to characterize the politicization of the faith of Muslims, it had been evolving in West Africa for decades. This development had been occurring parallel to, and independent of, the radical Wahhabite cells of Osama bin Laden. In light of September 11 and the events it triggered (e.g., the fall of the Taliban and Ba'ath regimes in Afghanistan and Iraq, and the ensuing European terrorism and Middle East insurgencies in reaction), it has become difficult, if not impossible, to study political Islam in West Africa without the spectral shadows of the tumbling World Trade Center towers and mental images of the toppling statue of Saddam Hussein.[1] This volume self-consciously frames itself within the post–September 11 context. It does so, however, while striving to balance the context imposed by a declared post–September 11 "war on terrorism" with the integrity of long-standing and autonomous trends in West Africa. The late Charlotte Quinn was quite correct in stating that "most African Muslims would not approve of the terrorist bombings in New York City and Washington on September 11, 2001, and would regard them as the work of extremists from whom they disassociate themselves" (Quinn and Quinn 2003:6).

I agree that "to see Islam in Africa from the sole perspective of the 'dangers' of Islamism would be a gross misrepresentation" (Bierschenk and Stauth 2003:12). Sanneh (1997) and Kaba (2000) have been most explicit about the nonviolent features of "radical Islam" in West Africa, the latter helpfully reminding us of the economic context in which a turn to religious answers for material problems has arisen. Among those who do sufficiently recognize the potential for conflict arising from West African Islamism, the perspective emphasizing internal factionialism rather than anti-Western unity is more on the mark: "The greatest threat to Western interests during the coming decade is not likely to come from an overwhelming wave of Muslim revolutionary change, despite the impact of September 11, 2001, events. Rather, Western interests will be challenged by internal instability generated by Muslim minorities who are denied a political voice or an acceptable standard of living" (Quinn and Quinn 2003:30).

Still, we must recognize that the literature on Islam in West Africa (like that of so many other fields) is increasingly tinged by the anxiety of what we can simply call "post–September 11ism" (see, for example, Glickman 2003; Lyman and Morrison 2004; Ellis 2005; ACSS 2003). This is in marked contrast with the most widely read pre– (and immediate post–) September 11 literature on political Islam (Esposito 1997, 1998, 1999, 2002; Piscatori 1983, 1986; Piscatori and Eickelman 1996; Roy 1994, 2004). This is a corpus that, notwithstanding requisite recognition of Nigeria, basically ignores West Africa. John Voll (1992a, 1992b) has been an exception, intellectually straddling the Sahara for decades. Few specialists of political Islam in the Middle East, however, reciprocate John Hunwick (1997), an eminent historian who looks at the wider world of Islam through the prism of Black Africa.

How, then, do we recalibrate a study of political Islam without relapsing into reductio ad Al-Qaidum as well as to elevate West Africa within intellectual consciousness of the wider world of Islam? My answer is to focus on the mutual transformation—sometimes subtle, sometimes not—

of West African societies as they interact with the postcolonial states that struggle to contain them.

Definitional and Positional Precisions

Definitions are always the sticky wicket of edited collections such as this one. So as to provide a common departure point for all of the authors—but explicitly not to impose a rigid conceptual grid—I proposed a working definition of Islamism adapted from the *Annals of the American Academy of Political and Social Science* volume on "Political Islam" (see Butterworth and Zartman 1992:9): "Islamism refers to organized activity and/or a systematic thought process that forcefully (but not necessarily violently) strives to bring politics into line with Islamic precepts. Such activity and/or thought process self-consciously positions itself within a wider, transnational movement of similarly-inspired political change."

This is a deliberately straightforward and relatively liberal definition, one that several of the contributors deliberately chose to modify, some to the point of virtual nonrecognition. Others invoke other definitions from other sources. So be it. I deliberately wanted us to start with a definition that does not inherently include the use of violent or illegal means to bring about Islamic ends, while not precluding such activities. I could just as easily have borrowed verbatim from Eva Rosander: "Islamism is a reformist and puritanical movement similar to previous ones which have appeared at intervals during early centuries, emerging as a reaction against the process of withdrawal from the Quran and Sunna, which form the main basis of the *sharia*" (Rosander and Westerlund 1997:4–5).

Islamism is a spectrum that spans both moderation and extremism, with many intermediary steps for line-drawing. This is certainly the case in West Africa, where the ethos of intensified politics toward Islamist ends still generally eschews wanton destruction of life and property. Indeed, as I have argued elsewhere, "it is perhaps at the margins of the Muslim world—in sub-Saharan Africa, for instance—that lies the greatest opportunity for shoring up a redemptive Islam" (Miles 2003:71).

Contrary to predictions of its imminent demise (or irrelevance), it is my position that—even in West Africa—the state still counts. No matter how important and resurgent a political factor, Islamism is still inflected and mediated by the ethnic composition, colonial legacy, political actors, governmental policies, and unforeseen contingencies unique to each West African nation in which Muslims constitute a significant size of the population. Especially when (with a bow to A. I. Asiwaju, dean of African partition studies) we examine neighboring states with borderlands sharing similar religious and ethnic profiles, we can see even more clearly the state dimension to otherwise global phenomena. Is Islamism in Niger but a mirror image (albeit in diminutive form) of that characterizing northern Nigeria? Do Islamist politics play themselves out similarly in Senegal and The Gambia? Can Mali contain unrest that Mauritania cannot?

Origins and Spread of Islam in West Africa

Readers desirous of detailed histories of the coming of Islam in West Africa can hardly do better than consulting Mervyn Hiskett (1984; see also part 2 of Levtzion and Pouwels 2000; Charlick provides a more focused account for the Sahel in this volume).

As early as the eighth century, Islam arrived in West Africa along the trans-Saharan trade route. North African Arabs and Sanhaja Berbers (Al moravids) first introduced the faith to Mande and Hausa business associates; they in turn converted others within their ethnic communities and trading circles. The most significant empires that were Islamized through this gradual spread of religion-via-commerce were Ghana (heyday in the eleventh century), Mali (strongest in the fourteenth century), and Songhai (fifteenth-century pinnacle).

Smaller Islamized polities in the Western Sudan included the Tekrur (subsisting along the Senegal River from the eleventh to sixteenth centuries), the Wolof (occupying the westernmost tip of the continent, at its prime in the fourteenth century), and the various Mande kingdoms (situated along and parallel to the Gambia River, especially in the sixteenth century). On the other end of Muslim West Africa (the Central Sudan) lay Kanem-Borno, situated around Lake Chad. Though peaking politically in the sixteenth century, Kanem-Borno remained a counterweight for centuries thereafter to the other important entities of the Central Sudan, the more-or-less fragmented seven Hausa states to their west.

Sharing religion (at least among elites—many peasants remained animist) did not guarantee political peace, however: the kind of rivalry and warfare that persisted between Kanem-Borno and Hausaland was emblematic of precolonial West Africa writ large, regardless of shared Islam. (For sure, various versions were practiced, itself a pretext for conquest.) After 1600 internal imperialism intensified among supposed coreligionists. Bambaras, Moroccans, and some Tuareg clans dismembered Songhai; other Tuaregs captured much of Kanem-Borno's territory. In the Senegambia the Wolof Empire splintered into smaller states, rearranging mixes of Mandinka, Tukulor, Wolof, and Fulani communities. Only the Torodbe Fulani, however, premised their newly emergent eighteenth-century Senegambian polities (Futa Jalon, Futa Toro, Bondu) on Islam per se.

Those cleric-led Torodbe theocracies were precursors to a broader wave of Toronkowa Fulani–inspired jihads in the nineteenth century. Beginning in 1804, Usman dan Fodio led a revolt against the allegedly oppressive and defectively Islamic Hausa leader of Gobir. Victory over Gobir was prelude to six years of warfare aimed at conquering and redeeming (for Islam) all the Hausa city-states. These were now consolidated into a single empire, ruled by Fulani emirs and called a caliphate, from the new capital of Sokoto. A century later, the Sokoto caliphate would be conquered and mostly incorporated into northern Nigeria by the British.

Within a decade of the Hausaland jihad, further to the west another Fulani, Ahmad Lobbo (bin Mohammed), followed dan Fodio's lead to erect another reformed Islamic polity, Macina. Unlike Sokoto, Macina would eventually succumb to French colonialism. So would Tukulor, which under El Hajj Umar al Futi absorbed Macina in the mid-nineteenth century to constitute another Islamic empire spanning from Timbuktu to Futa Jalon. To the east of the Sokoto caliphate, in Kanem-Borno, Muhammed al-Amin al-Kanemi adopted Fulani religious orthodoxy even as he resisted Fulani imperial overrule. Al-Kanemi's Islamist empire would eventually be split into British and French colonies, as would the Mandinka one (1870–1885) of Samory Touré.

Other nineteenth-century West African attempts at jihad worth noting are those of the Dyula El Hajj Mahmud in the Volta region in 1850; the Fulani Maba Diakhou in The Gambia in the 1860s; Amadu Ba in Jolof, 1869–1875; and, in the 1880s, Mahmadu Lamine, an anti-Tukulor Soninke. All four were killed in battle, the last three by forces led or reinforced by the French.

Despite the militant means of West African jihad, its longer-lasting aims lay in promoting Islamic universalism, literacy, and Sufism; enormous economic, demographic, and social change were by-products (Hiskett 1984: 241–243). Consolidation and (relative) uniformization of Islamic practice permitted Sufi brotherhoods, most importantly the Qadiriyya and later Tijaniyya, to spread throughout the region, the former beginning in the sixteenth century and the latter in the nineteenth century. Mahdist (millennarian) movements also periodically surfaced to threaten both clerical and political status quo. Colonial rulers (particularly the French) wavered between wariness and paranoia with respect to the mobilizational or subversionist possibilities of organized Islam. Ironically, the "pacification" and territorial reconfiguration that accompanied colonialism allowed for the expansion of Islam into (mostly rural) territories that had hitherto resisted it. Colonial overrule ensured that Islam would remain mostly a conservative institution.

In coastal colonies, where greater contact with Westerners, including missionaries, prevailed, Christianity also expanded. This was particularly the case in colonies along the Gulf of Guinea. Between the competing pressures of Senegambian and Sahelian Islam on the one hand, and coastal Christianity on the other, nonmonotheistic religions succumbed to pressures to convert—or at least to integrate, for the same syncretic tendencies that the Fulani purists decried and launched jihad to uproot reproduced themselves among Islamized communities no less than Christianized ones. Both colonial era tendencies—the expansion of Islam and Christianity and their syncretic character—carried over into the postcolonial era of West African history. This has also been the case concerning the overall geographical concentration of West African Islam.

Thus, a quarter of a century after independence and still today, the most heavily Islamized countries of West Africa are situated in the Sahel and Senegambia (see Miles 1990:218). Mauritania, which encroaches on both regions, is as much as 98 percent Muslim. So is landlocked Niger (whose territory encompasses the Sahara as well as the Sahel). Mali, Niger's geographical mirror image, has witnessed an increase in its Muslim population to about 90 percent. The two countries of the Senegambian cradle, Senegal and The Gambia, are at least 90 percent and 85 percent Muslim, respectively. Each of these five countries has a dedicated chapter in this volume that explores the transformation of state-society relations through the lens of political Islam.

So does Nigeria, whose Muslim citizens make up barely one-half of the country's total. But Nigeria's overall population (120 million) is so overwhelming that even a conservative estimate of 47 percent dwarfs, in absolute terms, not only the number of Muslims in Mauritania, Niger, Mali, Senegal, and The Gambia combined but also the total number of West Africans in those five countries. This would still be the case if we added to the theo-demographic mix Guinea, whose Muslim population is also among the highest in West Africa: 95 percent.

Below these statistical thresholds, the proportion of Muslims in West African nations dips from just under 40 percent (Burkina Faso) to as low as 8 percent (Togo). Our six country chapters thus well cover the West Africa in which Islam predominates.

Heuristic Underpinnings

There are two useful templates for contextualizing this book. The first is Elizabeth Hodgkin's invaluable but undercited 1990 overview, "Islamism and Islamic Research in Africa," which appeared in the West Africa section of an *Islam et sociétés au sud du Sahara* volume. Hodgkin, foreshadowing post–September 11 research interest in Muslim West Africa, writes: "The obsession of the West with 'Islamic fundamentalism' is distorting our perceptions of the Islamic world because we are tending to see everything in terms of 'fundamentalism' or 'anti-fundamentalism'" (Hodgkin 1990:74). Then Hodgkin both inverts and extends the insight: "the same distortion is happening in the Islamic world; Muslims are mirroring Western obsessions." To a lesser degree and in a different region, this phenomenon echoes the debate over the Iraqi insurgency: is "terrorism" in Iraq an authentic and indigenous phenomenon, or rather a spontaneous creation against Western troops sent there to eradicate it?

While sensitive to external Islamic events and powers (e.g., the cyclical influence in West Africa of Libya, Iran, and Saudi Arabia), Hodgkin (1990:78) wisely reminds us that "local political oppositions are more important than wider intellectual movements for the formation of individual organizations." We can rephrase another of Hodgkin's key points by saying that, even in the post–September 11 context, West African Islamism is less about importing Al-Qaida than about rejecting and marginalizing traditional sources of religious authority (Hodgkin 1990:84). The autonomy and specificity of Islamism in West Africa cannot be overestimated. There is also a "danger in labeling," she warns us. "The shades of attitude between what we may like to label an 'Islamist' and a 'non-Islamist' Muslim are many and delicate" (Hodgkin 1990:96).

Finally, Hodgkin highlights the contradictions in West African Islam. The faith is at the same time a solution to the continent's major problems (poverty, corruption, underdevelopment) as well as a threatened and minoritarian belief system. Islam preaches unity; Islamism creates divisions within Muslim communities. West African Islamism mobilizes a Muslim lumpen proletariat; it also triggers counter-Islamism. To better understand West African Islam after September 11, strategists need to incorporate Elizabeth Hodgkin's profound pre–September 11 analyses.

The second invaluable backdrop for the present collection is Eva Evers Rosander's and David Westerlund's analogous (though geographically broader) edited volume from 1997, *African Islam and Islam in Africa: Encounters Between Sufis and Islamists*. As a springboard to the present contribution, I note the continuation and intensification of key phenomena eruditely developed in that book, especially those that we reinforce herein.

While the editors of *African Islam and Islam in Africa* grant that the Sufi label per se is much more relevant in some countries (e.g., Senegal and Mauritania) than others (e.g., Niger and Nigeria), Sufism does serve as convenient shorthand for the indigenous and syncretistic style of Islam that has evolved in West Africa. In contrast, "Islamists" preach a much more orthodox, if not austere, version of the faith. Even if the labels are used in a novel way in West Africa, this dichotomy has simmered for more than a century.

As with all fundamentalist theopolitics (Miles 1996), a hallmark of Islamism in sub-Saharan Africa is line-drawing. Westerlund and Rosander focus on the rejection of allegedly overly innovative Sufi practices in the eyes of the orthodox Islamists. The case studies in the present volume attest to this ongoing tension between traditionalist Sufi (or quasi-Sufi) brotherhoods and rituals and their Islamist challengers.

Since September 11 the line-drawing within West African Islam has both accelerated and thickened. It has also been extended more broadly to the division between the *umma*—the larger community of Muslims worldwide—and the West: Mahmood Mamdani (2002) frames the West's binary view of Islam in terms of "Good Muslim, Bad Muslim." Such oversimplifying polarization has created a particular problem for West African brotherhoods and governments involuntarily caught in the middle of the war on terrorism. For it is not only the president of the United States who assumed a Manichean "you're either with us or against us" position in the wake of September 11. Islamists freely share this binary approach to loyalty. However problematic Samuel Huntington's (1996) theory of civilizational clash may be on a theoretical level, it may be taking on—with a little help from its friends *and* adversaries—the character of self-fulfilling prophecy.

Under the pressure of both Washington and Islamists, Muslims in West Africa are pressured to choose camps. Sufis, and the secular African governments under whose authority they typically lie, are cast, as they were during the colonial era, as collaborators with the unbelieving and exploitative West. If "Sufi cooperation with secular rulers in colonial and post-colonial sub-Saharan Africa [was] one of the reasons for the often vehement Islamist attacks against Sufi Muslims" (Westerlund 1997:311), then cooperation with Washington following September 11 revives accusations of treachery, if not heresy. Demonstrations against the invasion of Iraq in Kano, Nouakchott, and Niamey are not only aimed at the United States: indirectly, they put the governments of their own nations on notice. Western security analysts may not sufficiently appreciate it, but in West Africa, Sufis may be the linchpins of the war on terrorism.

Intra-Muslim demarcations in West Africa have also been greatly personalized since September 11, 2001. The choice of sides is not merely a theological question, it is one of profile: Osama bin Laden versus George W. Bush. Cheap posters of bin Laden make their way into the most remote of African villages (Miles 2003:69–70), rendering the mastermind terrorist just as famous—and, arguably, more admired—than the US president. Even where bin Laden's tactics are reviled, his persona is mesmerizing, if not magnetic. This is particularly true among young Muslim West Africans who, "facing unemployment and lost educational opportunities," are attracted to bin Laden's "skilled manipulation of the media and . . . his violent challenge to what he regards as American militarism and materialism, supposedly in the name of Islam" (Quinn and Quinn 2003:29). As someone with roots in Saudi Arabia, bin Laden has an intrinsic advantage over his born-again Christian nemesis for the Sahelian alhaji and Mecca-aspiring pilgrim.

Westerlund also identifies a number of "factors of discontent" that help to explain the rise of Islamism in Africa. Such factors include a postcolonial deterioration in economic conditions, breakdown in social services, autocracy in leadership, and the dead-end of secular, elitist ideologies. The clash of civilizations, as it is played out in West African Muslim societies, also entails the "problem of morality, loneliness, and psychological dissonance" (Westerlund 1997:316). It is in this context that Westerlund, Rosander, and others invoke the unsettled role of women in contemporary African society.

To these domestic and inward factors of discontent may now be added the globalized humiliation of Western (re)occupation of Muslim lands. West African Muslims need not be Ba'athist apologists to perceive the modern conquest of Iraq as an appalling demonstration of Western arrogance and imperialism. Quantifying the number of (mostly) youthful West Africans who have tipped toward Islamism as a result of the Iraq War is an impossible task (but see Schmitt 2005). To the ongoing immediate factors of West African discontent, however, must surely be added the external ones emanating from the Middle East.

Rosander places the Sufist-Islamist dynamic in terms of center-periphery relations. Far from the "more sacred . . . Arabo-Islamic" space, West African Islam has suffered, within the larger Muslim world, from marginality. It is not only a question of geographical distance or theological orthodoxy: it is also about money. "In relations between African Muslims and foreigners from the Arab (oil) countries, those who have the financial means dictate the Islamic discourse" (Rosander and Westerlund 1997:21). West African Islamism is thus also an attempt to realign this previous "backwater" within the context of the broader *umma*, the trans-state Muslim nation. Rosander and Westerlund do well to emphasize the dynamics prevailing between the so-called center of Islamization (the Middle East and North Africa) and its periphery (sub-Saharan Africa included). They helpfully acknowledge that "centres" and "margins" are subject to perspective. It is unfortunate that in terms of the world's interest, wealth and power (including the power to commit violence), rather than theology, religiosity, and humanity, have scoped out the territorial center of Islam and Islamism. Our volume focusing on West Africa is a small corrective to this marginalization.

Prior to September 11, competition between the Occident and the Gulf for the loyalty of West African peoples and government took the form of newer forms of Saudi and Iranian assistance (especially in the religious sphere) to balance USAID and European (especially French) foreign aid. Accelerated US security involvement in West Africa after September 11, in contrast, is more reminiscent of the Cold War. Only now, the desert and savanna areas once written off by the Pentagon as peripheral are seen as grist not for communist ideologues and operatives but Islamist ones. Whiteman and Yates (2004:374) underestimated West Africa's role in the "global war on terror" when they wrote, "In the wake of the attacks on the World Trade Center and Pentagon in September 2001, the problems of security in West Africa have been demoted from regional issues requiring 'small-scale contingencies of limited duration' to marginal concerns of a nation at war."

A Nyangian Perspective and Contemporary Response

Well before September 11, the phenomenon of "Islam and Politics in West Africa" was already taking a markedly new shape from that sketched out seventeen years prior in an essay by Sulayman Nyang (1984). In that concise but wide-ranging article, Nyang identified three marked historical stages in the relationship between Islam and state in West Africa. In the first stage, Islam represented an "immigrant religion," brought by trans-Saharan traders and adopted by local elites. Stage two witnessed the gradual adoption of orthodox Islam by erstwhile syncretizing practitioners of religion. This second stage culminated, according to Nyang, in jihadist wars of purification, such as those of the Fulani Sheikh Usman dan Fodio in Hausaland and of the Bambara by El Hajj Umar in Masina.

The third (and presumably final) stage occupied the bulk of Nyang's attention. This consisted of "the introduction of Western culture and the laying of the modern political, economic, cultural, and intellectual foundations of modern post-colonial African society on top of traditional African and Afro-Islamic culture"; in other words, "the Europeanization of African politics and society" (Nyang 1984:24).

Integral to this "Europeanization" was the grafting of Cold War considerations of ideology in West African polities: to wit, the rivalry between regimes of Afro-Marxism and those imbued with African capitalism. These, we read not that long ago, "are beginning to assume greater significance in African political discourse and activity" (Nyang 1984:24).

How quaint this now sounds! In such a short time, the destruction of the Berlin Wall and the crumbling of the Twin Towers has resonated far beyond Europe and New York, reshaping the contours of Islamic-state relations throughout Africa. Islamist politics by Nkrumah in Ghana, Senghor in Senegal, Modibo Keita in Mali, Sekou Touré in Guinea, and David/Dawda Jawara in The Gambia are rather different from those practiced today.

Rather than suggest a fourth stage to Nyang's intellectual scaffold, it is more useful to view our epoch in terms of reversion to Nyang's second phase: Islamist politics as both stimulus for, and response to, religious orthodoxy. Disillusionment with Marxism, capitalism, nationalism, and developmentalism has not resulted in the creation of any new ideology. Rather, it has reawakened a jihadist impulse—but one with a globalizing twist.

Growing familiarity with the wider Muslim world has seeped into even hitherto isolated pockets of rural West Africa. The relative ease of hajj nowadays—state-organized airlifts as opposed to overland caravans—has been the major factor, facilitating firsthand knowledge of both Saudi-style Islam and the truly international dimension of Islam as a world faith. These are all by-products of globalization, a phenomenon whose non-Western implications are often underappreciated. Through their active outreach in educational programming, satellite broadcasting, mosque-building, and even rebel-arming, a host of other Muslim states—Iran, Kuwait, Libya—have also etched grooves in the Muslim consciousness of West Africa. (In contrast, funding for American Cultural Centers has been slashed, even as US military assistance has boomed.) Israeli-Palestinian clashes are periodically reported upon in short-wave broadcasts in local languages. Afghanistan and Iraq filter into local discourse. Islam is not an afterthought to projects of state-building, modernization, and civil society. Islam provides the lodestone by which these other projects are judged.

Such is the context in which the distinguished contributors to the present volume are bringing to bear their deep knowledge and keen insights. They were asked to address a shared set of questions related to the rise of Islamism in West Africa. Initially, these dealt specifically with local perceptions of Al-Qaida and reactions to the group's attacks on the United States. Later, the local ramifications of the US-led invasion and occupation of Iraq were added to the agenda. Above all, the authors were to focus on broader, ongoing trends regarding Islamist politics in their countries of expertise. We then decided to cast our intellectual net even wider to include the greater politicization of Islam in West Africa and the resulting implications for the dynamics there between governments and societies. Hence, the main title enveloping our efforts: *Political Islam in West Africa.* While Islamism remains a central focus of our analyses, less "orthodox" instances of the dynamics playing out between West African Islam and polity are also examined.

Our collective profile is decidedly interdisciplinary, intergenerational, and intercultural. Contributors hail from the distinct disciplines of history, political science, and sociology but share an ethnographic sensibility. Between our veteran and more recently minted Africanists, we have scholars representing different decades of training and fieldwork. Victor Le Vine's contemporary analysis of Mali, for example, is enriched by his invaluable field notes from the early postcolonial years. Roman Loimeier, for his part, demonstrates the persistent power of classical historiography. Both Momodou Darboe and Leonardo Villalón returned to their field sites to update earlier versions of their chapters, while Cédric Jourde had to integrate a new military coup while working on his own draft. Robert Charlick deftly incorporates globalization theory in his analysis of an otherwise remote Sahelian society. It is no accident that he is our "lead-off hitter."

As mentioned previously, not every West African country with a Muslim population is featured here. Readers desirous of a general overview of Islam and politics in Burkina Faso, Gabon, Guinea, and Ivory Coast should consult Clarke (1987), Kaba (2000), and other sources referenced at the end of this book.

Scope of the Chapters

Niger is a good example of the disconnect between international imagery and grassroots reality, and Robert Charlick is a perfect guide. Between the politics over mythical Iraqi-bound "yellow cake" and popular images of a citizenry starving from drought and locust plague lies the emergence of an indigenous, reformist Islam. This is a movement that indeed has some implications for transnational Islamist networks and domestic Nigérien politics. Above all, though, it exemplifies, in an otherwise obscure locale, a global conflict over culture and identity. It is a microcosm of the long historical struggle, familiar to students of European evolution, between individual autonomy and obedience to authority. But rather than rejecting religion or nationality outright, reformists in Niger are reinterpreting Islam in a manner consonant with achievement-oriented and quasi-capitalist norms.

In "Islamist Identity and the Politics of Globalization" Charlick analyzes the local expression of Izala in Niger Republic. A movement spilling over from Nigeria, Izala in Niger operates within a quite different national context, one that is overwhelmingly Muslim and more uniformly impoverished. Nigérien religious reformists bristle against both pre-Islamic cultural practices and traditional Sufi Brotherhood hegemony. They demand freedoms that they perceive as inherent within Islam but that are undermined by indigenous hijacking of the true faith. Freedom to acquire capital is one of these (although, Charlick argues, Izala's preferred reforms exclude women from virtually all liberating changes.) Freedom to develop Islam independent from ethnicity is another distinguishing particularity of Nigérien Islamist reform.

In the context of the war on terrorism, to which their government has signed on, Nigérien proponents of Izala have come under added scrutiny, if not suspicion. Hence the standoff between an Islamic movement poised to incorporate the world economy but one that is also under global, anti-Islamist pressure. Such unresolved "contradictions . . . are the appropriate markers of transition," writes Charlick. "Toward what, it is too early to say."

Roman Loimeier's chapter on Nigeria situates Izala within its original national context, in which (unlike in Niger) Islam has had to coexist with a strongly represented Christianity. But a broader-reaching tension concerns the place of Islam among less orthodox Muslim polities. "The Quest for a Viable Religious Option" recasts a longstanding debate in West African Islam in contemporary terms: which of the three Islamic "oranges"—accommodationist, fundamentalist, or hybrid—is best?

In Nigeria, political Islam situates itself between the hybrid and fundamentalist "oranges." In the competitively fierce Nigerian religio-political arena, Izala comes across as a relatively moderate movement. The Muslim Students Society and Dawa, to cite but two Islamist competitors, jockey for fundamentalist status, ready to demand (as Izala does not) that sharia be imposed, as it were, from the top. Upon such differences the "oranges" themselves split: Loimeier gives ample examples of fission in the movements. In his section "The Muslim Internationale," he also draws attention to the important international dimensions of state-society relations in Nigeria. All of this is presented within an historical, colonial, and evolutionary context of Sufi brotherhoods in northern Nigeria, one whose continuing authority—as in Niger—is under question.

The Muslim populace, Loimeier suggests, is increasingly savvy and wary about the political uses to which Islamic rhetoric is put and the class inequity of sharia-based prosecution. One may disagree with his suggestion that the future of populist politics in Muslim Nigeria lies more in economics than theology. Still, it is harder to gainsay the growing disillusion with Islamism as the answer to Nigeria's complex problems.

If Nigeria has been struggling for decades to establish the proper role for Islam in electoral politics, in Mali the question is relatively new. In precolonial, colonial, and postcolonial times, Victor Le Vine convincingly shows ("Accommodation or Coexistence?"), the rulers of what became Mali have regarded Islam essentially as a social system endowed with extensive organizational structures with potential use for governance. Muslim leaders and subjects, for their part, were wary of instrumentalist power-wielders. Only after Amadou Toumani Touré's prodemocratic coup in 1991 have imams and Islamic organizations openly engaged with the polity. Between independence and democracy, under both quasi-communistic Modibo Keita and authoritarian Moussa Traoré, religious leaders circumspectly kept to "cultivating [their] gardens," as Le Vine colloquially relays from one informant cleric. The Malian *ulamaa* "kept their distance from power" and practiced "a kind of wary coexistence with cooperation only when it was unavoidable or too costly to refuse."

Since the transition to democracy, there has been a virtual explosion of civic associations, including religiously based ones. Charlick makes a similar point for Niger; in Mali, however, Islamic associations have been even more proactive about participation in electoral politics, backing Ibrahim Boubakar Keita in his ultimately unsuccessful bid for presidency. Radical Islamist groups (in particular Tablighi and the Groupe Salafiste pour la Prédication et le Combat) have also represented a much greater threat to stability in the country and region.

Interestingly, Le Vine concludes his chapter with a reference to slavery and human trafficking in Mali. These "taboo" topics, although increasingly mooted within the Western media, are rarely situated within the context of political Islam, in West Africa or elsewhere. By doing so here, Le Vine puts forth a different kind of challenge both to those who use, and to those who analyze, Islam for political ends: the place of Islamism within discussions of local human rights abuses. These provocative examples fit into an "overall picture of intra-Islamic and state-Muslim relations that," Le Vine explains for Mali in general, has "become more complex, shaded, uncertain."

The ambiguity to which Le Vine alludes for Mali is an even more problematic issue in Mauritania. There, according to Cédric Jourde, the entire nation's identity is up for grabs. Demographically, Mauritania is the most Muslim nation in all West Africa, surpassing even Mali and Niger in percentage of followers of Muhammad. Yet religion cannot transcend the ethnic dichotomy between a dominant Arabic-speaking Hassaniya (Moorish) community and an assemblage of non-Arabophone, Futanke (sub-Saharan) peoples. Democratization has done little to palliate these cleavages. Thus does Mauritanian Islamism operate, as per Jourde's title, between "Authoritarianism and Ethnicity."

Islamism is eschewed both by the Hassaniya power elite and the Futanke populace. The former remain even, under electoral politics, authoritarian to the core, denigrating the Islamists (and their would-be reforms) as strange to Mauritania society. The latter are hostile, as a matter of cultural identity, to the Islamists' arabizing agenda: unlike elsewhere in West Africa, in Mauritania use of Arabic is more an ethnic than a religious issue. Futanke also resent the Islamists for staying aloof from the brutal repression visited upon their communities beginning in the late 1980s. Here again, as with Le Vine's invocation of human trafficking and slavery, Islamist silence in the face of human rights abuses itself becomes an issue.

Why cede any ground to the Islamists when the state defines itself in terms of Islam? Such was the attitude of the authoritarian military who governed for most of Mauritianian independence. Formal adoption of democratic institutions in 1991, according to Jourde, did little to change this attitude—especially since real power remained among the same small coterie of men for whom, according to Jourde, stoking "dichotomous 'self-other' identities" is politically profitable. Mauritania is a fascinating example of a regime that baldly advocates a version of local Islam, castigating imported varieties as subversive to peace and tranquility. It is a convenient policy that plays to both the domestic and international fronts: especially after September 11, Mauritanian neo-authoritarian rulers became all the more popular among Western governments for holding the line against "foreign" Islam. After the invasion of Iraq, however, the pro-Western foreign policy became a domestic liability, prompting Islamist criticism and spurring even further governmental crackdowns. To what extent the leaders of the 2005 coup d'état will reverse governmental anti-Islamism remains to be seen.

As in Mauritania, in The Gambia an economically rickety neo-authoritarian leadership also adopted a convenient post–September 11 anti-Islamist stance to curry favor with the United States. Yet no one familiar with instrumental religiosity in The Gambia would be surprised. Certainly Momodou Darboe, author of "The Gambia: Islam and Politics," does not seem to be.

Darboe represents The Gambia as a fluid field of contested religions and denominations. Maraboutic Islam eventually overwhelmed Sonkinke nonbelievers, but animism persists. Christianity made inroads under colonialism; but it was divided between the Catholic and Protestant churches. Ahmadiyya, which considers itself Islamic, is viewed askance by traditional Gambian Muslims. And Wahhabism is now feared by all.

The Gambia is a fine West African example of religious symbolism converging with personal rulership. Independent Gambia's first president, Sir Jawara, is a case in point. Born a Muslim, Dawda Kairaba Jawara converted to Christianity as a youth, changing his first name to David. But when he entered national politics, he reconverted to Islam. What is more, to advance his electability, David/Dawda divorced his Christian wife to ensure that his First Lady was a Muslim, too. Yet compared to his successor, Jawara was a Muslim moderate. Yahya Jammeh, taking power in a 1994 military coup, enrobed himself in Islamic public works, policy, and dress, taking literally Darboe's observation that Gambian Muslims increasingly "wear their faith on their sleeves."

Darboe burrows into complex layers of struggle for legitimacy—political *and* religious—at various levels of Gambian society. Who controls which mosque, how do schoolgirls dress, which politicians do (and do not) consume alcohol: through such intricate details is the underbelly of Gambian theopolitics understood. Overlaying the local stage is the international. Libya, Pakistan, and Saudi Arabia have all seen their influence wax and wane in The Gambia, depending on circumstance. Such circumstances, as Darboe astutely reminds us, are to a large extent material in nature. They are also personalistic, at least as far as rulership is concerned. "A career in West African politics," Darboe concludes, "involves balancing allegiance to Islam with the realities of increasingly desperate economic conditions."

Diminutive Gambia's circumstances, of course, are in large part due to a Senegal that practically enwraps it. Are the parallels coincidental? These are the only two African Muslim nations whose premier politicians were Christian (although Jawara of The Gambia did convert back to Islam before independence). They are the only ones represented in this volume in which the veiling of females surfaces as a theopolitical issue.

In "Shades of Islamism on a Sufi Landscape," Leonardo Villalón traces the evolution of "maraboutic" Islam in the context of Senegal's highly institutionalized Sufi, qua Mouride, system. The 1980s and 1990s saw two interrelated changes on this theopolitical "landscape": (1) competitive electoral politics within a progressively democratizating polity; and (2) Islamist-inspired challenges to hitherto hegemonic Mouridism. Similar to our chapters on Niger and Mali, Villalón's work shows how heightened democratization in Senegal has created space for increasingly overt expressions of Islam within the political arena. Indeed, "the regime's flirtations with religion have also opened the door to new religious postures." But, Villalón cautions, we must avoid adopting simplistic, binary lenses in apprehending these new postures: it is not a simple matter of "moderate" Mouride Sufism versus "dangerous" global Islamism. The "dynamic forms and manifestations" of Senegalese Sufism are "adapting in ways that have heavily blurred, if not completely erased, the distinction between 'traditional' Sufi and Islamist groups." Importantly, the organization and leadership of the Mourides is being contested within the brotherhood itself.

Villalón frames his chapter around two specific changes in Senegalese politics and religion: the 2000 election of Abdoulaye Wade as president, and the emergence of younger, more "modern" and political Islamic groups from within the Mouride bosom. Foremost among these are the Moustarchidine. Other Senegalese student- and youth-oriented religious movements echo the preoccupations of Izala, as described by Charlick in Niger and Loimeier in Nigeria. Villalón points to their "anti-Westernization stance" and desire to "modernize" and "rationalize" indigenous structures of Islam.

In the final chapter I revisit my colleagues' treatments of political Islam in their respective country assignments with the aim of rethreading them even more thematically. I do so under six rubrics: (1) democratization, (2) Islamic reformism, (3) the Brotherhoods, (4) anti-Westernization, (5) gender, and (6) external influences. For readers desirous of a manageable compendium of other sources relating to political Islam in contemporary West Africa, a broad bibliography (which also includes the references in this and all other chapters) follows the concluding chapter.

Note

1. Imagine the ambivalent irony experienced by Donal Cruise O'Brien, whose manuscript on the symbolic confrontations of African Muslims with their states was set to go out to his publisher on September 11, 2001 (Cruise O'Brien 2003).

2

Niger: Islamist Identity and the Politics of Globalization

ROBERT B. CHARLICK

A BATTLE IS BEING WAGED TODAY IN THE WEST AFRICAN SAHEL (THE REGION between the Sahara and the grasslands of the Sudan) for the hearts and minds of ordinary Muslims. From a Western and particularly US point of view, this battle is related to our deepest concerns about anti-Westernism with its implications for security, terrorism, and eventually our economy with our growing dependence on African oil. Westerners have tended to see it as a form of fundamentalism, a rejection of globalization and of various aspects of modern life.

From the point of view of those participating in the battle on the ground, the conflict appears much different, as part of an effort to deal with real-life issues and to define an identity that at once embodies the cherished and distinctive values and practices of the past with the requirements and opportunities of globalization. Islam is not new to this region. Nor is the rise of Islamist movements, including jihadist movements and other expressions of "reformist" Islam that involve sharp and sometimes violent conflict, new, having been a prominent feature of the spread of Islam in West Africa in the early nineteenth century. In this chapter I will examine the evidence that the level of violence and threat is increasing, situate this conflict in the context of "political Islam" as a longstanding phenomenon in this region, and attempt to understand the appeal of Islamist doctrine, its internal contradictions, and its implications for the future of globalization. I will do this by focusing on one segment of Nigérien society, the Hausa people, and particularly the Hausa of Niger's most important secondary commercial center, Maradi.

Often this identity struggle has been framed as parochialism versus universalism. *Globalization* has come to mean many things, but in the context of this chapter I will define it as the integration of capital, technology, and information across national borders in a way that is creating a single, capitalist free market. *Islamism,* in contrast, is often characterized as a backlash antiglobalizationist movement, promoted particularly by those "brutalized or left behind by this new system" (Friedman 1999).

My principal thesis is that Islamist movements, like Izala (Jama'at Izalat al-Bid'a wa-Iqamat as-Sunna, or Movement Against Negative Innovations and for Orthodoxy), may be understood, at least in part, as the assertion of a unique identity within the globalization process as people seek to join a broader world economy on their own terms. From this perspective I suggest that the conflicts that are occurring with increasing regularity are expressions of two societal and global change processes—the rejection of older social and normative constructs, particularly the basic norms and structure of "traditional Hausa society," and the rejection of Western-dominated modernization by those who seek to make use of their resources to claim some of the power in the social change process. As I attempt to show, these conflicts now involve not only national debates and transnational (terrorist) movements, but also the day-to-day life of ordinary Nigérien at the local level. These conflicts are especially impacting the roles and socioeconomic relationships of women as the integration of markets and societies are creating accelerated pressures for change in gender relationships.

Although this is a controversial interpretation, it is one situated in an emerging broader debate about the adaptation of global culture in Africa (van Binsbergen et al. 2003). What is at stake is not solely the practices and preferences of a small sect of Islam in the Hausa hinterland, but a growing conflict over culture and identity that has economic and political as well as social and cultural implications.

Islam in Niger

Niger is a Muslim nation with well over 90 percent of its population identifying strongly with Islam.[1] Today there are fewer than 50,000 Christians in Niger and a rapidly declining number of animists in various stages of Islamization. The dominant ethno/linguistic group in Niger, the Hausa, are so thoroughly Islamized that the very definition of what it means to be Hausa incorporates being a Muslim. In a study of two villages straddling the Nigerian-Nigérien border, William Miles found that 95 percent of villagers interviewed in Nigeria and 89 percent in a village in Niger considered that their religion was the first or second most important element of their identity (Miles 1994). In fact, people who share the Hausa language and most other cultural attributes with the Hausa but who are not Muslim are considered *anna*, *arna*, or *maguzawa* (pagan) and not Hausa. Other important ethnic groups, such as the Tuareg, a Saharan people who are a subgroup of the Berber, were Islamized early in the second millennium and are entirely Muslim.

Islam in the Sahel has in fact always been "political," influenced from every vector. First brought to the region by the Almoravids and the Tuareg from North Africa, Islam was further spread by the merchants and political agents of the Mali empire—particularly in the fringes of the Songhai culture, which includes the modern-day Zarma people. Later influence of the Middle East and of Sudan on the people of the Bornu and Manga cultures in eastern Niger is evident in their histories and in the founding myths of the Hausa city-states to the south (Hogben and Kirk-Greene 1966:145). Finally, the Islamic jihads of the early nineteenth century both in northern Nigeria and in the high plateau of Guinea influenced Islam in present-day Niger through the introduction of both refugees and stricter, reformed notions of Islam.

Islam in Niger is rooted in the culture and shares some common elements while not extinguishing local differences (Nicolas 1978). The most important strain of Islam traditionally in Niger has been Tijaniyya, a Sufi brotherhood of Sunni Islam. Tijaniyya was widely adopted in Niger, in part because it offered a simplified ritual and a less thorough understanding of Islam by the mass of its adherents. At the same time, Tijaniyya as practiced in Niger emphasized tolerance of other Muslims (Zakari 1998, cited in Robinson 2005). Historically these diverse strains of Islam have not been in open conflict with one another. The only real manifestation of violence involving Islam historically was associated with opposition to colonialism, and then mainly on the part of Sanusiyya, which was never a major form of Islamic organization in Niger (Niandou-Souley and Alzouma 1996). The same cannot be said, however, for either the diehard practitioners of pre-Islamic cults, such as *anna/arna* (Faulkingham 1974), who ridicule Muslims for their "passivity," or more recently for the Islamists who argue that only their interpretation of the Quran preserves the essential truth and purity of Islam.

Historically, then, Islam in Niger developed in an African context quite different from that of the Arab world and historically did not transform the cultures it impacted in such a way as to cause them to lose their distinctiveness (Niandou-Souley and Alzouma 1996:250). This is a particularly important point with regard to the issue of Arabization. Despite the tradition of educating children in traditional *makaranta* (informal Islamic schools run by local marabouts), Hausa children never learned Arabic nor were they alienated from their customary practices. Women in Niger thus enjoyed greater freedom than in Arab countries, including the relative acceptance of the status of "free women," a term given to unmarried adult women often equated by outsiders with prostitution (Cooper 1995). In the practice of rituals associated with Islam, such as marriage and naming ceremonies, much of the pre-Islamic ritual was retained and no references were made to the Arab world (Niandou-Souley and Alzouma 1996). In recent years, however, this has begun to change with the infusion of larger investments from Arab countries in Niger's educational system. One manifestation of this has been the explosive growth of madrasa secondary schools, which teach both academic and religious subjects in French and Arabic. The creation of the Islamic University at Say, financed by the Organization of the Islamic Conference (OIC) and with instruction entirely in Arabic, attempts to offer an alternative career track to the usual and more prestigious education in French. This increasing expression of Arab language and culture in Nigérien Islam is now taking the form of a growing anti-Western sentiment among both elites and ordinary villagers and is supported by the emergence of Izala as a self-conscious expression of an alternative to both Western influence and the constraints on Arabization posed by traditional Hausa norms and practices. These developments, of course, have important political implications.

Political Islam and Islamism

Islamism is often defined as an organized activity or a systematic thought process that forcefully, but not necessarily violently, strives to bring politics into line with Islamic precepts. In contemporary West Africa this definition needs to be modified because in countries like Niger all forms of Islam, new and older, have at one time been "forcefully political" in the sense that they have stridently attempted to influence state policies. The difference between bringing state policies "in line with the Quran" and the complete integration of religion and the state is small. As we shall see, this is well illustrated by the distinction between attempting to declare Niger a state under sharia law and the resistance on the part of all Islamic organizations in Niger to the Family Code.

Today in Niger there are at least three strains of Muslim thought: the traditionalists, the reformists, and the rationalists (Meunier 1998). The *traditionalist* perspective has been dominant historically in Niger and has been a pillar of support of "localism" particularly for traditional Hausa political leadership. It is composed mainly of followers of marabouts in Sufi or mystical brotherhoods—notably Qadiriyya and Tijaniyya. In Maradi, ever since the early nineteenth century Tijaniyya has been the dominant brotherhood.

The *reformists* are principally Sunni groups that seek to "purify" Islam and return it to its literal reading of the "word," therefore rejecting all of the legal schools of Islam and notably the Malikite school that has historically been dominant in Niger, as well as all the other Sufi "deviations." In this chapter I shall refer to people holding this position as "Islamists" or "reformists." It is this group that is often viewed as the proponents of "political Islam"; however, I contend that they are but one of the tendencies attempting to influence and structure the state. In fact, all three tendencies not only have political agendas today but have had them for at least 200 years—when, in the early nineteenth century, Tijaniyya was spread by El Hadj Omar's jihad and Qadiriyya by Usman dan Fodio, "reformists" in their era. In Maradi, the most important group of reformists has been the Yan Izala, a school inspired by Salafist doctrine with strong connections to Saudi and Nigerian imams (Kane 2003b).

The *rationalists* are those marabouts and their followers who condemn radical reformist Islam and consider Islam as a personal religion and not as a social movement, while rejecting many tenets of local Hausa culture. Many of the leaders of this tendency have been educated in French schools, and many follow the Malikite legal tradition of Islam. Nonetheless, they have their own political agenda, which is to harmonize as much as possible Islam with modern European conceptions of the state-religion balance by insisting on a clear separation of mosque and state in Niger, if not the French formulation of the state *laïcité* ("secularity"). From a functional point of view the important distinction is not between their aspirations to "be political." It is between their conception of the state and whether Islam means controlling the state directly.

Islam, Politics, and the State

French colonial policy in Niger accommodated itself to Islam in general while suppressing to the maximum possible extent any independent associational life, including religious associations (Charlick 1991, Miles 1994). As a consequence, until recently the Sufi brotherhoods attempted to "stand aloof from politics," at least in terms of partisan positions (Robinson 2005). Islam in Niger, however, has always been the subject of intense political disputes. Michael Horowitz (1983) argues that the relationship between Islam and the modern state in Niger has been the subject of a "recurrent dialectic" between forces favoring localization and differentiation and those favoring uniformity. To the extent that French colonial officials and subsequent governments of independent Niger came to rely on local leaders despite their "nation-building" aspirations, they in fact came down on the side of localism and diversity. Leaders of the nationalism movement in Niger, for example, were uniformly on the side of localism, favoring the notion of a secular developmental state while leaving to local religious leaders (imams, marabouts) and wealthy merchants associated with the "brotherhoods" the diverse practices of Islam. This was true of both the Parti Progressiste Nigérien (PPN) leadership under President Hamani Diori and its main rival, the Union Démocratique Nigérien/Sawaba (UDN/Sawaba) under Diori's cousin Djibo Bakary, a party whose express ideology was supposedly more "socialist" or modernizing.

In the 1980s, however, the struggle for the soul of Islam in Niger erupted, even before the advent of political liberalization and democratization. During the debate over the national charter, a preconstitutional document issued in 1987, there was already discussion about the role that Islam should play in defining a more liberal state. Many of Niger's young educated bureaucratic elite wanted the country to be modeled more clearly on a Western (French) model and to adopt the language that would render Niger a "secular state"—to whit, that "no religion, no belief can arrogate the power of the State or interfere in its affairs" (Idrissa 2003).[2] At the Sovereign National Conference in July and August 1991 there was hardly any debate on the principal of secularity, though the exact wording of this in the future constitution was subject to considerable pressure. The decision made by conference president André Salifou was to omit any mention of Islam in the constitutional draft. Islamic organizations across the board strongly opposed this decision, claiming that it ignored the essential role that Islam had played in the forging of Nigérien culture, and attacking Salifou and many of the conference participants as anti-Islamic. They subsequently carried this argument forward throughout the 1990s as an attack on the overly Westernized political class. This has accorded the Islamists the opportunity to cloak themselves in the robes of both antiimperialism and opposition to atheism, two positions that resonated well with at least part of the politically conscious population. It led as well to the call for the adoption of sharia as the only way to reconcile the Nigérien state with the true principles of Islam (Niandou-Souley and Alzouma 1996; Sounaye 2001).

All three constitutions for the democratically constituted Third Republic (1992), the Fourth Republic under the dictatorship of Ibrahim Mainassara Baré (1996), and the reconstituted democratic Fifth Republic (1999) have employed identical language to deal with this issue. They state that one of the fundamental principles of the Nigérien state is to be "the separation of the State and religion," thus avoiding the formulation that the republic is to be *laïque* (secular). They nonetheless affirm the clear intention to preserve the free exercise of religion and not to declare there to be a "state" religion.

The formal legal separation of mosque and state, however, has been far from the reality of the Nigérien state since independence in 1960. It has not inhibited political leaders from mobilizing support by making pronouncements, using state resources, and posting slogans that call this separation into question. The military regime of President Seyni Kountché, for example, actively cultivated its ties to the Muslim world by courting Arab petro dollars, improving relations with Libya, authorizing the construction with Islamic Conference funds of the Islamic University at Say, and hosting the Islamic Conference in Niamey in 1982. It posted signs in the capital pronouncing "Our God, Allah; Our book, the Koran; our Prophet, Mohamed" (Horowitz 1983; Nicolas 1979). This same billboard returned to its pride of place outside the presidential palace following the democratic election of the "Forces of Change" government of Mahamane Ousmane in the early 1990s.[3]

Pressure in the late 1980s to return to some kind of electoral politics in fact followed the familiar form that it had in the 1930s and 1940s nearly everywhere in West Africa: it began with the formation of cultural associations. In the case of Niger these associations were not only protopolitical parties representing ethnoregional interests; some had strong overtones of religious revivalism as well as ethnic identity. This was clearly the case of the Association Mutualiste d'Animation Culturelle et Artistique (AMACA), formed in the Zinder area, and of similar associations in Maradi (Madallah) and in Tahoua that became the core of Ousmane's political party, the Convention Démocratique et Sociale (CDS). These associations not only militated for a greater political role of the East (broadly speaking, the Hausa) but also were carriers of a message of rededication to Islam, a core Hausa value (Lund 2001; Charlick et al. 1994). Not surprisingly, many CDS-elected leaders and appointed officials, including notably President Ousmane and the mayor of Maradi, Kané Sallou, made a point of their devotion to Islam in their political functions.[4]

In addition, since independence in 1960 every government has privileged one religious association, the Islamic Association, as a partner and advisory body to the government. This was clearly part of the corporatist nature of the state, authorizing until the advent of the Third Republic and competitive democratic elections only one Islamic association. With the democratic opening following the holding of the Sovereign National Conference and the installation of the transitional government, new associations were allowed to form and be legally registered. Several were subsequently banned when they were considered to be too radical or political. The current government of Niger under the Fifth Republic seems to have reaffirmed this longstanding practice and preference for corporatist institutions in establishing a single Nigérien Islamic Council (NIC) to deal with religious conflict and presumably to "advise" the government.[5] Finally, every government, including the current democratically elected regime, devotes time on state-run radio and television to Islamic religious programming, including by the Islamists. These acts led University of Niamey (Abdou Moumouni University) sociologist Souley Adji to declare in 1992 that "Niger has become a kind of Islamic Republic in secular packaging" (in Sounaye 2001).[6]

Local Manifestations of "Political" Islam

At the local and village level, Islam has been a major part of the governance process for generations. In many regards, Islam in Niger was always a local matter, and so too will be reactions to the new challenges posed by the "reformists." For this reason the contemporary practice of Islam and the patterns of resistance to "reformist" Islam vary considerably from one area and city to another even within the same ethnic community and country.[7]

Among the Hausa it is beyond question that part of the authority of the *sarki* (chief) has been based on his status in the Islamic faith as "emir" or representative of Allah on earth. *Sarakuna* (members of the noble status group), therefore, have always been more than secular authorities, the basic tier in a civil administration. As representatives of Allah on the earth, they must be accorded deference and respect, and they are looked to to intercede with the heavens in times of severe distress, such as droughts. This basis of political organization is nowhere more evident than in Faulkingham's study (1974) of a succession dispute in Madawa (south-central Niger). In the struggle for a village chieftaincy, the Sarki finally resolves the issue by chastising a complainant for challenging him, stating that "you have offended me, the spirits and Allah." This text is particularly interesting because the authority of the Sarki is justified based not only on Islam but also on spirits (*iskoki*), a Hausa belief in supernatural forces linked to earlier nature spirits that is clearly not a part of the belief system of orthodox Islam. The synthesis of spiritual authority and authority of the nature spirit world is but one of the many forms of syncretism that Islam takes even in present-day Hausa Niger (Horowitz 1983, Islam and Customary Law Section:7).

Village headmen have not carried this same special status, and therefore their capacity for dominance in political acts is dependent on a much broader range of skills and attributes. They have, however, been buttressed in their authority and decisionmaking by the local clergy (marabouts) and the holy scripture (the Quran) itself. As Lund (1998) amply documents, local land disputes are frequently resolved, at least in part, by compelling witnesses to swear on the Quran. It is widely understood and accepted that false swearing on the Quran can result in death or in other corporal punishment, such as being forced to contract the dreaded disease of leprosy.

Hausa villagers have reacted in diverse ways to the changing political and religious environment. In 1994 I observed the remarkable changes that had occurred in a Hausa village in Matameye, a county in the Zinder department in southeastern central Niger (Charlick 1974; Charlick 1994). Whereas twenty years prior the village I lived in had no masonry walls to separate and close off residential concessions, most of the households now sported them. In the earlier period nearly all the women worked on the family farm (*gandu*); now few ventured out to participate in this work. Instead they were partially secluded and vigorously involved in their own economic activities within the walls of their compounds. In 1969 the practice of *bori*, a possession cult, was prevalent in this village and was even led by the senior wife of the village's most important *mallam* (learned Muslim); twenty years later as far as I could ascertain *bori* was not being practiced there even covertly. The influence of Islamic "reformists," principally Izala missionaries from northern Nigeria, was clear in the changes in daily life and work but had not reached the point where villagers were pitted against one another over the practice of their faith or divided among several different mosques. Villagers spoke about making electoral choices based in part on their adherence to Islam, although this translated mainly into the symbols and colors that various parties employed. CDS, the dominant party in this area, had the fortuitous color of green, symbolic color of Islam. Neither at that time nor in any subsequent conversations that I had with villagers did I detect any enthusiasm for jihad or the kind of violence perpetrated by Al-Qaida. What is perhaps remarkable about this observation of change is that it occurred in a village recently converted to Islam from *maguzawa* (pagan Hausa) practices, including the political dominance of the village by *sarkin noma*, keepers of an ancient Hausa land cult.

Miles notes similar changes and dispositions in a Nigérien Hausa village he has studied intensely for more than twenty years, noting that affirming public support for Osama bin Laden would have been unacceptable both for internal reasons and because state authorities would not have tolerated it.[8] One factor that may distinguish these two communities from many others in Niger may be their proximity to the Nigeria border and now to Nigerian states that have officially adopted sharia and sanctioned elements of the Izala agenda.

Relationships between villagers in a much larger community in south-central Niger, Dogon Doutchi, seem to be significantly different. There, Adeline Masquelier (1999) reports that relations between the traditional Sufi brotherhoods and leaders of the Izala sect of "reformist" Islam have been marked by intolerance and conflict in their rhetoric or even in open and sometimes violent conflict between members of these communities. Similarly, the impact of a "modern" consumer ethos on the people of this community has led to a heightened conflict among the austere Izala followers and villagers, principally women, who want to continue the traditions of gift-giving and dowry that engender huge expenditures and that mark social success (Masquelier 2005a, 2005b).

The limited evidence available confirms that change has been occurring associated with the rise of "reformist" Islam elsewhere among other ethnic communities. Now that the Nigérien state has formally adopted a policy of decentralization, much more attention is being paid to the phenomenon of "localism" all over the country. In a recent study of a community near Gaya, in the southwesternmost corner of the country, Nigérien sociologists have discovered that Izala is attracting more adherents from among the strata of the population that is alienated from the practices of what they consider to be abusive state and traditional authorities (Moumoni 2004). In a telling quote from their research in the town of Bengou, a marabout commented, "Today the only justice you can count on is God's justice. A Muslim can only be judged by laws that are not inspired by the Qur'an. The people who have a little bit of power abuse it and make the poor suffer because they have little respect for God" (Moumoni 2004:13).

From this perspective, Izala represents not just a return to a purer form of Islam, but resistance and alienation from an illegitimate state. This political reformism, however, does not extend to women in this rural setting, where the struggle for scarce resources is being increasingly translated into the exclusion of women from economic activities outside the home that have traditionally been their major source of income. In the name of religious purity, women in this village are no longer permitted to work the salt pits and now are veiled.

A newly completed study comparing the attitudes and behavior of Tijani and Izala merchants in Maradi finds some significant differences between self-professed adherents of the "reformist sect" Izala and their Tijani neighbors. Adherents of Izala, for example, are nearly twice as likely to criticize such Hausa practices as drumming and dancing, the use of *gris-gris* (talismans), and animal sacrifices as their Tijani neighbors (Charlick and Hima 2006).

These are obviously too few observations of local level life in Niger to lead to any kind of research-based generalizations. They point out again, however, just how important it is to avoid such sweeping statements and study the development of Islam and Islamism at the local level.

Understanding Islam in the Era of Democracy and Rising Islamism

There is no doubt that since the collapse of the military regime in 1991, organized Islam has emerged as a major force in Nigérien civil society. By 1994, five officially recognized Islamic associations had been added to the single corporatist association, the Association Islamique du Niger (AIN) (Niandou-Souley and Alzouma 1995, Charlick et al. 1994). By the year 2000 this number had jumped to more than forty (Sounaye 2001). Only a small percentage of these associations are in fact associated with "reformist" or Islamist movements and views. Many are based on particular Islamic leaders (marabouts) and their followers. Although the level of organization and of policy influence of Islamic associations has no doubt grown, not all of these efforts reflect the rising of "reformist" Islam. From time to time a number of Islamic associations have coalesced around their opposition to a particular policy of the state. Opposition to the Family Code, for example, mobilized all of the official Islamic groups in 1993, as Leonardo Villalón has noted (2003:57). Together, these groups were able to build a lobby campaign from the village level to the National Parliament that stopped cold a major legal reform that had been in the works for over a decade. To the chagrin of the two major women's associations (the Rassemblement Démocratique des Femmes du Niger [RDFN] and the Association des Femmes du Niger [AFN]), a number of human rights groups, and many of Niger's international donors, this legislation never even got a full debate and vote.

For the most part Nigérien Islam continues to be dominated by a moderate form of Sunnism organized as Sufi brotherhoods, although they are far less powerful and organized in Niger than in Senegal or Mali. In many parts of Niger, and particularly in rural areas, Islam is very much a syncretist religion incorporating the magical and leadership powers of *malamai* (persons learned in some elements of the faith but with limited understanding of Quranic texts and Islamic law and medicine) and elements of pre-Islamic ritual and beliefs. As Louis Brenner (1993a) has documented, these practices and beliefs are often attacked by the "reformers," who wish to purge Islam of what they see as pagan, essentially traditional African, cultural artifacts. Hence, "reformers" inevitably clash with these leaders and their followers in a kind of war between alternative non-Western cultures.

At the same time, it is undeniable that while support for Osama bin Laden and jihadist politics in Niger has not been widespread, the "reformers" have grown significantly in their numbers and impact, particularly since the transition to more liberal and "democratic" regimes in 1991–1992. This growth is evident throughout the east-central part of the country, particularly in the city of Maradi and the southern portions of Magaria and Matameye counties. This is attributable, in part, no doubt to the proximity of these areas to Zamfara, Katsina, Daura, and even Kano in Nigeria—areas of intense Islamization and imposition of sharia. The vector for this influence, however, is far more commercial than spiritual, connected to the impact of commercial relations between Maradi's large merchants and their counterparts in Hausa northern Nigeria, and to a lesser degree Zinder's merchant class with Kano and Katsina. Direct and indirect influence of the conservative brand of Arab and particularly Saudi-inspired Islam via the experience of the hajj to Mecca that nearly all of the wealthier Hausa merchants undergo is also evident in the entire area, judging from the proliferation of new mosques in the Saudi style and the increasing practice of purdah (seclusion of married women). Nonetheless, it is in Maradi where the growth of the "reformist" movement has been most intense, leading some observers to label Maradi as the hotbed of Izala, a form of strict Islamic interpretation (*al adini*) of the Quran. Maradi today is a town in full transition, with an important new neighborhood populated almost entirely by Izala members who are constructing an ever more self-contained life with their own schools, mosques, and businesses (Grégoire 1993:106–115; Meunier 1997).

It is evident, moreover, that the power and authority of the Nigérien state have been in sharp decline, opening up political space both for Islam as a whole and for Izala. The decade following the political transition to Niger's first real elected government in 1993 has been turbulent, encompassing the overthrow of the elected regime by the military, the assassination of one military leader by another, and the eventual return to a civilian government experiencing chronic challenges by factions within its own military and secret police. This has hardly been a recipe for building public confidence and an increased sense of legitimacy of the state. In this political space new actors, particularly the Islamic associations, have grown in stature and importance.

Abdoulaye Sounaye (2001) argues that the post-Kountché military regimes (Saïbou, Baré, and Wanké) have been even more accommodating to the Islamic actors than have been the elected civilian regimes of Presidents Ousmane and Tandja. There is some evidence that the civilian-elected government of Niger, particularly since the reelection of President Tandja and Prime Minister Amadou in 2004, has regained some legitimacy and strength and has countered the Salafist "reformists" more directly. When, for example, some "reformist" imams began to follow the lead of their fellows from Nigeria in urging Muslims to reject immunization against polio on the grounds that it was a Western plot to sterilize them, the Amadou government arrested them, placed them in jail overnight, and told them that if they persisted they would be prosecuted (Darling 2005). More important, in June 2000 Sheikh El Hajj Aboubacar Hassoumi, Sarkin Kiota and head of the Tijaniyya brotherhood in Niger, openly called for official recognition of sharia, going so far as to dispute the legitimacy of any government not based on these principles and stating that "once there is sharia in Niger we will be able to deem ourselves true Muslims." A few days later President Tandja traveled to Maradi and declared that "Niger is a secular and tolerant state. We evolve as such and remain Muslims."[9]

Tandja is, of course, overstating the real differences between the Muslim clerics and his government, as demonstrated by the continued close links between government and the Islamic associations, the use of state media to promote Islam and even radical forms of Islam, the practice of Nigérien politicians to publicly appear devout and observant, and even the reluctance with which the Tandja government deals with Islamists even when they overtly violate the law. Clearly, it is the Islamic associations that have emerged as the most powerful nonstate actor in Niger today, surpassing even the historically important student and union associations in power and influence.

Political Islam and the Rise of Religious Conflict and Violence in the Sahel

In recent years Niger has experienced a rising pattern of conflict as new values of the reformists have come in opposition to older established cultural patterns. Some of this conflict has taken the form of open resistance to decisions and programs of the government of Niger, and some has even become violent. Thus far, this resistance has not directly threatened the Nigérien state. It has, however, challenged it, thereby contributing to the further erosion of its tenuous legitimacy.

Earlier expressions of censure for what was perceived to be modernizing and Westernizing tendencies within Nigérien civil society predate that confrontation. When in 1991, for example, the Rassemblement Démocratique des Femmes du Niger (RDFN), a newly organized women's association, demanded the right to participate in the Sovereign National Conference to reconstruct the Nigérien state, some leaders of the association and some demonstrators were attacked and stoned in the cities of Maradi and Zinder. It was not clear at that time that these attacks were instigated by "Islamists" or fundamentalist sect leaders. The severely weakened Ali Saïbou government did nothing to protect the women. In 1993, shortly after the installation of a democratically elected government in Niger, a series of mass demonstrations were held to protest the government's campaign to promote the use of condoms for birth spacing and protection against the spread of HIV/AIDS. Again, Islamic associations attacked the campaign as being anti-Islamic and directly criticized the newly elected president, Mahamane Ousmane, who was considered by many to be a good Muslim from an important maraboutic family. Death threats were made against those who were associated with the family-planning campaign. Demonstrators disrupted training programs and conferences designed to promote the anti-AIDS message, and posters promoting the campaign were torn down in the capital. For some time, the government suspended all attempts to use the mass media, including radio broadcasts, to get the message widely diffused. This time the leaders of this effort to stop the campaign did seem to come from newly formed "reformist" associations.

It is in this context that one should view the first openly violent conflict between the government of Niger and a "fundamentalist" movement. In March 1994 government troops and Izala sect members clashed at the village of Koulouka (near Bani Bangou), leaving eight Nigérien soldiers dead. Apparently the newly elected government did not order military reprisals against the sect in the wake of this incident. Protest continued when in 1999 the government of Niger ratified the UN Convention on Ending All Forms of Discrimination Against Women. The demonstrations were peaceful, but an intense lobbying and public opinion campaign was mounted to influence the government to add reservations to its ratification. The government acquiesced, and in the eyes of some, including the French permanent mission to the UN, these reservations were so restrictive that they effectively rendered the initial ratification completely meaningless.[10] Nearly all of these reservations pertained to the rights and obligations of married women as governed by "custom and tradition."

In 1999 these Islamic groups protested the holding of the first International Festival of African Fashion (FIMA), held near Agadez in the Saharan region of Niger. But when the second festival was held near the capital, Niamey, in November 2000, the protests were far more serious. These protests, which included acts of violence, seem to have been instigated by urban-based Islamist groups. The protests then spread to the central Nigérien city of Maradi, where they became openly violent as protestors sacked and destroyed bars, brothels, hotels, guest houses, and even churches and facilities associated with the long-present Sudan Interior Mission. In the course of these protests demonstrators even attempted to burn alive the Iya of Maradi, a female ritual figure associated with the cult of *bori* in the area (Idrissa 2003). This represented a major change in the relationship between Islam, the state, and practitioners of pre-Islamic religions, especially women. Under the Diori and Kountché regimes the Iya of Maradi had actually been the president of the corporatist women's association (first the Union des Femmes de Niger [UFN], and then the Association des Femmes du Niger) in Maradi. Because the Iya represented women's participation and particularly in Maradi the participation of traditionally high-status women, the government had welcomed the involvement of this figure. Now, the Islamists were not only challenging the traditional inclusion of women, at least in symbolic politics, but the policies of the state itself (Cooper 1995: 867). This time the government came down hard, arresting sixty-three people and banning seven Islamic associations, including the principal Izala association (Adini Islam).

In October 2001, following the September 11 terrorist attacks on the United States, there were signs of support for Osama bin Laden and his movement in Niger, particularly in Maradi. Pro–bin Laden T-shirts and stickers sprouted up, including one sticker showing bin Laden triumphant underneath an image of airplanes crashing into the New York World Trade Center.[11] Some observers reported that bin Laden had become a kind of hero in Maradi. Others saw these images not so much as support for Al-Qaida but for Islam. The government of Niger, by then an elected civilian regime, acted to suppress these images and arrested two leaders of Islamic associations after they wrote a letter to President George W. Bush condemning the US attack on Afghanistan. Nonetheless, the Nigérien and some international media began to talk of the "bin Laden effect" that was strengthening the campaign by the Islamic fundamentalists to promote sharia law (AfricaOnline, October 12, 2001).

Following September 11 the United States became much more active in pursuing the war on terrorism in the Sahel with the formation of the Pan-Sahel Initiative (PSI) and the provision of military support to the Sahelian border states of Chad, Mali, Mauritania, and Niger. President Tandja emerged as one of the staunchest allies of the United States and supporters of the PSI. The primary target of the PSI was the Groupe Salafiste pour la Prédication et le Combat (GSPC), an Algerian-based splinter group of the Groupe Islamiste Armé (GIA). Although the GSPC is the only armed faction of the Islamist movement in the Sahel and has formally declared its alignment with Al-Qaida, making it officially a "terrorist" organization, it is unclear how closely linked to the core jihadist movement it is (ICG 2005a:7). As the GSPC spread its operations into the Sahel, it seems to have been based in northern Mali. There it conducted several criminal operations, including taking hostage thirty-two European tourists who were released only after the payment of 5 million euros in ransom by the government of Germany. During the course of 2004 the Nigérien army fought at least three battles with GSPC elements along the border between Niger and Chad and on the Niger-Malian border. The most important was in October 2004, when PSI-trained troops, backed by US Special Forces, engaged elements of the GSPC again on the Niger-Chad border, resulting in the death of forty-three fighters from the GSPC, including militants from Niger (Darling 2005).

Although the Tandja government faces serious internal challenges from the rising popularity of the Islamist movement and has been cautious in its domestic moves against the Islamists, it has attempted to play a balancing act that would preserve the authority of the state. On the one hand, it has cracked down on Izala religious leaders who have openly defied state policy. As noted earlier, one such incident involved the temporary jailing of imams from Niger who, following the lead of "reformist" imams in Nigeria, opposed the vaccination of children against polio, claiming that it was a Western plot to sterilize Muslims. On the other hand, it eventually ceded to pressure from these same imams when they objected violently to the presence of "foreigners" in several towns on the Niger-Nigeria border that were serving the sexual and other proscribed desires of the population on both sides of the border, in violation of Nigeria's new application of sharia (Kirwin 2005). Tandja may only have taken this step because it involved mainly noncitizens of Niger.

Neither has the situation of Nigérien women improved in the face of heavy pressure by Muslim and so-called reformist groups. In fact, in June 2006 Niger became the first African country to totally reject the Protocol to the African Charter on Human and People's Rights, specifically rejecting its stipulations on women's rights (Cheruiyot 2006). Pressure from the Islamists was so great that fully 77 of the 113 deputies to the National Assembly did not even show up for the debate, apparently not wanting to incur the wrath of these organizations.

What Do the Reformists Want?

Izala and other forms of Salafist Islam present in the Sahel today seem to have as their primary objective the forging of a new autonomous identity. This identity, I argue, is distinct from that of traditional Islam in that it attempts to delink Islam from its ethnic community and to elevate the "culture of the self" (Roy 2004a). For some followers of reform, this means rejection or at least separation both from traditional Hausa cultural norms, practices, and institutions and the norms, practices, and institutions associated with Westernization. These beliefs they share with Islamists in general who "perceive the problem of the Muslim world to be not insufficient modernization, but an excess of modernization—and even modernization itself" (Lewis 2005:48).

Until recently, the dominant discourse for development in Niger has been the "modernization" of Hausa society associated with Westernization. Despite the fact that nearly all of Niger's Western-educated class retain close ties to village-level society, these individuals have accepted many aspects of Westernized modernization, including the use of the French language, an appreciation for a number of individual human rights, and even a significant alteration of gender relations. Abdourahmane Idrissa (2003) calls these individuals the "Francophone elites."

In recent years reformist Islamic movements have emerged to challenge this vision of the Nigérien state and society. At one level the message that the Yan Izala (the followers of Izala) spread can be interpreted as rejection of everything either Hausa or modern in the name of a purified, monotheistic Islam (Grégoire 1993). For example, Izala rejects the organization of Hausa society based on hierarchy, titles, and gerontocracy. It also condemns traditional Hausa rituals that involve redistribution of wealth, such as baptisms, naming ceremonies (*sunna*), and elaborate wedding celebration parties (*tam-tam*) (Sounaye 2001). My recent fieldwork in Niger supports these conclusions, as Izala members of Maradi's merchant class were more than twice as likely to disapprove of large expenditures for weddings and baptisms, for example, than were Tijanis. Izala merchants generally denigrate these practices as well as *bori* (possession cults) and the *maguzawa* (pagan Hausa) redistribution ritual of *dubu* on religious grounds, arguing that they are pagan, pre-Islamic, and "irrational" beliefs and practices.[12] Like other Salafists, Izala adherents reject the idea of the marabout as a spiritual leader both because it advocates a personal relationship with God and because they view marabouts as practitioners of occult arts and purveyors of mystical powers and magical medicines (charms called *gris-gris*, or *laya*). In addition, they reject the entire Sufi tradition of brotherhoods within Sunni Islam.

Ironically, in rejecting these values and practices Izala adherents can be viewed as supporting the essence of what they claim to reject—modernization—for they are railing against African values that they see as traditional and irrational and, above all, wasteful. In this sense "de-Hausafication" is the assertion of a new and foreign kind of "modern" world—one imported from the Arab world in its golden age.[13] At the same time Islamists reject many elements of what came to be understood as modern in the West—the idea of the secular as distinct from the sacred, and of liberal values with regard to the acceptance of equal and individual rights for all, including women, values that they argue are not derived from a strict reading of the Quran but rather from Western thought. So, for example, Izala opposes the idea of the secular school and the secular state. At the same time, some of what Izala rejects are the values and practices that limit the growth of native capitalism, particularly its waste of economic resources.

How far have the Islamists been able to advance with their social, cultural, and political agenda? The evidence thus far is mixed. In northern Nigeria the impact has been significant but has not led to the complete suppression of Hausa cultural practices and, presumably, attitudes and values that the reformers vehemently oppose (Miles 2003; Last 2000). In the borderland of southern Niger that impact may be considerably less (Miles 2003), yet it is certainly observable in the reduction of women's work outside the household, of redistributive rituals, and of the practice of spirit possession ritual (*bori*).

The response of the Hausa to Islamism has been complex and is still very much in process. Izala's task, the formation of this new identity, is an ambitious one, and one not easily or uniformly accepted in Hausa communities. Hausa society has historically been very syncretic, adapting and incorporating newer beliefs and values into older traditions. So, most of Maradi's wealthy merchants historically have belonged to the Tijaniyya brotherhood that was both Sufi in origin and socially conservative. Others belonged to the Qadiriyya, influenced by the jihadist movement to the south in the early nineteenth century. Both sects traditionally accommodated themselves well to Hausa traditional practices, including rituals of redistribution. Over the years, the emerging class of wealthy older merchants in Maradi (the *alhazai*) have become stricter in their practice of Islam, particularly with regard to the rights of women, who have been increasingly veiled and secluded as an expression of the prestige and status of their husbands (Cooper 1995). It is notable, then, that the Izala Islamists have particularly singled out this group for their scorn in criticizing their "impure" (polytheistic) form of Islam. But even among followers of Izala some of the same syncretist practices have been noted, particularly in certain neighborhoods of Niamey, where they continue to incorporate such Hausa traditions as the building of personal networks and even adhering to Islamic brotherhoods as part of their social integration into modern urban life (Sounaye 2001). Other observers note that, at least in some rural Hausa communities, there is sharp resistance to the reduction or elimination of gift exchanges (particularly around marriage rituals), as these threaten common ways of establishing social standing in the community (Masquelier 2005a). In other communities—particularly in rural areas—few people seem deeply attached to many of the practices, especially pre-Islamic practices that Izala condemns (Miles 2003). Rituals like *dubu* and the practice of extensive networks of gift exchange (Nicolas 1965) have largely fallen into disuse or have been greatly reduced by thirty-five years of difficult economic times in this region. Nor is the notion of change and reform of Islam a new idea in the Sahel. Although the appeal of Usman dan Fodio's nineteenth-century purification movement never had the same impact in the Hausa refugee states of Niger (Gobir and Maradi) as it did in the states of Kano, Daura, and Katsina to the south, it did transform Islam even there.

Even more critical is whether a poor country like Niger will tolerate and even benefit economically from the informal resistance to the strict Salafist moral code, thereby limiting its reach, or whether adherence to the "norms and identities" of the Nigérien nation-state will suffice to limit this religious movement (Miles 2003). And there is the question of the ascendancy of economic opportunity over puritanical values. Not far from the Izala stronghold of Maradi are several border towns that cater to the human desires now held illegitimate in the sharia-ruled states of northern Nigeria.[14] How should the toleration of these "towns of convenience" be viewed? Are they a reflection of a state that is willing to permit an affront to the values of the Islamic reformists for strictly economic gain? Or should it be seen rather as part and parcel of the longstanding Hausa informal toleration of prostitution and alcohol use in a society that has incorporated *giya* (beer) and *gidan magaji* (houses of prostitution) into its Islam?[15]

Of major interest from a socioeconomic point of view is the fact that Izala seems to have several different audiences. On one level, it has attracted the support of the young merchants of Maradi. On the other, it has garnered significant support from people who are socially marginal in traditional Hausa society, like the urban unemployed, former students of Western-type schools, and farmers who have become landless or nearly landless (Meunier 1998:88). In Nigeria, many leaders of Izala are drawn from the lower tier of the civil service. The question is, what unites three such diverse audiences? The ethnographic literature on the motivations of Izala followers in Maradi is not rich. A new preliminary study of the attitudes and practices of Maradi's merchant class may shed some light on these motivations (Charlick and Hima 2006). Work that has been done in Nigeria (Kane 2003b) is far richer but, as Miles (2003) has pointed out, takes place in a context that is significantly different.

The evidence that is available, however, suggests two hypotheses. One is that Izala's appeal is to categories of people who are attempting to assert their value and worth largely outside the framework of traditional Hausa culture and values. Each of these categories sees itself as limited by the way the old Hausa culture allocates status largely through title and material wealth. The other hypothesis is that each is trying to create a new basis of earning status and prestige by making a new niche within Hausa society, based on a different set of values they hope to get Hausa society to adopt. Piety and service to one's fellow devout Muslims becomes a way to succeed for marginal people who stand little chance of achieving within the old value system. For Olivier Meunier, reformist Islam is a way to reorder status and prestige in Hausa society. He states that the "Wahhabist ideology allows them to get out of this traditional framework that they cannot control" (Meunier 1998:119–120, my translation). It allows its young followers to integrate into urban life, independent of both the state and the brotherhoods. At the same time, success for the followers of Izala in Maradi is still measured to a significant degree in terms of economic success and the reinvestment of wealth into social capital and even political power (Meunier 1998:120).

The Rise of the New Hausa Capitalists

In the mid-1960s the foremost European student of the Hausa of Maradi, anthropologist Guy Nicolas, stated that his research led him to the conclusion that unless there was a profound change in the values and thus the practices of the Hausa they would be incapable of advancing economically and raising the standard of living of the Hausa people. The greatest incompatibility between Hausa culture and "development," he argued, was the virtual imperative of participating in gift-giving. Nicolas went on to state that "it seems that there is no partial solution. . . . It will be necessary to substitute one complete system of values for another."[16] His studies and those of other social scientists suggested that the existing pattern of social organization and practice of Islam served to limit the growth of capital. It did so in two fundamental ways. First, members of the old merchant class of Maradi (the *alhazai,* or wealthy merchants who had been to Mecca) quickly hit the upper limit of their ability to accumulate capital because Hausa social norms virtually forced them to redistribute a great deal of their wealth. In his 1986 study, Emmanuel Grégoire came to this same conclusion, arguing that these practices "constitute . . . with tradition, a brake on the establishment of new social relationships similar to those that exist in the West, where the economy is entirely detached from society" (1992:168). Second, the older system of values ordered social status in a way that was disadvantageous to the merchant class, consistently assigning them a ranking considerably below that of traditional title holders and marabouts.

It might have come as a surprise to Nicolas and a generation of social scientists and policymakers focused on development, then, to see how that transformation may be taking place. In recent years we have seen the appearance in Maradi, the commercial capital of Niger, of a new reformist community centered on an emerging class of young merchants. Less than a decade after Grégoire's initial analysis, he began reporting on a new phenomenon: that followers of Izala, especially in Maradi, were promoting a concept of Islam that favored capitalist development and an accompanying culture of individual wealth (Grégoire 1993). By rejecting the values of Hausa society involving redistribution of wealth, these merchants could hope to grow their enterprises in ways that their older colleagues could not, expand their scale of operations, and compete on a broader scale. Grégoire hinted that the older merchants, members mainly of Tijaniyya Sufi brotherhoods, were actively combating these new beliefs, in part because they recognized the economic threat that the beliefs represented. My recent fieldwork, based on a much larger set of interviews in Maradi, largely confirms these views (Charlick and Hima 2006). Masquelier's research also supports this view when she notes that the older established merchants and Hausa notables ridicule the younger Izala followers as "tightfisted, selfish individuals who turn their backs on social obligations" (1999:233).

All of this suggests that underlying the search for a new identity is a deeper struggle for reordering power and prestige in Hausa society. Meunier (1998) sees this as the reversal of the old pattern, legitimatizing the role of merchants as leaders of the community. In a few short years Maradi has seen the development of an entire neighborhood complete with its own institutions (schools, for example), manifesting the rise of this new class. These new institutions are explained, of course, in terms of piety and faith, but they are much more than that. They are schools for the new economic class, fostering a religious education that is more "responsive to the expectations of an urban population inculcated with values that are foreign to the local culture . . . [and] a more rational style of Islam that matches better their economic activities" (Meunier 1998:14,120, my translation). This reformist Islam is less time-consuming in its ritual demands. It sets forth simple and clear rules that permit its followers to avoid a lot of supposedly superfluous prayer rituals practiced by the brotherhoods. It sanctions keeping more of one's own capital, and it may even serve to help them become more active participants in a globalized capitalist economy without accepting most of the elements of Westernization. If this in fact proves to be the case, it is even possible that the logic of this new identity will spread to the intellectuals and young bureaucrats who, in the interest of their own capital accumulation and social reproduction, seek a non-Western rationale to escape some of the limits of obligations to the extended family and community. The political implications of the rise of this new culture with its new assignment of prestige and status could be profound, but they are unlikely to replicate the Western experience where a rising capitalist class helped, along with labor, support institutions of liberal democracy.

The Problem of Islamic Globalization

At this stage in the development of the phenomenon, and with only partial empirical evidence for what the leaders and followers of Izala are striving for, it is difficult to judge what the long-term impact of Islamism in Niger may be. Only now is more research at the local level being conducted and reported (e.g., Charlick and Hima 2006).

Understanding the relationship between these very local adaptations of "reformist" Islam and globalization, however, is not merely one of data. It is also one of concept and language. So much of our way of conceptualizing change, as development, is wrapped up in the assumptions of cultural Westernization and the historic impacts of industrialization. The Western modernizing experience embodied the struggle not only for an improved standard of living but for rights. With rights came access to knowledge and eventually to at least some power. Will the evolution of Hausa capitalism lead to the progressive inclusion of Africa's backwaters, like Niger, into a more globalized economy? Will that inclusion also carry with it a gradual expansion of rights and sharing of power?

There are serious challenges to this pathway, even from the seeming internal contradictions in Islamism. The current evolution of things is replete with contradictions both from within Islamism and from without, and particularly in the domain of gender relations.[17] For example, reformist Islam promotes a kind of egalitarianism that openly denies the authority of individuals with high traditional status and seniority. It also strongly supports literacy and the diffusion of knowledge, even for women, a norm that traditional Hausa society certainly did not promote in the poor lands of the Sahel (Miles 2003; Meunier 1997; Masquelier 1999). Followers of Izala say that they want ordinary people to be able to access the wisdom of the Quran while freeing themselves from the potentially exploitative and often ignorant intermediaries. While Izala promotes egalitarianism at one level, this does not extend to the position of women in general. As Imam Ayesha states, "Women's subordination to men and control by men is emphatically a part of the Islamist program" (quoted in Miles 2003). Izala leaders are no more favorable to a more liberalized family law and even the broad affirmation of women's rights than have been other Islamic groups in Niger.

There are forces at work, however, that may create internal pressures for change. We are witnessing the ongoing battle over the imposition and interpretation of these new norms. Barbara Cooper (1995) points out how Izala's attacks on women through the demonization of their organizations and leaders (the Iya of Maradi, for example) are further steps in their loss of power. Masquelier (1999, 2005a) demonstrates how Islamism further controls the bodies of women and how it strives to deny them the accumulation of material wealth associated with giving them "excessive" gifts as part of the courtship and marriage rituals. Pearl Robinson (2005) even posits the possibility that Tijaniyya's increasing engagement in politics may be an opening for "female empowerment" as it struggles to confront the challenge of Izala and Islamism. The fact that some women may be drawn to Izala because they have more opportunities to study and because they can benefit in their own economic activities free now of the burdens of family farm labor may say too little about how far individual rights and women's rights may be able to advance under this kind of Islamic capitalism.

How, for example, will the fact of being literate and able to study affect women? Will they accept the roles that Izala leaders assign to them mainly as the educators of their children, limited in their economic opportunities by a new division of labor accompanying partial or progressively more total seclusion? And will the structure of the family as an economic enterprise in Hausa culture be completely transformed by the withdrawal of women from the family farm workforce? Will families be able to absorb such costs in so poor a land?

Beyond the local level, global forces also serve to limit Niger's choices. This has been painfully obvious in the past in terms of the limited discretion poor African countries have in their foreign and economic policies (Charlick 1994). But it also may be becoming more obvious in terms of how governments deal with Islamist movements. So, it is argued, President Tandja's crackdown on Izala poses serious internal problems within Niger but is dictated at least in part by the decision to become one of the most active partners of the Bush administration in its war on terrorism.

On the one hand, globalizing forces seem to be contributing to the Islamist movement, pushing its followers to become more fully part of the world economy but on their terms. On the other, the struggle for political control of the globalization process is continuing to demand of weak states like Niger that they line up against the Islamists, even at high internal political costs. The one conclusion that the data do appear to make clear at the moment is that Nigérien Izala is not likely to be violent or an important ally of the Islamic jihadists who are at the heart of many anti-Western terrorist movements (Charlick and Hima 2006; ICG 2004). Contradictions and the lack of resolution are the appropriate markers of transition. Toward what, it is too early to say.

Notes

1. Estimates run from 80 percent in official US Central Intelligence Agency documents (Central Intelligence Agency, *The World Factbook*, 2004, www.cia.gov/cia/publications/factbook/index.html) to 98.7 percent based on the 1988 Recensement Général de la Population (Niamey: Ministère de Finance).

2. My translation of *La Charte Nationale* (Niamey: Secrétariat Général du Gouvernement, 1987), p. 24.

3. Personal observation in July 1994.

4. Based on personal observations and interviews conducted in July and August 1994.

5. Décret 2003-313/PRM/MI/D dated November 14, 2003.

6. My retranslation of the quote offered in Sounaye 2001.

7. Personal communication from Adeline Masquelier, October 20, 2005.

8. Information is drawn from an unpublished briefing document that Miles presented to the Seminar on Niger, sponsored by the US Department of State, Bureau of Intelligence and Research, October 11, 2002.

9. As quoted in Reuters, reported in *Kakaki* on July 10, 2000. Sheik Hassoumi was speaking to the Islamic newspaper *As Salam* at the time.

10. The representative of France to the UN High Commission on Human Rights, for example, argued in an official objection that Niger's reservations "completely vitiate the undertaking of the Republic of Niger and are manifestly not authorized by the Convention." See www.unhcr.ch/html/menu3/treaty9_asp.htm.

11. Personal observation. Ironically, this sticker on trucks and bush taxis often replaced the highly suggestive picture of Madonna in her metal bra.

12. See Charlick and Hima 2006. The dubu, or one thousand, in Hausa is a ritual that was practiced by a pre-Islamic clan of super farmers called *sarkin noma* in Niger that was suppressed by the colonial administration and independent governments and fell into virtual disuse.

13. On the notion of "de-Hausafication" see Miles (2003). The argument about the "foreign nature" of Islamist values is developed by Brenner (1993b) and Grégoire (1993:111), who argue that Izala has come to West Africa and Niger through Saudi and Sudanese missionaries and through the influence these missionaries have had on the Hausa of Nigeria.

14. Bach (2003) calls these towns "dividends of shari'a" (see Miles 2003). I believe the term "towns of convenience" is a bit more descriptive. Kirwin (2005) describes three such towns in the department of Maradi.

15. Kirwin (2005) suggests that the existence of these "towns of convenience" may reflect the willingness of the leaders of Niger to become a "courtesan state," or at least that they have little option but to tolerate it.

16. While these notions are implicit in much of his works (1965), these quotes are drawn from an unpublished document "Comptes rendu de la session de travail des cadres de l'animation en pays haousa," 1969:8. My translation.

17. This point is well developed in Masquelier (1999).

3

Nigeria: The Quest for a Viable Religious Option

ROMAN LOIMEIER

IN HIS ARTICLE "THE LOVE OF THE ASKIA FOR THE THREE ORANGES," WHERE he alluded to an old fairy tale motif (as well as an opera by Prokofiev) that thematizes the problem of choice, Humphrey Fisher (1993) posed a question that continues to bother Muslims in sub-Saharan Africa, and northern Nigeria in particular, until today: which of three options of Islamic government would the ruler of the Sudanic empire of Songhay, Askia (Alhaji) Muhammad Turé (r. 1493–1528), eventually choose to legitimize his rule? The first option was represented by the religious scholars affiliated with the imperial court of Gao. These were known for their accommodating positions and their acceptance of African customary religious practices.

Conversely, he could try to draw legitimacy through an alliance with a North African religious scholar, Muhammad b. Abd al-Karim al-Maghili (d. 1504), who had become known for his uncompromising theological positions and could be called a "radical scripturalist." Finally, Askia Muhammad Turé could refer to the established traditions of Islamic learning as embodied by the religious scholars of Timbuktu, who also represented a scripturalist, yet local, tradition of Islam.

Muslims in what is northern Nigeria today are confronted with similar questions: how to choose among several options for the development of their society along Islamic lines. In contrast to the early sixteenth century, when Askia Muhammad Turé had the choice between "three oranges" only, Muslims in northern Nigeria are asked to make their choice among a spectrum of different "fruits," a multitude of expressions and translations of Islam. These different realizations of Islam are the result of an enlarged historical scale that in turn reflects the processes of social, economic, and political transformation. In these processes of change, the corpus of Islamic traditions of learning has grown considerably and so has the number of interpretations of possible societal models. Eventually, however, Muslims in northern Nigeria will have to come to a conclusion as to which "orange," which of the different realizations of Islam, will be the most viable for their future.

The Historical Context: Networks of the Qadiriyya and the Tijaniyya

Whereas historical northern Nigeria—Hausaland and Bornu—experienced a long process of Islamization that led in the late eighteenth century to the widespread acceptance of Islam as the most important (if not the only) paradigm for the organization of society, deeper knowledge of the scholastic canon of Islamic learning remained confined to a small intellectual elite of religious scholars.[1] From the late eighteenth century, these traditions of Islamic learning acquired a new quality, however, through the emergence of Sufi brotherhoods (*tariqa*, pl. *turuq*) as agents of change. When in the ancient kingdoms of Hausaland religious scholars took over political power for the first time in the history of Islam in this region of sub-Saharan Africa by becoming, from 1804, the rulers of the Sultanate of Sokoto and its emirates, established traditions of learning and translocal links thus experienced a respective enlargement of scale.[2] The leaders of the jihad, Usman dan Fodio in particular, were namely affiliated with the Qadiriyya Sufi brotherhood and saw Abd al-Qadir al-Jilani as the "patron saint" of their movement (Brenner 1988:47). As a consequence, close links with the regional centers of the *tariqa*, particularly the Kunta in Timbuktu, were established and cultivated. For the time being, affiliation with the Qadiriyya remained, however, an affair of the scholarly elite. Yet though the Qadiriyya was established as a *tariqa* in northern Nigeria by the early nineteenth century, brotherhood activities and teachings did not become an issue in Islamic education and the Qadiriyya did not assume the function of an "official ideology" for the empire (Brenner 1988:44).

Religio-political competition started, however, in 1831, when the Senegalese scholar Alhaji Umar Tal came to Sokoto and was subsequently able to win a number of scholars for the Tijaniyya, a new *tariqa* that claimed spiritual supremacy over all other Sufi brotherhoods. The ruling elite in Sokoto saw the Qadiri legacy of Usman dan Fodio and the jihad endangered by the growth of a competing *tariqa*. In the context of this struggle for spiritual hegemony, the Sultan of Sokoto was prepared to depose local rulers, such as the Emir of Zaria, Abdulkadir, who had dared to publicly proclaim in 1854–1855 his affiliation with the Tijaniyya and to reject the supreme spiritual authority of the sultan. Only when the Sokoto caliphate was integrated after 1903 into the British colonial realm and became part of the colony of Nigeria were Tijani scholars free to propagate their affiliation.

After the disruption of the wars of conquest, colonial rule came to mean a greater degree of peace and stability, fostering travel and exchange among Muslim communities in West and North Africa. Although both British and French authorities remained nervous about alleged Mahdist or jihadist (and later Wahhabi) activities, and consequently tried to control religious activities in their respective colonial domains, the number of traveling scholars increased considerably in the twentieth century.[3] As a consequence, a further enlargement of scale and multiplication of corresponding options took place, even if still confined to different variations of what Louis Brenner (2001:17ff) has called the "esoteric episteme," the broad spectrum of different expressions of Sufi Islam. In particular, the religious scholars connected with the Tijaniyya strove to intensify their network links with the centers of their *tariqa*, a move that was answered by respective initiatives of the Qadiriyya.

In the case of the Qadiriyya, a great number of traders based in the commercial emporium of the north, Kano, helped to establish new links with Qadiri centers in the trading communities of Northern Africa—in particular, Ghat and Ghadamis, but also Tripoli, Tunis, and the Fazzan, where centers of the Qadiriyya-Arusiyya and the Qadiriyya-Salamiyya existed (Adamu 1968:47–48; Ahmed 1986:207). With respect to the Tijaniyya, the first *silsila* (spiritual chain; pl. *salasil*) of the Tijaniyya as introduced by Alhaji Umar Tal in the mid-nineteenth century was quickly complemented by a number of new *salasil* that established links with the centers of the *tariqa* in Fes (Morocco) and Ayn Madi (Algeria). Of particular importance was the link with the center of the Tijani diaspora in the Hijaz, as led by Alfa Hashim (d. 1931), a nephew of Alhaji Umar Tal who had emigrated, in 1903, after the collapse of the Tukulor empire in the late 1890s, to the Hijaz (Paden 1973:82). Pilgrims from northern Nigeria, in particular, made a point to renew their *salasil* through Alfa Hashim, who thus became the hub of Tijani activities in the Hijaz.

One of the first Tijani scholars to come to Nigeria after 1903 was the Mauritanian Sheikh Abd al-Wahhab Ujdud, also known in northern Nigeria as "Sharif Ujdud." He came to northern Nigeria in 1909 and was instrumental in renewing spiritual links for the Umarian branch of the Tijaniyya of local Tijanis. This process was characterized as a *tajdid*, a renewal of spiritual allegiances through personal contact with a renowned sheikh of the *tariqa* who would claim possession of a specific *silsila* within the *tariqa*, a link that was preferably not known before, and came to mean thus an increase in *baraka* (blessing power) for the respective "holder" of such a *silsila*. Competition for *salasil* and the diversification of *salasil* in fact were to become a well-respected activity for scholars of both the Tijaniyya and the Qadiriyya in northern Nigeria in the twentieth century (Paden 1973:89). Alas, these activities of Tijanis as well as Qadiris were still characterized by the fact that they touched only a small group of scholars and students.

The Reformers: Ibrahim Niass and Nasiru Kabara

This character of *tariqa* affiliation was to change, however, through the activities and teachings of Ibrahim Niass (1900–1975) and later, Nasiru Kabara (1925–1996), who respectively opened the teachings of Tijaniyya and Qadiriyya for all Muslims, thereby transforming both traditions into religious mass movements. These movements, which could be seen as an expression of the changing political, economic, and social conditions of the colonial era, were to influence northern Nigeria's religio-political development. From the 1950s *tariqa* networks were to become conveyor belts for political activities, the mass mobilization of voters, and thus primary tools of power in the hands of increasingly influential scholars. The leaders of these Sufi networks started to compete for followers. Greater numbers of disciples of the network in the 1950s increased the buying and selling power of religious scholars. The movements of reform that were started first by Ibrahim Niass (Seesemann 2004) in Senegal in 1930 and northern Nigeria in 1945 and later, as a direct reaction, by Nasiru Kabara (Loimeier 1997a) in Kano beginning in the early 1950s were again connected with a renewed quest for spiritual *tajdid* and the establishment of new translocal links with the centers of the respective brotherhood. The different networks of the Sufi brotherhoods were not only characterized, however, by their respective endeavors to reform established modes of teaching within both the Tijaniyya and the Qadiriyya. Other traits also intervened, such as the way in which they approached teaching and audiences, their theological argumentation, and their stress on specific features of the ritual (such as praying with arms folded—*qabd*—versus arms outstretched—*sadl*) (Loimeier 1997a:80f). These features of the ritual were central to the politics of identity of these different religious groups. As a result of intra-*tariqa* disputes since the 1930s, the further expansion of different realizations of the "esoteric episteme" can be attested. The move toward the fragmentation of religious authority that had started with the competition between the Qadiriyya and Tijaniyya Sufi brotherhoods in the nineteenth century was accentuated, in addition, by the competition between the different networks and branches of the individual Sufi brotherhoods.

The success in the 1950s of the Tijaniyya-Ibrahimiyya as a religious mass movement in northern Nigeria had a number of consequences for the development of this branch of the *tariqa*. As membership in the Tijaniyya-Ibrahimiyya came to mean membership in a religiously respected network that was open to any Muslim willing to join without being constrained to undergo the tedious and time-consuming process of religious learning, the Tijaniyya-Ibrahimiyya became a network for traders and entrepreneurs who saw this affiliation as a channel to further economic activities as members of a transnational religious network. Such a network could provide important political and economic contacts as well as spiritual protection by virtue of shared membership in a spiritual family (Tahir 1975; Hiskett 1980:103; Paden 1973:86).

The network of Ibrahim Niass was to become, in fact, so important in not only religious but also economic and political terms that he was invited in 1962 to become a member of the Rabitat al-'Alam al-Islami, the first reformist Muslim world organization. Niass remained a member of this organization until his death in 1975 (Schulze 1990).[4] As I observed in Kano in the 1980s, the spiritual activities and rituals of the Tijaniyya-Ibrahimiyya were effectively used by politicians, traders, and entrepreneurs to discuss and advance, in and outside the mosques of the *tariqa*, their worldly as well as spiritual affairs. These networks of trust have since become an umbrella for all kinds of religious, economic, and political activities. These focus not only on northern Nigeria but on Kaolack/Senegal, where Ibrahim Niass's residence, Medina-Kaolack, has become a major center for regional pilgrimages, as well as a center of studies in search of knowledge and recognition. These activities continue today under the leadership of Niass's successors, in particular, Hassan Cissé. Cissé has established close links with the diasporic communities of the Tijaniyya in the West, especially London and New York (Gray 1988:52; Loimeier 2001:389–390; Villalón 1995:141) but also in such new frontiers as South Africa (Jeppie, interview 2004).

What has been said for the development of the Tijaniyya-Ibrahimiyya may be repeated, with slight difference in emphasis, for the Qadiriyya-Nasiriyya. For in the 1940s and 1950s Nasiru Kabara developed the Qadiriyya after the model of Ibrahim Niass. In order to be able to claim leadership for the local networks of the Qadiriyya, he started to collect the *salasil* of the different local branches of the Qadiriyya. Then, in 1949, he established a direct link to the Sammaniyya in the Sudan. Finally, he made a pilgrimage (*ziyara*) to Baghdad in 1953, visiting the grave of Abd al-Qadir al-Jilani and establishing a direct link with the local leader of the

Qadiriyya, Sharif Ibrahim Saif ad-Din al-Jilani (Kabara 1981:113). Nasiru Kabara had acquired thus the largest number of *salasil* of all Qadiri scholars in Kano as well as northern Nigeria, and he was the only one to have established a direct link with Baghdad. This direct link with Baghdad was to help him enormously in the ensuing years to establish his spiritual supremacy within the Qadiriyya, first in Kano, then in northern Nigeria. In 1978 the Sultan of Sokoto, who had until then been regarded as the supreme leader of the Qadiriyya in Nigeria, recognized Nasiru Kabara's ascendance by handing over to him Usman dan Fodio's sword and charging him to lead the struggle against the reformist movement of the Izala that had started, in the late 1970s, to attack the Sufi brotherhoods as *bida*, un-Islamic innovations.

In addition to his success in northern Nigeria, Nasiru Kabara was able to renew old scholarly ties with Libya and to establish, in the 1980s, a link with Mu'ammar Qaddafi. In late 1986, Salim Warfalli, a Libyan Qadiri and a leading member of the Libyan Jam'iyat ad-Da'wa al-Islamiyya, visited Nasiru Kabara in Kano and started negotiations about closer ties as well as the publication of Kabara's Hausa translation and exegesis (*tafsir*) of the Quran.[5] This visit was followed by a more formal visit in 1987, when the Libyan delegation took part in the celebrations of the *mawlid*, the birthday of Abd al-Qadir al-Jilani, in Kano and opened a Nigerian office of the Jam'iyya. In spring 1988, Kabara finally responded to these Libyan initiatives and met Qaddafi in Libya (Kabara, interview 1988). In February 1988, the links between northern Nigeria and Libya were strengthened when Bayero University Kano (BUK) conferred an honorary doctorate on Qaddafi (*Süddeutsche Zeitung,* February 2, 1988). The alliance between Qaddafi and the Qadiriyya-Nasiriyya was of mutual interest: Nasiru Kabara acquired not only a donor prepared to publish his *tafsir* of the Quran as well as official recognition of his religious links with the centers of the Qadiriyya in Libya, but also support for his struggle against the Izala. Qaddafi, for his part, could claim to have won a valuable local ally for his struggle against the Saudi regime as represented, locally, by the Izala group and Abubakar Gumi. In 1981, after a series of polemical confrontations, Saudi Arabia had declared Qaddafi a heretic and infidel. In 1982, this expiation (*takfir*) again led to an appeal to Muslims, by Qaddafi, to "liberate the Kaba" (Loimeier 1997a:289).

Nasiru Kabara was eventually able to successfully defend the Qadiriyya against the attacks of the Izala and to provide it with a relatively high degree of internal cohesion. This unity survived his death in 1996 and the succession of Qarib Allah b. Nasir Kabara (b. 1960), who continued to cultivate close links with Libya (Bari 1997:40). In contrast, after the demise of Ibrahim Niass in 1975 and the rise of the Izala in the late 1970s, the Tijaniyya experienced a serious crisis. This was accentuated by the recrudescence of numerous autonomous local networks of the *tariqa*. To this day, they try to cultivate their own independent links with the different centers of spiritual authority. These include Fes, Ayn Madi, Cairo, and the Hijaz to the north and east, but also Kaolack and Tivaouane to the west, in Senegal. These different networks have developed distinctive positions as far as the attacks of the Izala on the theological tenets of the Tijaniyya were concerned. Thus, there was a "die-hard" faction led by Dahiru Bauchi (b. 1929), who simply refused to discuss the tenets of the Tijaniyya. Yet there is also an "accommodating" faction led by Ibrahim Salih (b. 1939) from Maiduguri (Loimeier 1997a: 274–276).

Ibrahim Salih emerged in the 1980s as a leading figure in the Nigerian Tijaniyya. He earned widespread recognition on account of his prolific writing as well as his efforts to defend the Tijaniyya against the attacks of the Izala (Loimeier 1997a:271ff). In addition, he became famous for his efforts to collect as many *salasil* of the Tijaniyya as possible. He thereby established links with, first, the scholars of the Tijaniyya in Bornu (in particular Sheikh Abu al-Fatih), and then the leading scholars of the *tariqa* in Cairo, especially Muhammad al-Mustafa and Muhammad al-Hafiz al-Misri. The latter two had by the 1950s and 1960s become the most prominent scholars of the Tijaniyya in Egypt. In 1970 Ibrahim Salih formed a personal link with Ibrahim Niass in Kaolack. Last but not least, he acquired a direct link with Maula Idris al-Iraqi in Fes. That solidified his personal and direct affiliations with virtually all major centers of the *tariqa* (Salih, interview 1988).

Ibrahim Salih's fame was also due, however, to the fact that Nigeria's head of state at the time, General Ibrahim Babangida, regarded him as his personal *malam* (teacher, spiritual guide). In addition, he was able to establish a network of spiritual and economic links with Chad, the Central African Republic, Sudan, and Saudi Arabia, where he became known for his powerful amulets (Loimeier 1997a:272–276). In 1985 Salih also rose to become the Nigerian chairman of a transnational initiative of the Tijaniyya.

Supported by the Kingdom of Morocco, this movement strove to reevaluate Tijani writings so as to present an "acceptable interpretation" of the most controversial dogmatic positions of the *tariqa*, as derived from the teachings of Ahmad at-Tijani. This Moroccan connection had been established in the context of a conference on the Tijaniyya in Fes. Organized by the Moroccan minister of religious affairs, it convened hundreds of scholars of the Tijaniyya from all over Africa. The conference resulted in the subsequent establishment of an Association of Ulama of Morocco and

Senegal, as well as a corresponding Association of Ulama from Morocco and Nigeria. Both were well supplied with Moroccan funds. This move may have been connected, as in the case of Libya, with a corresponding Moroccan political agenda in sub-Saharan Africa. Morocco's efforts to win local allies for its annexation of the Western Sahara was posited as a major reason (Kane 2003b:171).

The Modernizers: Abubakar Gumi and the Jama'at Nasr al-Islam

Competition between the Qadiriyya and the Tijaniyya was superseded in the 1970s by the rise of a new religious movement, namely the Jama'at Izalat al-Bid'a wa-Iqamat as-Sunna, or Izala. This movement has come to stand for another Islamic option in northern Nigeria—in Louis Brenner's terms, a "rationalistic episteme," characterized by Izala struggles against all kinds of "un-Islamic innovations."

The success of Izala as a religious mass movement in northern Nigeria in the 1970s and 1980s is related to the transformation of northern Nigerian society in the colonial and postcolonial period. It is also tied to the emergence of a Western-educated and urban Muslim population no longer willing to accept seemingly obsolete, costly, and time-intensive social and religious customs. The development of Izala in northern Nigeria must be situated in a wider sociopolitical context connected to the politics of modernization, as started by the British colonial administration and continued in the 1950s and 1960s by the first (and only) prime minister of the northern region, Ahmadu Bello (d. 1966).

Bello's policies of modernization were not conceived only as policies for the economic development of the north. His administrative, political, and religious reforms essentially sought to end the established political and religious authority of both emirs and Sufi scholars. He aimed to replace accepted forms of political and religious authority with a modern administration that would bring about far-reaching judicial reforms as well as social change.[6] These policies of modernization led to the emergence of a first generation of Muslim reformers who rejected Sufi influences and sought to establish their own translocal and transnational links. In particular, they sought direct connections with Medina and Mecca, as well as other centers of Muslim reform in Egypt and Pakistan. Membership in Rabitat al-'Alam al-Islami and other Muslim transnational organizations was one method; mediation through teachers from Pakistan, Egypt, and Sudan was another.

On the religious level, Ahmadu Bello found support for his policies of modernization in a young religious scholar. In the 1940s Abubakar Gumi

(d. 1992) had fought, like Ahmadu Bello in the 1930s, a personal struggle against the Sultan of Sokoto (Tsiga 1992:40ff). As deputy (and later chief) Qadi of the northern region, as personal adviser to Bello, and as holder of an array of other official functions, Abubakar Gumi was able to form, in the 1950s and 1960s, a small but growing group of Muslim reformers. Together with Bello and the Kaduna-based modern political elite of the north, they came to constitute the so-called Kaduna Mafia.[7]

The organizational framework of the Muslim reformers in the new religio-political setup of the north was the first reformist organization, the Jama'at Nasr al-Islam (JNI), established in 1962. JNI was supposed to support, in religious terms, the politics of modernization of the new elites of the north, as well as to act as an umbrella organization for all religious groups in the north, irrespective of their religious affiliation. As such, the JNI was not only to religiously legitimate the politics of modernization but also to coordinate the building of mosques and schools, to organize the hajj and Islamic *dawa* (mission), and to enhance religious unity in order to overcome the spiritual authority of the Sufi scholars. In order to achieve these goals, Abubakar Gumi, who had established contacts with Saudi Arabia in the context of a number of pilgrimages to the holy places beginning in 1955, organized links with Saudi Arabia, Kuwait, and other Gulf states. These soon started to channel money into Islamic development projects in northern Nigeria.

In 1962 Gumi was a founding member of the Rabitat al-'Alam al-Islami. In the ensuing year he rose in the Rabita to become a member of the Supreme Council for the Islamic University of Medina, where in the 1970s many graduates from Nigeria continued their studies. He also became a member of the World Supreme Council for the Affairs of Mosques and of the Legal Committee of the Rabita. A major success in Gumi's efforts to use Saudi capital (both spiritual and financial) was the reorganization of the hajj. In 1956 Gumi became the first Nigerian Pilgrims' Officer in Jidda; in 1974, Nigerian members of the allegedly heterodox Ahmadiyya movement were finally banned from taking part in the pilgrimage (Loimeier 1988:201ff; 1997a:160).

Efforts to tighten control over mosques in Nigeria misfired, however. In the 1970s not all Nigerian Muslims were prepared to accept Abubakar Gumi's ideas and supreme guidance with respect to administration and organization of their mosques—even when presented as advice of the Supreme Council for the Affairs of Mosques.[8]

In competition with the efforts of Muslim Nigerian modernizers to establish links with Saudi Arabia and the Gulf states, Egypt, which had its own political and religious agenda with respect to African states, also started in 1962 to support the JNI. This took the form not only of funds but also, more importantly, grants for studies at al-Azhar University (Paden 1986:534). In the quest for the diversification of external sources of support, new contacts were continually cultivated. From 1974 on, Sudan, Pakistan, India, and Malaysia also became donors. As Gumi's monopoly of access to external sources of funding eroded, so did his role as a national player.

The assassination of Ahmadu Bello during the military coup of 1966 and the subsequent political rise of the Nigerian army further lessened Gumi's position as spokesman of official Islam in Nigeria. In the years to come, he lost exclusive access to power in Kaduna. Meanwhile, leaders of the Sufi brotherhoods were able to reassert their public influence and to even take control over the management of the JNI in the late 1960s and early 1970s. As a consequence, Gumi was no longer able to rely on the institutions of the state in his efforts to fight the *bida*, the un-Islamic innovations, in the guise of the Sufi brotherhoods. Rather, he turned to other means of struggle: public sermons, pamphlets, and the radio.

Gumi was in fact the first Muslim activist to launch a radio program. In 1967, after five years of delivering a public *tafsir* (exegesis of the Quran) in the Sultan Bello Friday mosque, he began transmitting his *tafsir*s on Radio Kaduna. Only in 1977 did other religious scholars follow suit, with Umar Sanda Idris (1929–2002), a scholar of the Tijaniyya, followed by Dahiru Bauchi in 1980.

As Sufi scholars gained public support through the media, Abubakar Gumi resorted to the establishment of a new Muslim mass organization in his struggle for reform of Islam. Thus was born Izala, under the official tutelage of Ismaila Idris (d. 2000). Headquartered in Jos, with the moral backing of Gumi and massive financial support of local and Saudi donors, Izala was the first reformist mass organization in northern Nigeria to seriously disrupt Sufi brotherhoods, especially the Tijaniyya (Loimeier 1997a:207ff; Kane 2003b). Izala fought against a broad range of customs labeled un-Islamic: innovations, such as amulets; saint veneration; supererogatory prayers; conspicuous consumption; and customary funeral ceremonies. In more general terms, Izala fought against the "esoteric episteme" symbolized in the position of the Sufi sheikh as the mediator between the faithful and the Prophet. Instead, it insisted on direct access to the sources of the faith without an intermediary, on the ritual in its pure and simple form, and a modest style of living.

Izala thus came to represent a new religious option. This one not only broke with established forms of religiosity but constituted a comprehensive socioreligious program. It thereby incarnated the aspirations of a new category of modern educated Muslims in the north who sought theological blessing for a process of distancing from established forms of religiosity and seemingly obsolete forms of ritual.

As a consequence, disputes between Izala and the Sufi brotherhoods were not only expressed in political, social, or economic terms; more important, they diverged on theology. Sound theological argumentation was the precondition for legitimization of the reformist program of Izala as well as the delegitimization of its opponents. Both groups presented their theological positions on radio programs and in public sermons, pamphlets, and programmatic texts. These included Gumi's *al-'aqida as-sahiha bi-muwafaqat ash-shari'a* (The Right Faith According to the Prescriptions of the Islamic Holy Law) and the respective responses of Nasiru Kabara and Sani Kafanga (see Loimeier 1997a). Different schools of *tafsir* that developed in northern Nigeria in the 1970s, representing different readings of the Quran, were also heard.

Until the early 1970s, northern Nigerian traditions of *tafsir* had been dominated by a scholastic *tafsir*. This *tafsir* achieved prominence during the month of Ramadan, when the recitation of the Quran and the respective *tafsir* assumes a particularly sacred character (Brigaglia 2004:125). In Kano, Nasiru Kabara has come to dominate the scholastic *tafsir* of the Qadiriyya: since 1953 he held the Ramadan *tafsir* in the palace of the Emir of Kano.

The Tijaniyya, by contrast, brought forth a number of its own *masu-tafsiri*, masters of *tafsir*, such as Sani Kafanga (d. 1989), Tijani Usman (d. 1970), Dahiru Bauchi (b. 1929), and Ustadh Yusuf Ali (b. 1949) (Brigaglia 2004:132, 153ff). The sacred character of the *tafsir* was abandoned in the 1970s, however, on account of such activists as Gumi and Ibrahim Datti Ahmad. When Abubakar Gumi died in 1992, Lawal Abubakar and Ahmad Muhammad Sanusi Gumbi, today leading representatives of Izala, took over from him in Kaduna; Ibrahim Datti Ahmad and Jafar Mahmud Adam came to represent Izala-ahl as-sunna radio *tafsir* in Kano and Maiduguri since the mid-1990s (Brigaglia 2004:356, 360).

These activists have contributed to the desacralization of the *tafsir* by linking their *tafsir* to religio-political contexts (Brigaglia 2004:127). The exegesis of the Quran has acquired a new direction and an object, and so does the master of *tafsir*, the scholar who presents his interpretation. Dahiru Bauchi, for instance, prefers to use his *tafsir* to fight, with Quranic references, against Izala. He has consequently developed a polemic style that aims to delegitimize his opponents as religious entrepreneurs (Brigaglia 2004:107, 174). The same is valid for the *tafsir* of Abubakar Gumi and, in more general terms, all public *tafsirs*. The burgeoning of radio *tafsirs* in the 1970s has since led to "exegetic duels" (Brigaglia 2005a).

When turning to the development of Izala since the 1970s, we see that their agenda has been dominated by issues of a predominantly national Nigerian social, economic, and political nature (Umar 1988; Loimeier 1997a; Kane 2003b). Only in the early 1990s have local branches of Izala started to develop in neighboring countries, such as Niger (see Charlick's chapter in this volume; Hassane 2002; Glew 2001:99–122; Miles 2003), Cameroon (Adama, interview 2004), and Benin (Abdoulaye 2003). Translocal and transnational affiliations seem to have thus played a comparatively small role for Izala. Ousmane Kane, in fact, describes Izala as a religious movement that was always characterized by its national agenda and its identification with the Nigerian federal state (Kane 2003b:237). It almost seems as if Abubakar Gumi's role as mediator of Saudi Arabian influences was sufficient as an external link for Izala. Indeed, its preoccupation with education and development of a reformed Muslim society in northern Nigeria appears paramount; political questions come second. Izala has thus stuck, so far, to a rather accommodating position in its relationship with the state and has not attacked it as have other Muslim activist groups. This rather quietist political character may be attributed, at least until Gumi's death in 1992, to its seeing itself as a primarily religious and social movement. It worked with the implicit support of state institutions, or at least the support of the political nomenclature of the north. It was not a movement of political opposition.[9]

Izala was thus always willing to tolerate northern Nigeria's conservative political status. It also supported the consolidation of the modernist northern elites, a position that was again compatible with Gumi's close affiliation with Saudi Arabia and its conservative politics.[10] Izala has thus become the most important Muslim movement of religious, social, and educational reform in contemporary northern Nigeria, and a major force of religious opposition to the Sufi brotherhoods. It did not become a revolutionary Islamist organization in political terms.

In the 1980s a number of disputes developed within Izala that eventually led to its disintegration in the early 1990s. These originally stemmed from internal fissures in local branches. In Kano between 1986 and 1988, an influential patron, A. K. Daiyyabu, managed to marginalize the established leadership, as led by Shaykh Sulaiman.[11] Daiyyabu also opposed the policy of economic liberalization of the Babangida government (which was supported by Gumi and Izala leadership). Daiyyabu's authoritarian style led to an internal coup and his deposition in 1990, by the National Committee of Ulama of Izala, as led by Ismaila Idris (d. 2000).

Daiyyabu's downfall did not lead to an end of internal quarrels, however. A number of local branches of Izala increasingly came to reject, in the early 1990s, the National Committee of Ulama of Izala. This they accused of representing the interests of the political authorities and to have lost, under the leadership of Ismaila Idris, its independence. By contrast, a number of local patrons under the leadership of Musa Mai Gandu, the national chairman of the Committee of Patrons, as well as Rabiu Daura, the chairman of the Ulama of Izala of Kaduna State, rejected such political instrumentalizations and supported the political autonomy of Izala. These dissident groups did not dare to attack the government openly. They did, however, start to criticize Ismaila Idris, questioning his sources of wealth. In June 1991 Musa Mai Gandu suspended the leading personalities of Izala in Jos from their positions for embezzlement of funds. He was subsequently counter-excluded by Idris's fraction in Jos. In summer 1991, each group openly campaigned against each other, cementing the split of Izala (see Kane 2003b:218ff). Izala did not recover from these internal disputes until the late 1990s, when a new generation of Izala adherents became eager supporters of the campaign for the introduction of the sharia penal laws in northern Nigeria.

The Activists: The Muslim Students Society, Dawa, and the Islamic Movement

As a consequence of the politically accommodating position of Izala, radical and revolutionary political positions developed in the 1970s in northern Nigeria. These were originally linked with the Muslim Students Society (MSS) and were primarily characterized by their activist attitudes with respect to political issues; socioreligious or economic issues came second. These activist Muslim groups may be seen to represent yet another option, even if their interpretation of Islam was defined by political and ideological considerations. Religio-dogmatic or theological questions were deemphasized, for the sake of political unity of the Muslims. Groups that emerged from an MSS-background were the Dawa group, as led by Aminu d-Din Abubakar; the Umma group (Kane 2003b:79; Ibrahim 1991:115–136); the Brothers (Ikhwan) of Ibrahim az-Zakzaki; and the Islamic Movement, led by Malam Yakubu Yahaya. Both the MSS and the Umma group—as well as the Ikhwan, the Islamic Movement, and Dawa—have rejected the conservative political positions of the Izala and its affiliation with the "corrupt" Saudi establishment. They also condemn the series of corrupt Nigerian military regimes. Since the Iranian revolution in 1978–1979 they have advocated more radical, sometimes revolutionary, political solutions for northern Nigeria. For a long period of time, these groups were confined to the campuses of the universities, in particular, Bayero University Kano, Usman dan Fodio University–Sokoto, and Ahmadu Bello University (ABU)–Zaria.[12] Some of them were stigmatized as "Shiites" on account of their sympathies toward Iran and the fact that the Iranian government actively supported these groups.

Iranian efforts to rally support among Muslims largely misfired, however, in the mid-1980s. War with Iraq, nonimplementation of social reforms in Iran, and massive rioting of Iranian pilgrims in Mecca in the 1987 hajj season led to a certain disenchantment with the Iranian revolution among Nigeria's pro-Iranian radicals. As a consequence, some activist groups turned to Libya, and others to Saudi Arabia. Still others, especially the Muslim intellectuals connected with the Umma group, came to stress the historical legacy of Nigeria's indigenous revolutionary models, notably the Sokoto jihad.

On account of these foreign policy setbacks, Iran changed policies and eventually established a link with a leading scholar of the Tijaniyya, Dahiru Bauchi. Bauchi had become a major spokesman for the hardliners within the Tijaniyya. These not only tried to fight back Izala attacks but also refused to compromise Tijani ideas for the sake of a de-escalation of intra-Muslim religious disputes and Muslim political unity, a strategy that other Tijani scholars such as Ibrahim Salih from Maiduguri had chosen to follow. Since 1988, when Dahiru Bauchi actually visited Iran and gave interviews to *Sakon Islam* (The Message of Islam, an Iranian-sponsored newspaper in Hausa), Iran has diversified its links with Nigerian Muslim groups. Since then, Iranian influence seems to have increased, especially among the younger generation of Muslim radicals, the Ikhwan of Ibrahim az-Zakzaki, and the Islamic Movement of Yakubu Yahaya. For them, the Iranian revolution represented virtually the only Muslim power to effectively resist US imperialism and Westernization. Since the 1990s these groups have been able to garner supporters outside university campuses. This added constituency enabled them to challenge the military regime, beginning with the military governors of some northern states.

Ibrahim az-Zakzaki (b. 1953 in the Kwarbai quarter in Zaria; Loimeier 1997b:5–23; Kane 2003b:95ff) began studying political science at ABU-Zaria in 1976. There, he soon became the local chairman of the MSS and the leading organizer of a number of campus riots in the late 1970s and early 1980s (Loimeier 1997a:298ff). After a return from a journey to Iran in 1980, he became a staunch supporter of the Iranian revolution. As a consequence, his supporters, the Ikhwan ("Brothers"), were labeled by an unsympathetic press Yan Shia, Shiawa, or mini-ayatollahs. Az-Zakzaki, and later Yakubu Yahaya, nevertheless denied any religious connections with

Shiism and stressed that there were "no shiites in Nigeria, but only Islam" (*West Africa*, May 26, 1991; see also Bunza 2005). This statement was supported by Abubakar Gumi, who claimed that the supporters of the Islamic movement were not Shiites but "only admire what happened in Iran" (Sulaiman 1993:11).

Recently, however, some members of the Islamic movement of Ibrahim az-Zakzaki seem to have "converted" to Shiism in religious terms. Bunza (2005), for instance, claims that since the late 1990s members of the Islamic movement have openly acknowledged their "shiite inclination" and celebrate Ashura (i.e., the tenth of Muharram, the anniversary of the battle of Karbala) and Fatima's birthday. They have even started to ritually curse Abubakar, Umar, and Usman, the first three caliphs of Islam before Ali's short reign from 656–661. As a result of the increasing Shiite orientation of az-Zakzaki's group, a faction broke with the Islamic movement and established in Kano the Jama'at at-Tajdid al-Islami (Society for Islamic Renewal).

On account of his radical positions, during his time studying economics at ABU-Zaria, Ibrahim az-Zakzaki was imprisoned several times—in 1980, 1984, and 1987. After his release from prison in 1989 he was put under constant surveillance. Still, he was imprisoned throughout most of the Abacha period (r. 1993–1998). Although since 1987 he seems to have rejected violent means of political struggle, az-Zakzaki is still seen as the mastermind of Nigerian radical and activist Islam (Loimeier 1997a:302). He continues to attack traditional rulers. For instance, he derides the Sultan of Sokoto as Sarkin Gargajiyan Sokoto (*gargajiya* alludes to the un/pre-Islamic character of the kings of Hausaland before the jihad of 1804–1808). He calls for a jihad against the "system" from which every Muslim should withdraw (giving rise to the appellation for his followers as "Yan System"). The appeal to withdraw from an un-Islamic system is publicly represented as a long tradition in Islam, from the Prophet Muhammad to Usman dan Fodio to Ayatollah Khomeini and finally Ibrahim az-Zakzaki himself (Bunza 2004).

Ibrahim az-Zakzaki's major ally, Malam Yakubu Yahaya (b. 1954 in Unguwar Madawaki in Katsina; Loimeier 1997b:16; Sulaiman 1993: 11–12), studied at the Arabic Teachers College in Katsina until 1983. He then joined Ibrahim az-Zakzaki in Kano and Zaria in 1984 established the closely affiliated Islamic Movement (Harakat al-Islam) in Katsina.[13] In the early 1990s the Islamic Movement took the lead in a number of highly politicized conflicts with military governors of northern states. Colonel Madaki in Katsina state was one of them. Due to his authoritarian and rather undiplomatic style of government, Madaki became a negative symbol for the arbitrary character of the Nigerian military regime that the Islamic Movement sought to fight (*West Africa,* September 29, 1991). In the aftermath of a number of violent clashes with the Nigerian security forces in 1990 and 1991, Malam Yakubu Yahaya was imprisoned and sentenced to death. To date, however, the verdict has not been executed.

Serious clashes between followers of the Islamic movement and security forces again occurred in 2002 in the Pindiga emirate of Kaduna state and in Yauri emirate. Under the leadership of Malam Tukur, Malam Abdullahi Bello, Malam Shuaibu Tela, and Malam Abubakar Danfulani, members of the Islamic movement disturbed Friday prayers and abused the traditional rulers (Bunza 2005).

While the Ikhwan and the Islamic Movement have been rather consistent in their politically radical orientation as well as pro-Iranian affiliations, Aminu d-Din Abubakar and the Dawa group present a different picture: Aminu d-Din Abubakar (b. 1947 in the Sheshe quarter in Kano) originally studied higher education at the School of Arabic Studies in Kano in 1967, where he graduated in 1970. For a short period of time he became a student of Nasiru Kabara (see Loimeier 1997a:247–250, 288; Kane 2003b:75ff). In 1971 he started to study at Bayero University Kano, intermittently working as a teacher. He graduated in 1979 with a bachelor's degree. Since 1975 he has acted as tne leading spokesman of the MSS at BUK, and he used to translate the Friday sermon into Hausa. It was during this period of time that he seems to have become familiar with the writings of the Egyptian Muslim Brothers, in particular Sayyid Qutb. Still, like many young Muslims, he was drawn toward the Iranian revolution.

In 1979 he moved to Kaduna, where he came into contact with Abubakar Gumi. The latter apparently convinced Aminu d-Din to change his affiliation. As a consequence, Aminu d-Din Abubakar turned against Iran and accepted, in 1982, Saudi support for the construction of his mosque in Sulaiman Crescent in Nasarawa/Kano. In addition, he became a major leader of the Izala in Kano. He was never, however, as outspoken against the Sufi brotherhoods as were other Izala leaders.

Aminu d-Din Abubakar shifted affiliations yet again, breaking ties in the mid-1980s with Abubakar Gumi as well as the Izala. Though he accepted Kuwait and Emirate support for a short period of time, he rejected that of the Saudis. The organization that Aminu d-Din set up, Dawa, soon became the most important activist group in Kano. It refused to adopt the radical position of Izala toward the Sufi brotherhoods but still propagated and legitimized a reformist agenda. Aminu d-Din Abubakar accepted a number of official positions and in 1983 became principal of the Gwale Arabic Teachers College.

In 1987 he again shifted alliances, this time by establishing links with Libya. Aminu d-Din's biography may be presented thus as a showcase for the rapid change of affiliations and the "games" Nigerian Muslim scholars are willing to play. At the same time, his example shows that Nigerian religious scholars are rather keen on remaining the masters of their own careers. Today, Aminu d-Din Abubakar has become the chairman of the Kano State Hisba Committee, which monitors the implementation of the sharia penal law in Kano state (Peters 2003:49).

The confusing multifacetedness and increasing fragmentation of northern Nigeria's religio-political spectrum was furthered by the emergence of yet another group of militant Muslims. More than any others, these were prepared to resort to violence in their struggle against the Nigerian state. In January 2004 a group of approximately 200 self-styled Taliban followers attacked police stations on the Nigeria-Niger border. In a series of further attacks on police stations in Bornu state in September 2004, the Nigerian army was able to kill 27 Taliban, while some managed to flee to neighboring Cameroon (Brigaglia 2004:240–241; *Süddeutsche Zeitung,* September 25–26, 2004; *informationszentrum dritte welt,* August/September 2004; Paden 2005:170, 187–188).

For sure, violence is a sad part of Nigeria's political culture—and not only in the north, as widespread acts of vigilante terrorism all over Nigeria attest. The Taliban incident, however, shows that northern Nigeria may have reached a new level in the escalation of religio-political violence.

Interestingly enough, the first link between Nigeria and the Taliban was not established in Nigeria but rather in Washington, DC. In April 2002 the Center for Religious Freedom of Freedom House published a paper entitled "The Talibanization of Nigeria: Shari'a Law and Religious Freedom." The paper demonstrated how the example of the Taliban regime in Afghanistan was used by the American Christian political right in a post–September 11 climate of fear to establish an analogy between Afghanistan and the Nigerian political context. In particular, the introduction of the sharia penal laws in northern Nigeria since 2000 and subsequent clashes between Muslims and Christians were interpreted as a gesture of defiance on the part of Muslim extremists—even though most of these conflicts were localized and did not have their origins in religious differences. Indeed, "the vast majority of Nigerian Muslims do not subscribe to extremist ideals and . . . are deeply disappointed with political and religious leaders' appropriation of the sharia agenda" (Human Rights Watch 2004).

It is noteworthy that a considerable number of Muslim-Christian clashes have occurred in one state (Plateau), where sharia was not even applied. Plateau state conflict was mostly linked to disputes over land and access to resources between old populations and immigrant groups. Conflicts in Nigeria, if registered at all beyond the local level, are interpreted in different ways and levels of politics and instrumentalized for a variety of reasons. As a consequence, an economic conflict in a Plateau local government area may assume an "ethnic" character on the Plateau state level and a "religious" character on the Nigerian national level (Loimeier 1992). Conflict in northern Nigeria should thus be seen as an ever-changing cocktail of ethnic, economic, political, and religious motivations that may be easily remixed.

The Clash of Religions

The dynamics of religious and political change in northern Nigeria have not only been influenced by intra-*tariqa* disputes. Nor does the common struggle of the Sufis against the onslaught of Izala tell the rest of the story. Radical and activist Christian (mostly Pentecostal) movements have united under the umbrella of the Christian Association of Nigeria (CAN) to actively and aggressively proselytize in all parts of northern Nigeria. They have been particularly successful in the so-called Middle Belt areas, the territories of the north that had not been central lands of the Sokoto caliphate but that had been used as slave-raiding areas in the nineteenth century. In the twentieth century, the populations of the Middle Belt region continued to feel threatened by claims of political supremacy as formulated by the Hausa-Fulani administrative elites, as well as encroaching Hausa-Fulani settlement. They have consequently joined Christian churches in considerable numbers and thus shaken northern Nigeria's image of being purely a Dar al-Islam. In fact, major areas of the north have become religiously mixed, and some areas in the Middle Belt have become predominantly Christian. Many Muslims consequently fear that their role as the major religious group in the Federation of Nigeria is under jeopardy.[14]

The rise of this interreligious conflict scenario became particularly visible in the Kafanchan riots of 1987, probably the first violent disturbances in northern Nigeria that were interpreted in a Christian-Muslim conflict paradigm as a manifestation of "Muslim jihadism" or "Christian crusaderism" (Loimeier 1997a:295ff; Hock 1996). This Muslim-Christian crusade-jihad conflict paradigm resurfaced more and more frequently in the 1990s and the early years of the twenty-first century with a number of serious riots and clashes in Plateau and Kaduna states. It has brought about the emergence of what Klaus Hock has called an "Islam-Komplex," an almost paranoid obsession that tends to portray Muslims (or Christians, respectively) as the ultimate source of all things evil. It is a syndrome of feeling threatened by the other, and is easily activated in periods of crisis (Hock 1996:6–7).

The refusal of *tariqa* candidates to support Izala candidates (and vice versa) contributed to some spectacular victories of Christian candidates in Muslim majority areas in the 1987 local government elections. This neutralization of the Muslim vote paved the way for Christian majorities in some local councils. As a consequence of these Christian advances, *tariqa* and Izala leaders shelved their disputes and agreed in 1988 to form a coalition of convenience in order to better resist the Christian "crusade" in the north (Loimeier 1997a:308). These alliances of convenience may have led to a considerable pacification of intra-Muslim disputes. Still, they should be seen as temporary, subject to revocation at any time. Change in the political context may again lead to a redefinition of religio-political discourses and disputes. Inasmuch since the 1950s religious movements in Nigeria have become mass movements, they have also become more susceptible to the dialectics of social and political change. This includes the social, political, and economic aspirations of their clienteles.

The rise of activist Christian groups to political prominence has had far-reaching effects on the positioning of the different Muslim factions in the north and a renewed stress on the need to overcome religious disputes for the sake of political unity. Muslim repositioning, expressed in such meetings of reconciliation as between Abubakar Gumi and Nasiru Kabara in 1990, led to the emergence of new Muslim national umbrella organizations. Foremost among these are the Council of Ulama and the Nigerian Supreme Council of Islamic Affairs (NSCIA). These organizations pressed for the "introduction of the Islamic calendar, the establishment of sharia courts of appeal, the introduction of Islamic religious education for all Muslim students and the introduction of Muslim school uniforms" (Loimeier 1997a:310). A group of Muslim intellectuals and functionaries, often affiliated with the Umma group, soon came to dominate these new Muslim bodies. They stressed the unity of the Muslims in the north as a precondition for political success. The constant propagation of the ideal of Muslim political unity has become a major problem in Izala's efforts to fight the Sufi brotherhoods. Religious argumentation inherently implies the othering of Muslim religious opponents as *kafirun* (unbelievers). It has correspondingly strengthened those groups that have always argued in primarily political terms while accepting the basic "Islamic" nature of all Muslims.

In the early 1990s these changes in the religio-political setup of northern Nigeria became even more accentuated, as many representatives of the old generation of scholars, such as Abubakar Gumi, Sani Kafanga, and Nasiru Kabara, died and were replaced by a younger generation of Muslim religious and political leaders who were confronted with a different social, political, and economic context. The return to civilian rule in 1999 after the authoritarian rule of General Sani Abacha (1993–1998), and the rise to power of General Obasanjo, the first Christian from southern Nigeria (Abeokuta) to win democratic elections in the federation (with 62 percent of the vote), forced Muslims in the north to rethink their pattern of internal competition and dispute (Miles 2000). The pressure to achieve Muslim unity was kept alive, at the same time, by activist and radical Muslim groups such as the MSS and the Islamic Movement. These have continued to point out to Muslims that internal disputes, as cultivated by the Izala and the elder generation of Sufi leaders, would lead to *fitna* (strife, chaos) and subsequently support the further spread of Christianity. The shift from intra-Muslim rivalries to a larger conflict between Muslims and Christians is complicated, however, in that religion is not the only motivation for dispute and that questions of land distribution, political rule, and ethnic rivalry continue to contribute to the cocktail of potential conflict.

The "Muslim Internationale"

There is thus a new group of Muslims who have started to move beyond old Sufi-Izala dichotomies by stressing the need for Muslim unity in the face of Christian "crusaderism" in the north. By so doing, they implicitly deprive Izala of their own proper legitimation in their struggle against Sufi brotherhoods. Their most notable leaders are Muslim intellectuals such as Ibrahim Sulaiman (ABU-Zaria), Umar Bello (Center of Islamic Studies, Sokoto), Usman Muhammad Bugaje (Islamic Trust of Nigeria, Zaria), Muhammad Sadiq al-Kafawi (Center of Islamic Legal Studies [CILS]; ABU-Zaria), Ibrahima Na'iya Sada (CILS, Zaria), and Aliyu Dauda and Danjuma Maiwada (both BUK). All are more or less closely affiliated with the Umma movement (see Loimeier 1997a:311; Kane 2003b:79; Ibrahim 1991), in addition to being a younger generation of Muslim students who graduated from northern Nigeria's universities in the 1990s. They have become outspoken local leaders of the MSS and their affiliated organizations. These Muslim intellectuals deemphasize the importance of affiliations with translocal players such as Saudi Arabia, Iran, Kuwait, the Gulf states, Pakistan, Libya, Egypt, and Sudan. Rather, they stress the legacy of the Sokoto jihad as a model for Nigeria's Islamic revolution. Outside support is still welcome, yet the younger generation has not developed particularly close ties with any of these countries. Much more important for the development of Muslim political discourse in northern Nigeria than specific regional affiliations is the development of a "Muslim Internationale."

This has arisen in the context of a number of international conferences organized by Muslim world organizations like the Organization of the Islamic Conference (OIC). One example is a conference on Islam in Africa at the Islamic University of Uganda in Mbale in December 2003. This new form of organization and networking seems to have started with a first Islam in Africa conference in Abuja in December 1989. The Abuja conference attracted numerous delegations from all over Africa. Also in attendance were well-known Muslim opposition leaders and intellectuals, such as Rashid al-Ghannushi from Tunisia, the Sheikh al-Azhar, and delegations from Iran, Saudi Arabia, and Great Britain (Loimeier 1997a:317).

Ties and networks of these Muslim "internationalists" have largely formed in the context of their respective studies at al-Azhar, the Islamic University of Medina, the universities of Khartoum and Umdurman, and the Islamic University of Mbale in Uganda. Teachers from these countries, in particular Sudan, are often employed by the Africa Muslim Agency, a Khartoum-based internationalist Muslim body established in the 1980s and funded by Kuwait. The Africa Muslim Agency has spread rapidly in East Africa and employs teachers from a broad spectrum of Muslim countries such as Morocco, Libya, the Sudan, India, and Malaysia (Morier-Genoud 2002:123ff). Other transnational Muslim organizations of importance for the Nigerian context are the Muntada al-Islami Foundation, the Haramayn Foundation, the International Institute of Islamic Thought, and the World Assembly of Muslim Youth (WAMY) (see Bunza 2004:54). Local and national networks of Muslim intellectuals, linked with local and national Muslim organizations such as the MSS and the Islamic Movement, are also linked globally through the "old boys' networks" of the different universities and colleges.

Networking through academic and bureaucratic institutions is not entirely new to the Nigerian context. Indeed, it began in the colonial period when the first modern Islamic institutes were established. These modern Islamic institutions were closely connected, not only in structure and scope or with respect to their religious and political tasks but also with respect to the personal links that were to develop among the graduates of these institutions. In Nigeria, the first modern Islamic institution was the Northern Provinces Law School (est. 1934 in Kano), which became in 1947 the School of Arabic Studies (SAS). Its purpose was to train teachers, qadis, and clerks for the modern colonial administration, education, and legal services. Beginning in 1954 the SAS offered an expanded madrasa curriculum and developed to become northern Nigeria's first college for higher Islamic education. This was a model for the Sokoto Arabic Teachers College, founded in 1963, as well as a whole series of Arabic colleges established after 1979 in Gombe, Kano, Maiduguri, Katsina, and elsewhere in the north (Umar 2004:99ff).

Modern Islamic institutions of higher learning were also not a purely local, northern Nigerian phenomenon. They followed the earlier, colonial-era development of Islamic institutions modeled on the Bakht ar-Rawda College, established in 1931 near ad-Duwaim (c. 150 km south of Khartoum) in Sudan. The Bakht ar-Rawda College was inspired by still earlier British Indian models of modern Islamic education and professional training. In its turn, the Nigerian SAS served as a model for the establishment of the Zanzibari Muslim Academy, established in 1951, as well as Islamic colleges in The Gambia, Brunei, and Malaysia. A central feature of modern Nigerian institutions was thus the central mediating role of Sudan, first in the form of the Bakht ar-Rawda College and then through the universities of Khartoum and Umdurman, as well as the Africa Muslim Agency, and finally in the guise of Sudanese teachers who came to teach in northern Nigeria or contributed, as directors of schools and in other administrative tasks, to the development of modern Islamic institutions in northern Nigeria. These academic links were cultivated in the context of conferences. In 1960 a first African conference on Islamic education united thus a number of Muslim scholars from northern Nigeria, Sudan, and Zanzibar in Kano to discuss issues of educational reform (Muhammad 1992:6). Since the 1960s, these ties have become an important factor in intra-African Muslim academic networks that have moved today into their second or third generation (Umar 2004:101).

These new forms of Muslim organization on the nongovernmental level have been denounced by Christian organizations as manifestations of an "Islamic threat" or "proof of Islamist internationalist networks of terror." It is a convenient strategy to delegitimize Muslim political positions and discourses in a climate of mistrust and rumor. A few months after the 1989 Abuja Islam in Africa conference, for instance, a fake communiqué from that conference was published. Among other false claims, it said that Muslims would demand that Nigeria be declared a member of the OIC as a "Federal Islamic Sultanate" and that all Western forms of legal and judicial systems were to be replaced by sharia (Loimeier 1997a:318). In an aborted military takeover in April 1990, the coup leaders, mostly army officers of Middle Belt origin under General Gideon Orkar, proclaimed in their radio announcement the "excision of five Northern states, Sokoto, Katsina, Kano, Bauchi and Bornu," from the federation in order to stop the discrimination of the non-Muslim populations in the rest of the federation (*Newswatch*, May 7, 1990).

Muslim-Christian disputes thus characterize the religio-political development in northern Nigeria to a considerable extent. As a consequence, any kind of event is likely to trigger responses in the form of Muslim-

Christian accusations and counteraccusations based on mutual perceptions of marginalization. In such a climate of suspicion, all is necessarily subject to political and religious interpretation. Such interpretations tend to confirm, as a Catch-22, the paradigms of mutual fear of the "other."

By Way of Conclusion: Is Sharia the Solution?

Since 2000, a new field of conflict has been added to the long list of Nigeria's religious and political problems: the introduction of the sharia penal law to twelve of the northern states.[15] The announcement to introduce the penal laws of sharia by the governor of Zamfara state, Ahmad Sani Yerima (an ABU graduate and a supporter of the Izala movement and, more recently, of the Ahl as-Sunna group), on October 27, 1999, and the enactment of the new and "complete sharia" legislation in Zamfara on January 27, 2000, set off a wave of enthusiasm for sharia and forced other politicians to follow suit. Yerima was presented as a hero, supposedly reestablishing, 100 hijri years after the end of the Sokoto empire (1320, or in modern style, 1903), the rule of Islamic law. The introduction of sharia penal law was supported by a plethora of Muslim groups and organizations and a majority of the Muslim population of northern Nigeria.[16] They saw in the introduction of sharia a chance to reestablish justice where all other systems of law had failed (Last 2000:141, 149).

According to Murray Last, the introduction of sharia penal laws can be seen as a form of decolonization of the legal system and a return to a system of law as recommended by God. At the same time, it was seen by the population as a way to fight corruption and bad government, immorality, and ostentatious wealth: sharia was a new option when all others had failed (Last 2000:141).

However, the introduction of the sharia penal law has been criticized by a number of Muslim personalities and organizations in northern Nigeria. These critics include those with a record of opposition to the northern Nigerian religio-political establishment since the 1970s. They also number those who fought, for different reasons, against the religious and political program of the Izala (Danfulani 2005:28, 49ff). Ibrahim az-Zakzaki, for instance, argued that inasmuch as it was politically motivated and not introduced in a proper Islamic way, the introduction of sharia was illegal (Brigaglia 2004; Bunza 2004:61; see also interviews with Ibrahim az-Zakzaki in *This Day,* March 14, 2000, and *Africa Today,* December 1999). This argument was shared, if for different reasons, by Dahiru Bauchi, leading scholar of the Tijaniyya Sufi brotherhood, and a number of Muslim women's associations, such as the Federation of Muslim Women's Associations in Nigeria (FOMWAN) and Women in Nigeria (WIN) (Paden 2005:125f).

When looking at other opponents of the introduction of the sharia penal laws, we encounter other familiar faces. One is the Sultan of Sokoto, Alhaji Muhammad Maccido, who had replaced the controversial former sultan, Ibrahim Dasuki, a close associate of Abubakar Gumi, who had been deposed in 1996 by the military government (Loimeier 1997a:324). Sultan Muhammad Maccido remained conspicuously neutral in 2000 when the sharia penal laws were introduced in Zamfara state. All he said was that "adequate enlightenment on sharia should have been carried out by its proponents before its full adoption" (Danfulani 2005:28, 52). Bala Usman, a leading representative of a Marxist tradition of thought at ABU–Zaria, rejected the introduction of the sharia penal laws. So did Sanusi Lamidu Sanusi, an outspoken Muslim intellectual (Ben Amara 2005:67ff). Baobab, a women's rights group in Lagos led by Ayesha Imam, also weighed in (Mahmud 2004:88; Peters 2003:49).

The introduction of penal law in Zamfara state (incidentally, Abubakar Gumi's state of origin) added to existing anxieties among the non-Muslim populations of the north, particularly in those states, such as Kaduna and Niger, where Christians formed a considerable part of the population. These anxieties were fed by the fact that the most outspoken supporters of the introduction of "complete sharia" were well-known members of the northern political and economic establishment. It was they who had influenced the political and economic development of the north from the 1960s until General Obasanjo's accession to power in May 1999. Among them were former presidents Shehu Shagari and Muhammad Buhari; JNI leader Usman Jibrin; secretary-general of the Nigerian Supreme Council of Islamic Affairs (NSCIA) Alhaji Lateef Adegbite; and wealthy businessmen Alhaji Ahmed Chanchangi, a well-known patron and financier of Izala and relative of the former Sultan of Sokoto, Ibrahim Dasuki (Danfulani 2005:28, 66; Loimeier 1997a:227). Backing by these politicians supports the claims of those who argue that the introduction of the sharia penal laws has essentially been a political maneuver as well as highly unconstitutional.[17]

The impression that "complete sharia" is instrumentalized for many purposes is supported by the fact that a number of Muslim groups seem to see the introduction of sharia penal law as a chance to enforce, as Yan Hisba (vigilante groups controlling the implementation of sharia regulations), their own concepts of Islamic law and order, often in a rather arbitrary way.[18] The actions of the Yan Hisba have in fact opened a wide field for the misuse of power that has led to recurrent civic dispute, killings, and riots in the Middle Belt areas and Christian diasporic communities in the far north.[19] Since the introduction of the sharia penal laws, at least ten people have been sentenced to death (even if only few cases, such as those of Amina Lawal and Safiya Hussayni, have gained international notoriety), dozens have been sentenced to amputations, and floggings have been a regular occurrence (Human Rights Watch 2004:2). Defendants usually have no access to legal representation. Badly trained judges of quickly established lower sharia courts (formerly the area courts) often fail to inform defendants of their rights, and they even accept confessions extracted under torture. Almost all the convicted are poor and often female, with little knowledge of legal procedures in general and sharia penal laws in particular. According to many Nigerian Muslims, these trials violate the principles of sharia itself (Human Rights Watch 2004:2).

With the obvious misuse of sharia, Muslims have started to complain about the biased nature of verdicts. These seem to clearly disadvantage the weak and poor, and to violate one of the basic, popular assumptions in the context of the introduction of the sharia penal laws—namely, that all Muslims, including the rich, would be punished on equal terms. As a result, many Muslims have started to say that the sharia penal laws in application today are not sharia proper but political sharia. They furthermore point to the politicians' failure to implement those economic and social reforms that would alleviate poverty in northern Nigeria (Human Rights Watch 2004:4)

By 2005, the application of sharia penal laws seemed to have lost steam. Although sharia penal laws remain in place in twelve states, no other state has introduced them. Political will to enforce sharia penal laws is waning, especially when it comes to the application of the *hadd* punishments.[20] With one exception, all death sentences as well as numerous other verdicts for criminal offences as imposed by lower sharia courts have been cancelled by sharia courts of appeal for procedural reasons (Human Rights Watch 2004:4f, 25ff). Of dozens of amputation sentences, "only" three have been carried out, and none since mid-2001.[21] Even cases of Yan Hisba harassment seem to have decreased, perhaps because male adulterers now visit prostitutes in nonsharia states or have acquired Christian identities (and identity cards) in order to be able to drink alcohol (Last 2000:143; Human Rights Watch 2004:79).

As a result, a majority of Muslims now think that sharia may no longer be a viable option. A local Muslim voice from Kaduna asserted that "Muslims are fed up with sharia." At the same time, Muslims were ashamed to say, "We don't want sharia. . . . Challenging the government is like challenging Islam. . . . There is a fear of being misunderstood, so people keep quiet. They would be seen as blasphemous" (Human Rights Watch 2004:89).

In sum, Nigerians have become disillusioned with the way in which sharia has been implemented so far. The state governments of the north that introduced sharia are increasingly perceived as not being sincere in application. Religion is transparently instrumentalized for politics. Even religious scholars who had originally supported the introduction of the sharia penal laws turned against the way in which they were applied in 2003:

> The penal code of Northern Nigeria was working well until some states like Zamfara began agitating for sharia. Their motives were purely political. It had nothing to do with religion. The real needs of the people are health, education etc. The politicians did nothing about that. Instead, they made a big fuss about sharia. There is manipulation by politicians. . . . The call for sharia contributed to violence and social tension between Muslims and non-Muslims, and even among Muslims themselves. (Human Rights Watch 2004:90, 94)

Will it be possible to either abolish, suspend, or amend sharia penal laws? Or would it be advisable to improve the training of judges in lower sharia courts and improve legal procedure?[22] The first initiatives to amend sharia penal laws were initiated in March 2002 by the attorney general of Nigeria and minister of justice, Kanu Agabi (Human Rights Watch 2004:101). Nonetheless, the federal government has been so far reluctant to interfere directly in sharia states lest it antagonize the Muslim electorate in the north. These voters had contributed considerably to the victories of President Obasanjo in both the 1999 and 2003 presidential elections.

At the same time, politicians and state governments of the north still see sharia as a way to increase political legitimacy. Some politicians, such as Ibrahim Shekarau of Kano, were able to win elections in 2003 for being "more principled" than their predecessors or other state governors with respect to the implementation of both full sharia and popular welfare programs. "Saying no to implement sharia would have constituted political suicide" (Human Rights Watch 2004:92). Sharia has become a symbol of identity of the Muslim north. Northern Nigerian Muslims feel they should not sacrifice it to national and international pressures or "Western values."

Sharia has thus become a symbol of resistance to the encroaching Westernization of northern Nigeria. According to Nafiu Baba Ahmed, the secretary general of the Supreme Council for Sharia in Nigeria, "the introduction of the sharia shows the yearning of the people. They are not happy with having a foreign system imposed on them." A Yan Hisba leader from Kano added, "We have our own value system and religion. Just because the west doesn't agree, it doesn't mean it's wrong" (Human Rights Watch 2004:103).

Under these circumstances, it seems as if sharia will stay for some time and remain a platform for the negotiation of religion and politics.

Last but not least, the sharia debate seems to have led to yet another turn in the dialectics of religio-political development in northern Nigeria. A younger generation of Izala seems to be mobilizing for the implementation of the sharia laws through different Yan Hisba groups (Brigaglia 2004:243). Particularly outspoken and active among the diverse Yan Hişba groups is the Ahl as-Sunna movement. These are young, radical Muslims who were socialized as members of Izala in the 1980s. After the death of Abubakar Gumi and the split of the organization in 1991–1992, they regrouped under this new name, meaning People of the Sunna (Kane 2003b; Brigaglia 2004).

Members of the Ahl as-Sunna movement still maintain some tenets of the Izala, such as the struggle against *bida*, yet they are careful to stress the need for Muslim unity. They consequently put great emphasis on the struggle for the implementation of the sharia penal law (Kane 2003b; Brigaglia 2004). The link between Izala and pro-sharia politics seems to be most clear in Zamfara state. The governor of this first sharia state, Ahmad Sani Yerima, was closely associated with the Izala (Brigaglia 2004:244). In Kano, this link is not as evident, as the local Izala groups seem to have been marginalized in the early 1990s as outsiders and disparaged as *yan shege* (bastards). Their radical religio-dogmatic positions were nevertheless adopted by the local Ahl as-Sunna as it emerged from the Dawa group of Aminu d-Din Abubakar.

The Ahl as-Sunna in Kano could thus be regarded as the localized and more respectable manifestation of the Izala. But it is still closely linked to the implementation of the sharia. Ahl as-Sunna leaders Yakubu Musa, Ibrahim Datti Ahmad, and Ustadh Jafar Mahmud Adam are in the forefront of Yan Hisba activities, even as they continue to fight against the Sufi brotherhoods.[23] The struggle for the implementation of the sharia penal law must be seen thus as a discourse reflecting essentially local, northern Nigerian preoccupations and agendas. At the same time, the struggle for the implementation of sharia penal law seems to have stimulated the emergence of a new generation of Izala in the guise of an Ahl as-Sunna movement more at home with local dialectics of development than international agendas.

Over the past two hundred years, the scope of options among different models and translations of Islam in northern Nigeria has undergone considerable enlargement and diversification of scale. Yet none of these different realizations of Islam has yet produced a convincing political model. Recurrent experiences of instrumentalization of religion for politics have had a sobering effect on a growing number of Muslims; the sharia debate is but one recent example. In the end, Muslims in Nigeria may reach a stage of complete disillusion with respect to the different models of political Islam offered by disparate social, religious, and political forces. Ultimately, they may turn to societal models that are less defined by religion than by economy.

Notes

1. According to Philipps (1985:44), "Islam . . . was accepted [by the late eighteenth century] by all, even by those who never practiced it, in the sense that they believed in its power and sought its blessing in such forms as amulets and charms."

2. For a recent presentation of these old translocal links see Reese (2004); older studies are Haarmann (1998) and an-Naqar (1972). The term *translocal* is used here to refer to the networks of religious scholars or movements that in discourse as well as agency do not necessarily refer to a state or nation (such as Nigeria) but rather stress religious or ideological links beyond state and nationality while transcending purely local orientations.

3. For the development of the pilgrimage in northern Nigeria, see Loimeier (1988).

4. The inclusion of Ibrahim Niass shows that the Rabita was always prepared to sideline dogmatic considerations for the sake of political interests.

5. The Jam'iyat ad-Da'wa al-Islamiyya was set up in 1972 as a Libyan Islamic World Organization that would be able to counterbalance corresponding Rabita activities. For more on the Jam'iyat ad-Da'wa al-Islamiyya, see Mattes (1986).

6. These policies of modernization were also reflected in local poetry. See Umar (2002:96).

7. For the development of the Kaduna mafia, see Takaya and Tyoden (1987).

8. For the development of the Rabita, see Schulze (1990).

9. The Izala were indeed tolerated and even actively supported by both the Shagari (1979–1983) and Babangida (1985–1993) administrations and experienced adverse treatment only during the short regime of General Buhari (1984–1985). See Kane (2003b:208–210).

10. Abubakar Gumi's political positions were formulated clearly in a famous interview with Gaskiya Ta Fi Kwabo in 1982 in which he made clear that in order to consolidate the paramount political role of Muslims in Nigeria, Muslim women had to be mobilized for the next elections. Moreover, he famously declared, "politics was more important than prayers" (*siyasa tafi muhimmanci da salla*); otherwise Christians would come to dominate the federation. This statement made clear that Gumi foresaw Muslims in power in Nigeria in 1982. Accordingly, he saw no need for Muslim political opposition (Loimeier 1997a:166–167).

11. For Daiyyabu's career, see Kane (2003b:112ff).

12. Ahmadu Bello University (ABU)–Zaria has been, since its founding in 1962 as the first university in northern Nigeria, a fertile breeding ground for all

kinds of radicals, both religious and political. It was the first platform for well-known Marxists such as Bala Usman and later, as we shall see, Muslim activists like Sheikh Ibrahim az-Zakzaki.

13. An important branch of the Islamic movement was Sokoto. There, two religious scholars who had formerly been affiliated with Izala, Sheikh Abubakar Jibrin and Sheikh Abubakar Tureta, joined Ibrahim az-Zakzaki in the early 1980s. The two sheikhs were able to gain control over the most important Izala mosque, Farfaru. Meanwhile, followers of Izala under the leadership of Sheikh Sidi Attahiru Ibrahim (Sokoto) had to resettle in a new mosque on Ali Akilu Street (see Bunza, 2005). Sidi Attahiru soon broke with Izala and established his own organization, called Ahl as-Sunna (People of the Sunna). It failed, however, to gain more than regional importance. As a result of these internal disputes, Izala was seriously weakened in Sokoto state (Loimeier 1997a:241).

14. Pentecostal activities are also seen by some mainstream Christian observers as a threat to the political and religious stability in northern Nigeria. See Danfulani (2005:54–55).

15. Zamfara (January 2000), Niger (spring 2000), Sokoto (spring 2000), Gombe (May 2000), Kano (June 2000), Kebbi (July 2000), Jigawa (August 2000), Katsina (August 2000), Yobe (August 2000), Bauchi (February 2001), Bornu (June 2001), and Kaduna (November 2001, yet only confined to Muslim areas). Four other states were preparing sharia penal codes of their own but have not enacted them so far. For an extensive presentation see Peters (2003), Last (2000:142–152), and Human Rights Watch (2004). Journalistic sources consulted on this and other dimensions of political Islam in Nigeria include iz3w (*informationszentrum dritte welt*), *Newswatch*, *Süddeutsche Zeitung*, *This Day*, *The Pen*, and *West Africa*

16. Other aspects of sharia, in particular, Islamic personal law, had always been in force in northern Nigeria in colonial as well as postcolonial times. Only Islamic penal laws were abolished or modified by the British after 1903.

17. The constitutionality of the sharia penal laws will not be discussed as it does not directly concern our argument here. Also, the issue has been discussed extensively by Peters (2003), Ostien (2003), and Human Rights Watch (2004).

18. The Yan Hisba (from the Arabic root *hisba,* i.e., examination, control) were usually legitimized by a reference to Quran 3:104, which calls on each Muslim to "enjoin what is right and to forbid what is wrong."

19. For Yan Hisba activities, see Human Rights Watch (2004:16ff); for an extensive overview of the events as such, see Peters (2003:51ff) and *informationszentrum dritte welt* (August/September 2004:14–15). Riots first occurred in Kaduna and Kano in February 2000, followed by Gombe in May 2001, Bauchi and Jigawa states in June and July 2001, and Kaduna in 2002. For an extensive account of the Kaduna riots, which resulted in hundreds of deaths, see Danfulani (2005:17ff) and Peters (2003:54ff). See Peters (2003) and Human Rights Watch (2004) also for a detailed account of verdicts under sharia penal law.

20. *Hadd* (pl. *hudûd*) punishments are the punishments for those crimes that are explicitly mentioned in the Quran: extramarital sex (*zina*; punishable by flogging or death by stoning), robbery (*hiraba*; death by hanging, amputation, or banishment), theft (*sariqa*; amputation), false accusation in a case of zina (*qaf*; flog-

ging), apostasy (*irtidad*; death), and the consumption of alcohol (*shurb al-khamr*; flogging). In northern Nigeria, apostasy is not acknowledged as an offense according to the sharia penal laws. For an extensive discussion, see Peters (2003) and Ben Amara (2005).

21. By 2005, only one case of a verdict of amputation for theft had reached the Federal Court of Appeal (FCA). FCA is the first non-Islamic level of appeal beyond the upper sharia court of appeal, and it is the last level of appeal before the Supreme Court.

22. The Human Rights Watch report on the application of Islamic penal law in northern Nigeria contains a list of recommendations for the resolution of the political crisis in Nigeria. See Human Rights Watch (2004:6ff).

23. In 1987 Sheikh Jafar Mahmud Adam from Bornu won the Nigerian national Quran memorization competition. He then went to Saudi Arabia to continue his education, returning to Nigeria in 1996 before leaving again, this time to study in Sudan. He finally established himself in both Maiduguri, his hometown, and Kano, where he became both the imam of the Dorayi mosque and leading representative of the Ahl as-Sunna. Ibrahim Datti Ahmad (b. 1962) is a medical doctor and the imam of the BUK Friday mosque. In the 1980s he was a presidential candidate. In addition, he heads the Supreme Council for Sharia in Nigeria, established in 2000. Adam and Ahmad take turns performing radio *tafsir* in Kano (Brigaglia 2004a:153, 360; Brigaglia 2004b).

4

Mali: Accommodation or Coexistence?

VICTOR LE VINE

CONTEMPORARY MALI, THE EARLIEST CENTER OF ISLAMIC LEARNING IN SUB-Saharan Africa, has remained a secular nation-state, demonstrating an interesting synergy between postcolonial ideologies and traditional religious authority. Like its two predecessors, and despite the fact that about 90 percent of the country's population is Muslim,[1] the constitution of its "Third Republic" proclaims the state to be "democratic, laic, and social."[2] The First Republic, led by its socialist president, Modibo Keita, took pride not only in the country's secularism but also, during the late 1960s, in its increasing ideological tilt toward Maoist China. Modibo[3] was ousted in November 1968 by a military junta led by Moussa Traoré, who within a year had himself installed as president of Mali's "Second Republic." Traoré cast aside Modibo's socialist trappings, but instead of moving toward some sort of Islamic republic, as several of the country's prominent religious leaders had demanded, he retained the country's secular vocation. Traoré, who turned out to be even more autocratic, corrupt, and detestable than Modibo, was himself removed by a coup in March 1991, to be followed by the country's first democratic multiparty elections in June 1992, a new popularly elected president (Alpha Oumar Konaré), and the (still secular) constitution of the "Third Republic."

It is not that Modibo, Moussa Traoré, or their successors deliberately disregarded Islamic interests in their regimes or were themselves unbelievers or unobservant Muslims; not so: both Modibo and Traoré were practicing Muslims (though not ultraorthodox), but as Modibo chose to subordinate religious observance to socialist zeal, so Traoré chose defense of his secular prerogatives as ruler over the political challenges of the country's religious establishments. Modibo, in fact, even distanced himself from the antireligious doctrines of his Marxist models, choosing to include Islam within his party's program, claiming that "There is no religion more socialist than the Moslem religion" (Hazard 1969:2).[4] That effort (and his occasional hymns of praise for Malian tradition and faith) had no payoff for him; the country's religious leaders, while having no hand in his ouster or calling for it, nevertheless "gradually and unanimously withdrew their support from his regime" (Clark 1999:163).

Even Moussa Traoré, not known for his piety but who apparently sought the sympathy of Mali's religious leaders by giving his regime a veneer of religiosity, appeared at the second of his two trials ostentatiously clutching a large Quran to his bosom. (The gesture availed him little, as he was again convicted of crimes committed during his tenure as president.)[5] And Alpha Konaré and Adamou Toumani Touré, respectively the Third Republic's first and second presidents, themselves observant Muslims, apparently chose to uphold the country's secular constitutional tradition rather than open the door to unpredictable (or perhaps unmanageable) religious contestation if openly confessional parties were allowed onto the electoral lists. Thus, in conformity with Article 28 of the Constitution, which mandates that political parties "must respect the principles of national sovereignty, democracy, territorial integrity, national unity, and secularism [*laïcité*]," no religious parties were formed or contested the 2002 presidential and national legislative polls, or the 2004 local elections. However, despite the absence of religious parties, the 2002 elections marked the active, open entrance of Muslim leaders, marabouts, and imams onto the political stage as partisans for the first time in over forty years.

All this notwithstanding, the religio-political challenges of the country's several Islamic doctrinal/ideological strands remain as more or less permanent features on Mali's political landscape—as they have since the country's independence in 1960, and before. By and large (with the possible exception of the chimerical Tuareg Islamic state of "Azawad"[6] and some recent incidents of communal violence) those challenges have been peaceful and within the framework of Mali's traditions of pragmatic inter- and intrareligious and mosque-state relations. However, the recent appearance on the Malian (as on the larger Sahelian) scene of more militant and aggressive Islamist elements has generated some apprehensions that Mali's secular and pragmatic democratic vocations may be in danger (ICG 2005a; 2005b). I will broach that development later in this chapter; first, however, some background on Islam in Mali is needed to set the stage.

The Spread of Islam in Mali and Its Latter-day Effects

By general agreement among the most authoritative historians of Islam in Africa, Islam came to the region that is now Mali during the latter seventh and early eighth centuries when the Arabs began and completed their conquest of north Africa. At first the agents of that penetration were traders and travelers; they were subsequently followed by missionaries, by themselves or as members of nomadic or immigrant populations, armed sects or brotherhoods, or conquering armies. The general outlines of the penetration needs no rehearsal here; there is ample literature on the subject. What is important for the purposes of this chapter, however, are two aspects of equal importance to the politics of modern Mali: first, the appearance of states and leaders that became icons—part of the founding myth—of the modern history of the country and of Malian political identity; and second, the early development of the traditions of religious tolerance that have become important keys to Mali's contemporary political life and its democratic vocation.[7]

First, the name Mali itself. It was hardly accidental that the Mali Federation, effectively a merger of Senegal and the former French Sudan, was so named. (Originally Upper Volta—today's Burkina Faso—and Dahomey—today's Benin—were slated to be members, but they backed out.) According to William Foltz, it was Leopold Sédar Senghor, the poet-president of Senegal, who "himself proposed the name . . . thus reviving Soudanese memories of their exalted past, memories kept alive in the folklore and songs of the extended Mande linguistic family" (Foltz 1965:104). Foltz added that "In one sense this was a major personal sacrifice for the Senegalese leader, for it gave added personal prestige to Modibo Keita, who has some claim to be a lineal descendant of Soundiata Keita, the founder of the Mali Empire, and who adopted Soundiata's personal motto, 'Death rather than Dishonor,' as his own" (Foltz 1965:104).[8]

When the federation broke up in 1960 after only sixty-three days of existence, it was almost inevitable that Modibo would name his federal state "Mali" (he had first called it the Sudanese Republic). Senghor's feelings about the collapse of the federation aside, his gift proved a munificent one, at least for Modibo and Mali, for Modibo had thus recaptured for himself, and for his country, the extraordinary symbolism of the old name and his (putative) association with its past glories. There was more: Sundiata and his conquest empire, which only became Muslim during the late thirteenth century, nevertheless owed a great deal to the cultural and administrative gifts of local Muslims and opened the door to penetration of the faith, a history that arguably found its distant echo in the "one faith" element of the national motto. By adopting the name, Modibo not only nominated himself to the ranks of Mali's heroic historical icons—for example, the Malinké Keita royal lineage was Muslim, and Modibo was presented as the "father of the country"—but also, by implication, placed the country among the constellation of Muslim states.

In 1965, during a brief stay in Bamako, I was allowed to look through a collection of primary and secondary school textbooks, in particular those that dealt with Malian history and "civic instruction," that is, citizenship training. Not surprisingly, the books, for both primary and secondary levels, devoted many pages to singing the praises of Modibo Keita and reciting his deeds and genealogy; they also dwelled at length on the three great medieval conquest empires in the Western Sudan, Ghana (sixth–late eleventh centuries), Mali (1230–ca. 1400), and Songhay (ca. 1485–ca. 1592), plus the two others that arose during the nineteenth century led by El Hadj Omar (1854–1864) and Samory Touré (1879–1898).[9] The books also lavished praise on an array of iconic national heroes; not only Modibo Keita but also Sundiata, celebrated in D. T. Niane's epic as the model of the triumph of good over evil; Mansa Kango (Kankan) Musa, the legendary Malian emperor whose golden pilgrimage to Mecca so astonished the Arabs; Askia Mohammed, emperor of Songhay, whose series of jihad*s* spread Islam over the growing expanse of his empire; and El Hadj Omar Tall and Samory, nineteenth-century jihadists and military opponents of France's empire-building campaigns in the Western Sudan. Reportedly the current crop of school books cover much the same ground, propagating an ever-growing list of national heroes, including contemporary leaders supposedly descendants of Sundiata—that is, of course, Modibo (despite his fall from power and mysterious death in 1977), plus (in 2001) former prime minister Ibrahim Boubakar Keita and former president Alpha Omar Konaré.[10]

Ghana remains in the pantheon of Mali's historical icons, despite the fact that the name was appropriated for modern Ghana, because at its apogee (mid-eleventh century) it gained renown for being the center of the West African gold trade and extended from the Niger River into Senegal, and because it was the first of the Sahelian medieval empires to become Islamized, albeit by the invading Almoravids, a militant eleventh-century sect originating on the banks of the Senegal River.

It is no surprise that Mali, like many new states in Africa, went about reconstructing an heroic past for itself, borrowing freely from its real and mythical past. What is interesting is that that project, notwithstanding the country's ostensibly secular vocation, deliberately included—and includes—so much reference to Islam, as a model of governance (Sundiata), as a regional power, as a proselytizing influence, and as a cultural icon, all themes with clear reference and relevance to the contemporary political scene.

Are Cultural Pluralism and Tolerance Aspects of Mali's (Historical) Political Culture?

An often overlooked fact about Mali's history is that it was not until the twentieth century that Islam became the religion of most Malians, spreading from the northern and central Islamic strongholds to mostly southern rural populations—to "pagans," animists, adherents to traditional cults and religions, Christians—all long resistant to Muslim proselytization. Even some central towns were part of that trend. For example, Nicholas Hopkins, reporting on his research in Kita, in southwestern Mali (ca. 100 miles west on the Bamako-Dakar rail line), notes that its "pronounced Muslim character" was a "fairly recent development," citing Maurice Delafosse to show that in 1912 the Kita administrative *cercle* (district) as a whole was just over 1 percent Muslim and estimating that though there had always been Muslims in residence, the town itself "must have [then] been 15 to 20 percent Muslim" (Hopkins 1972:52–53). Also, Richard Warms, writing about the district and town of Sikasso (in southeast Mali), makes much the same point, though he puts the period when large portions of the local population began to embrace Islam as toward the end of the nineteenth century and the beginning of the twentieth (Warms 1992: 489–491, passim).

All this may certainly attest to the tenacity with which non-Muslim populations in Mali clung to their traditional beliefs, but it may also be evidence of long-established patterns of pragmatic, peaceful coexistence by whose rules the dominant Muslim rulers of the region kept the allegiance and cooperation of subordinate, historically conquered non-Muslim peoples –the jihads of Askia Mohammed, El Hadj Omar, and Samory notwithstanding. The historical record supports both propositions.

The leading historians of the western Sudan appear to agree that Islam, when it first appeared, was brought by traders and missionaries, and when it was adopted by the rulers of the three great medieval empires, it remained very much an elite cult, practiced by the ruling class but not enforced upon the subject populations.

In Ghana, before it was conquered by Almoravids, who presumably had strong ideological incentives to spread the faith, the pace of Islamization proceeded slowly among the pagan populations and tended to stress the cultural, rather than the purely religious, aspects of Muslim life. (Not so with the Almoravids, whose conquests northward to the Maghreb took on a much more militant, even jihadic, character as they sought to stress the stricter mandates of their leaders' teachings. It was the Almoravids, more than any other factor, that accelerated Muslim conversion in Ghana.) According to Nehemia Levtzion,

> In Ghana, the Muslims lived under the auspices of a non-Muslim king who invited Muslim traders to the capital and employed literate Muslims in his court. According to the geographer al-Zhuri, writing in 1137, the people of Ghana converted in 1076. This must have happened under the

> influence of the Almoravids. . . . In 1154, according to al-Idrisi, Ghana was a Muslim state and still among the most powerful in the Western Sudan. (Levtzion 2000:65)

However, as Muslim as Ghana became, the patterns of rule and the spread of Islam followed paths of gradual influence, which itself turned out to be the template for subsequent expansion. As Levtzion observes (of Ghana and later, Mali),

> [The Arab historian] Al-Bakri's account, like other traditions, emphasizes the rulers as early recipients of Islamic influence, and therefore also the importance of kingdoms in the process of Islamization. Indeed, Islam did not penetrate into segmentary societies even when and where Muslim traders and clerics were present. . . . The common people, even when integrated into the new states, did not undergo radical social and economic changes that called for a readjustment of religious life. Their way of life remained harmonized with the rhythm of the traditional religion: its fertility rites, ancestor worship, and supplication of the deities. (Levtzion 2000:66)

In his discussion of phases of Islamization in Africa, J. Spencer Trimingham summarizes the character of Islamic diffusion during the 1050–1750, period (involving Ghana; Mali, and Songhay), which he characterizes as "slow and largely peaceful":

> The feature of this period is the adoption of Islam as a class religion—the imperial cult of the Sudan states like Mali Kanem as the cult of the trading and clerical classes. Just as various religious strata existed side by side in the mosaic of Sudanese religion, so when Islam came on the scene there was no feeling that it was incompatible with African religious outlook, and, strange as though it may seem, Islam was incorporated into the Sudanese religious scheme. Religious life was characterized by accommodation, or more correctly, by a dualism or a parallelism of the old and the new—the African idea of the harmony of society maintained itself against any idea of Islamic exclusiveness. Consequently, Islam's elements of challenge to traditional life were largely neutralized. (Trimingham 1980:100)

During the next period, from 1750 to 1901, which saw the emergence of theocracies and states in which Islam was the state religion and jihad a frequent form of state and imperial expansion, enforced Islamization in what is today the Malian realm tended to sweep up members of outlier Islamic cults and brotherhoods, close down fissiparous groups, and establish increased elements of Islamic practice such as observance of Muslim holidays, establishment of *kadi* courts in all larger towns, and the opening of religious schools throughout the state. Otherwise, the old patterns persisted, despite the militancy of the new rulers. To be sure, the pace of Islamization increased everywhere in the Malian region, but again, not yet to the point when the majority of the population turned to Islam, which happened during the twentieth century.

There is much more to this point. For example, John Hunwick states that the accounts of the great Arab traveler Ibn Battuta, who visited Mali in 1353 during the reign of Mansa (King) Suleiman, "show clearly that while Islam was firmly established at the time, the ruler also respected local custom with a remarkable tolerance. Indeed it seems clear that he dealt with his non-Muslim subjects in quite a traditional fashion, at the same time observing Islamic festivals and religious practices" (Hunwick 1965:119). Traditional practices like prostrating oneself before the ruler and covering the head with dust "persisted side by side with typically Islamic ceremonials. Just as Ibn Battuta was shocked by the fact that young women walked naked in the streets while taking food to the sultan during Ramadan so was the North African theologian Al-Maghili shocked to learn that girls customarily went naked until the time of marriage in the city of Jenne until the fifteenth century" (Hunwick 1965:120).

The point, of course, is that at least until the latter part of the nineteenth century, Islam tended to be considered more as instrumental to effective rulership than as a matter of conviction. The evidence certainly permits the conclusion that the *mansas*, emperors, kings, and other rulers of the western Sudan saw Islam as an elite culture worth supporting and practicing because it provided a pole of popular obedience and a set of tested organizing principles, both of which enhanced their authority and scope of action as rulers. Moreover, such observance and practice of Islam permitted wide latitudes of tolerance and useful syncretisms with traditional observances and beliefs, thus adding to its attraction. Finally, it also stands to reason that this long history of Islam/state cohabitation and tolerant rulership became part of what Malians came to expect of all their rulers, be they Muslim or not, religious or secular in orientation. What the French acquired, then, were time-tested elements of a Malian political culture that allowed them a surprising amount of latitude in using Malian talent to construct their (French) version of the conquest state.

France and "Accommodation" in the Western Sahel

Starting from their bases in Senegal, in twenty years—between 1880 and 1900—the French completed their conquest of what became French West

Africa, and in particular, the Sahelian expanse from Senegal to Chad. Propelled by a febrile nationalism inspired by the humiliating French defeat at Prussian hands in 1871, French naval officers (at the time, the navy was in charge of France's colonies), leading columns composed mainly of African levies, headed east, sweeping all resistance before them, determined to help give France the empire that would guarantee its return to world-power status. The African opposition, from both chiefs and peoples, was often ferocious and sometimes protracted, but in the end, the Tukulor empire of Ahmadou, son of its founder, El Hadj Omar; Samory and his conquest state, who resisted the French advance for seven years; the sultan of Zinder; the Damel of Cayor (Senegal); and others all fell to the superior firepower of the French, helped sometimes by a "divide and conquer" strategy whereby local chiefs or *almamys* were persuaded to join the French against their particular enemies.[11]

With Mauritania yet to be pacified, the defeat of the Mahdist adventurer Rabeh of Bornu-Sudan at Koussouri (today on the Cameroon side of the Chari River, then near or on Lake Chad) on April 22, 1900, marked the end of France's West African conquests. Besides capturing one of the largest territorial empires ever put together (combined, French North Africa and French West and Equatorial Africa comprised about 90 percent of Africa's northwestern quadrant), what in fact did France acquire, particularly in West Africa and the Malian domain?

In French West Africa (formally constituted in 1895) the French found themselves masters of a population of somewhere between 8 and 12 million, already depleted by years of war, disease, and the slave trade. By 1925, when the first reliable official demographic data appeared, it had grown to about 13.5 million, which suggests that the lower estimate is closer to the actual figures.[12] Establishing administrative systems, pacifying the die-hard remnants of the Tuareg and Timbuctu resistance (Boni 1971:183–194), and taking sociodemographic and economic stock ranked high as items on the early colonial agenda. Also, and more pertinent to this discussion, in Mali, Niger, and Chad the French faced the problem of dealing with substantial Muslim populations, many of whom had been involved in resisting the French advance or lived in areas or communities where the memory of resistance was still fresh.

Among other political assets, the French were informed by their experiences in Senegal and (later) in Mauritania, where after overcoming local resistance to the occupation, they came to a variety of accommodations with the leaders of the Sufi brotherhoods—*tariqa* (plural, *turuq*)—notably the Tijaniyya, the Qadiriyya, the Hamawiyya, the Hamaliyya, and the most difficult to win over and eventually the most durable as an ally, the

Muridiyya.[13] One notable convert to accommodation was the Tijani leader Malik Sy, who by 1912 came to advocate complete allegiance to France and its colonial regime. In an unsolicited text (or so the French claimed) that was widely circulated, Malik Sy advised as follows:

> Support the French government totally. God has given special victory, grace, and favor to the French. He has chosen them to protect our persons and property. That is why it is necessary to live in perfect rapport with them. . . . Before they came we were living in enslavement, murder and pillage. Muslims were no better than infidels on that point. Had they not come we would still be in that state. . . . Know that the French have given great assistance to our religion and to our country. The Intelligent will understand that.[14]

The French also had the use of what Donal Cruise O'Brien calls "the Algerian model":

> The French authorities in Algeria, France's first African colony, were by the mid-century discovering the uses of Sufi brotherhoods in a variant of administrative 'indirect rule'. . . . The Algerian model was then to be of great significance in the establishment of France's sub-Saharan administrations at the end of the nineteenth century. The colonial government, in tacitly recognizing the Islamic brotherhoods for reasons of administrative expediency, in order to collect the necessary impositions (in blood, sweat, and taxes) without undue disturbance of the peace, also helped to alter the basis of Sufi authority. The cohesion of reputedly loyal brotherhoods was reinforced, while the reputedly disloyal were pursued and chastised. (Cruise O'Brien 1988:20–27, passim)

"Pursued and chastised," it must be added, by both the enforcers within the brotherhoods and by the French, if that disloyalty was also seen as a threat to the colonial regime. To be sure, such cooperative activity tended to be limited, that is, focused on the major brotherhoods and their leaders, but it did have wide impact across the expanse of France's Sahelian domains. It must also be added that however cooperative became the religious leaders in Senegal, Mauritania, and the Sudan, French rule had its harsh side, particularly when it came to levying troops (for service in Europe during World War I), recruiting forced labor for public works, collecting duties and taxes, imposing the special colonial legal system (the *indigénat*), and removing uncooperative chiefs and local rulers. To be sure, Africans often found ways to evade or avoid the more odious impositions, or to manipulate French colonial officers to their ends, but there was usually no way around the occupation or its strictures.[15]

In any case, it remains that the French occupation, for all its harsher aspects, actually served Islam—without intending to do so—by generating a cascade of conversions throughout the French western Sudanese territories, an observation convincingly argued by Mervyn Hiskett and other scholars of the area (see Hiskett 1984:276–301 and Clark 1999). Colonial modernization, by Hiskett's estimate, resulted in many more conversions in some seventy years of colonial rule than had occurred in the area during the nine preceding centuries (Hiskett 1984:181, Cruise O'Brien 1988:14).

Besides the cooperative leaders and marabouts of the Sufi brotherhoods (in Mali, particularly those of the Tijani *tariqa*), who were encouraged to recruit new members by a colonial administration that admired their ability to command absolute obedience, the vectors of the wave of conversions, and of French-African cooperation, included

- The construction of roads and railroads, notably the Dakar-Niger railroad, which connected coastal Dakar to Bamako and the Niger River and facilitated the spread of the new administrative arrangements
- The opening (with French blessing) of numerous Quranic schools (madrasas) by local *tariqa* teachers
- A much more rapid exchange of people between Muslim and non-Muslim areas, as well the transport of goods and services between the coast and interior
- The return and dispersion of West African troops (many of them veterans of the famously misnamed *Tirailleurs Sénégalais*) to the interior after World War I, many of whom had been converted while in the service, and who brought back both Islam and (often) politically and religiously radical perspectives on France and Frenchmen.[16]

Then there was the surprising (to the French) fact that many of France's new wards in the region actually saw French rule as less restrictive and onerous than that of the Umarian and/or Samorian states, and thus gave at least nominal obedience to the new occupiers.

There had also been an important shift in French attitudes, which initially had been hostile to Islam and suspicious of the motives of Muslim leaders. Having just finished fighting jihadist forces and meeting with fierce resistance all the way, at the beginning of the twentieth century the French were in no mood to tolerate religious opposition, tending to see sedition and conspiracy behind every unfamiliar Muslim bush. Here, the work of such scholar-administrators as Maurice Delafosse and Paul Marty was crucial in changing the perspectives of French public opinion, the colonial ministry in Paris, and the West Africa administration. Delafosse and Marty, the most influential of the several such researchers sent into the African field to assess the ways and moods of the conquered peoples, wrote extensively (according to Clark)

> about the Muslim brotherhoods in Senegal and the French Soudan as forces for peace and stability rather than resistance . . . [and] generally viewed the large brotherhoods rather favorably. The French also openly endorsed the Muslim leaders they controlled and gave their sanction to succession decisions. Thus, individuals acceptable to the secular state continued to lead the Tijaniyya in both Senegal and the French Soudan. . . . As long as the marabouts instructed their followers to work and cooperate fully with the secular state, the administration did not interfere in religious matters. Brotherhood leaders likewise did not interfere in political matters and decisions. Each group had its own separate interests, yet most often concerns and interests of the political and religious authorities converged.[17] (Clark 1999:158)

In sum, once the remaining resistance had been crushed, the French found the occupation much easier to impose than they had expected, in part because they could enlist both compliant religious leaders and sentiments of accommodation in their cause.

Transitions: French-Muslim Relations Toward and at Independence

The distinguished French colonial administrator Robert Delavignette, who had spent many years in French West Africa and the Cameroons between 1927 and 1946, in one of his many books on his experiences in service devoted numerous pages to a view of colonial rule that emphasized the need for a firm and pragmatic but respectful relationship with native institutions and beliefs (Delavignette 1950). In effect, he advocated and practiced "accommodation," and in fact frequently used the term itself in his essays about colonial administration. Delavignette was a worthy successor to Maurice Delafosse, linguist, ethnologist, and colonial administrator who died in 1926, a year before Delavignette took up a post in Senegal, and who had gained renown for his many excellent studies of West African peoples and cultures. Delafosse, like Delavignette after him, was a practicing exponent of accommodation.

Delavignette undoubtedly represented the best of French policy toward West African Islam before and after World War II, and his departure from the scene—as of most French officials and *commandants de cercle* (district officers) from Senegal, Mauritania, Mali, Upper Volta, Niger, Cameroon, and Chad—marked the coming of independence and the transfer of state-Islam relations to African hands. Such practices, administrative mores, and colonial adaptations of local political cultures as had been more or less part of the long-term relationships between Islam and the state under the French rule were now the charge of the new—and usually unpredictable—African regimes, to keep, change, or eliminate.

For all that, however, the latter part of the colonial period had also brought some highly significant changes (under French law) to the region's Muslim populations—as it did to all the others. Excepting the citizens in the *Quatre Communes* of Senegal (who became citizens during the 1840s), they were now "citizens," not subjects, and could give their civil allegiance(s) as they chose; they could (again excepting the *Communes*), and did, vote for representatives who could speak for their concerns, an extraordinary departure from the codes of obedience that bound most of them; their religious leaders found their way onto institutions of governance (local legislatures, local councils, and the like), or into official positions (judges, teachers, mayors, councilors, high-level civil service jobs); old institutions like slavery and forced labor had been largely abolished, and individuals could now move, sell their labor, seek schooling, and marry as they saw fit. The authorities now gave considerable latitude to the formation of new associations, including religious ones, something that had been difficult to do without official sanction. By 1960, when most Francophone West African territories became independent, it was expected that most of these changes, plus the guarantee of *laicité* (all of which represented radical departures from the old colonial ways and relationships), would also find their way into the new states' constitutions and laws, which is what happened.

Islam and the New Mali, 1960–1992

Though Mali's 1960 constitution promised democratic governance, as was noted earlier, it took some thirty-one years for that promise to be fulfilled. Modibo Keita equated his brand of socialism with democracy; however, there was never any question that the hard-line Marxist regime he operated was only rhetorically democratic and socialist, by proclamation in the ideology and doctrines of his single mass party, the Union Soudanaise–Rassemblement Démocratique Africain (US-RDA). Communist in all but name, operating upon Modibo's command, the US-RDA and its official governmental siblings ruthlessly suppressed all opposition, to the point of murdering the regime's most prominent critics, razing villages whose elders were guilty of dissent, and eventually, in 1968, activating a 3,000-man "Popular Militia" on the model of China's Red Guards, in effect to punish alleged "counter-revolutionaries" and terrorize the countryside.[18] It remains, however, that Modibo took care not to antagonize the country's religious leaders, even (as noted earlier) finding ideological consonance between African Socialism and Islam, all for good reasons. For one, Modibo's US-RDA party drew much of its support from the Malinké ethnic areas, the base of the ancient Mali empire and core of the Tijani *tariqa*. "In a sense," writes Irving Markovitz (1977:159), "the strategy of the Union Soudanaise was to create a coalition between the descendants of the Malian and Songhai Empires previously dominant in the area." Here is Modibo in 1961, offering praise of Mali's "unique" traditions in a speech to the graduates of the first accelerated national journalists' class:

> What is the basis for the bloody evolution that characterizes the history of other continents? It is the existence of feudal systems that ravaged the people and found accomplices in feudal religious orders which rendered them apathetic and insensitive. . . . We had feudal systems [in Mali], but they were unlike those of the past. Feudalism here (one can say) presented itself as more humane, even close to being democratic! . . . It is the same with religion. Here there never were, nor are, feudal religious [orders] seeking to plunge [the] people into the kind of lethargy that permits their exploitation.[19] (Keita 1962:10, my translation)

The point is that however strongly committed Modibo was to creating a Soviet-style African Socialism, he had to deal with a society that was still largely traditional in its social and religious orientations, and consequently had to tread carefully in pushing his regime's centralizing efforts in the Malian hinterlands. For another, as Kenneth Grundy observes, "The Malians place great faith in the efficacy and adaptability of socialism to the African milieu. In theory, African Socialism is simultaneously a modern approach to economic problems and a continuation of the traditional way of life. It is the adaptation of the 'existing cooperative tendency to [a] modernized structure'" (Grundy 1964:177).[20]

Note that "adaptation" and "cooperative" are the key words here; in sum, the older state-Islam accommodation patterns, developed over time and reinforced by the French, carried over without serious change into the new era. Andrew Clark is to the point:

> In both Senegal and Mali, colonial policies toward Islam, which had proven effective and durable, continued after independence. The secular

> state, which had to consolidate its power among the brotherhoods' leadership and their followers, did not interfere in religious matters and avoided antagonizing such a key constituency. Political authorities continued to encourage certain festivals and traditions, including local pilgrimages within the countries. Secular and religious education remained separate, and Arabic language instruction was offered in the public schools. Political and religious leaders gave their mutual sanction to any leadership change. (Clark 1999:160)

The new accommodation between Modibo's regime and Islam, as it turned out, broke down as Modibo's Marxist economic experiment failed and the country suffered from the US-RDA's heavy-handed attempts to coerce loyalty, enforce unworkable centralization, and mobilize peasants and youth for make-work infrastructural improvement projects, the so-called Human Investment (*Investissement humain*) and Civic Service (*Service Civique*) campaigns. In the end, the marabouts and other religious leaders withdrew their support and, at least initially, welcomed the coup that removed Modibo from power on November 19, 1968. As for Modibo, he was arrested on the day of the coup and held in detention until early 1977, dying suddenly on May 16, 1977, under what are still suspicious circumstances (Imperato 1989:69, 154; Imperato 1986:172).

Moussa Traoré understood that Modibo had failed to craft credible working relations with the country's religious leaders, and for that reason Traoré not only actively courted them but also strove to portray Mali as a Muslim country with a secular vocation that could also continue to cherish Muslim practices and traditions. Over time, and particularly during Traoré's second term in office, his regime became increasingly repressive, including making attacks on religious leaders, whom he came to see as threats to his rule. Some marabouts fled the country, and others were coerced into silence. In the end, as they had with Modibo's regime, almost all religious leaders withdrew their public support, and when Lt. Col. Amadou Toumani Touré and his cohort of seventeen officers staged their coup on March 26, 1991, the imams and marabouts joined in the public acclaim over the change.

Islam in the Return of Democracy

A military seizure of power with the express purpose of restoring civilian rule and democratic governance is rare enough; in fact the coup led by Amadou Toumani Touré was only the second such intervention in independent Africa.[21] Moussa Traoré had promised reforms leading to civilian rule and had in fact undertaken a number of steps in that direction, but then turned the other way to tighten his rule and clamp down on the opposition. If Toumani Touré and his officers are to be believed, that, and pro-democracy demonstrations in Bamako and elsewhere late in 1990, persuaded them to act. In any event, within four months of the March 1991 coup, Toumani Touré and his Transitional Committee for the Salvation of the People (CTSP) had organized a "Sovereign National Conference" that led directly to a new democratic constitution, the country's first genuinely free national elections, and, in May 1992, the presidency of Alpha Oumar Konaré.[22]

Under the regimes of Modibo Keita and Moussa Traoré, Mali's religious leaders gave occasional, limited endorsement of government policies but, following the well-trodden paths of earlier accommodation with France, kept their distance from power and tended to avoid open participation in official mobilizing campaigns. "Nous avons cultivé nos jardins" (we cultivated our gardens) is how one Malian religious leader, obviously referring to Voltaire's *Candide*, put it after having been asked about enlisting in Modibo Keita's Service Civique.[23] In effect, it was not cohabitation but a kind of wary coexistence with cooperation only when it was unavoidable or too costly to refuse. Such Islamic associations as operated did so locally, except for their primary national spokesgroup, the Association malienne pour l'unité et le progrès de l'Islam (AMUPI—the Malian association for the unity and progress of Islam), formed in 1980. At all events, this stance changed radically after the Toumani Touré coup and promulgation of the new guarantees—written into law by the (January) 1992 constitution and the electoral statutes—of political pluralism based on democratic participation.

For one thing, the transition to democracy triggered an extraordinary explosion of associational activity, including a variety of explicitly Muslim groups and organizations. Zeric Kay Smith, who tracked the number of civic associations officially registered with the Malian government, reported first a fourfold jump, from 81 (during 1980–1984) to 345 (during 1985–1989), to a startling 2,449 during 1990–1994 (almost 31 times the 1980–1984 figure), all the more remarkable in light of the fact that it took some fifty-six years to reach the 81 figure (Smith 1996).[24] There is no accurate count of the number of Malian associations with explicit religious or semi-religious purposes (almost all Muslim), but one official source estimated that by the end of 2005 approximately 10 percent of the combined national-level and local groups fell into that category, and that within the body of the 1,800 participants in the July–August 1991 Malian National Conference, there were forty-two registered political parties and 100 associations. Among these associations, at least ten represented religious interests (Counselor, interview

2005). Since 1990 at least 150 Muslim associations with national reach have been formed, of which twenty-one had registered voluntarily with the government by 2000 (Agence France Presse 2002).[25] By the beginning of 2002 Bamako also had a privately owned Islamic radio station offering both religious and nonreligious programming, including open criticism of government policies, something no earlier Malian regime would have tolerated. All this testifies to what amounts to not only an extraordinary efflorescence of Muslim associations but also the multiple appearances of Muslim social and political voices, both of which continue to this day. However, it was the series of six elections during 1991–1992 and, most important, the 1992 and 2002 presidential elections, that marked the emergence of Islamic groups onto the visible, active national political stage.

Various sources (some official) claim that Mali now has eighty political parties, more or less, none of which (by law) explicitly represent religious, ethnic, or social interests. Nineteen registered political parties ran candidates in Mali's January 1992 municipal elections, a number that grew to thirty-three entered for the 2004 communal polls. Twenty-three parties contested the February/March 1992 National Assembly elections, of which eleven won seats (sixteen gained seats in 2002), and there were nine main presidential candidates for the April 1992 elections, representing nine parties and factions (Vengroff 1993; Electionworld.org 2005).

The April/May 2002 presidential elections, won by Amadou Toumani Touré, were contested by eight main candidates representing five main parties. In January 2002, in order to contain the growing force of the Muslim associations and channel the increasingly audible voices of criticism from the mosques, the government convoked hundreds of Muslim leaders to Bamako's Palais des Congrès convention center and established the High Islamic Council (HIC) to represent both the older AMUPI and the new associations. The HIC did help keep the Islamic community more manageable, but only partially so because the religious leaders understood what the government wanted and were determined to maintain as much independent space as possible. Thus, the criticisms in the Friday sermons continued, AMUPI declared itself neutral in the presidential elections (and was thereby rewarded with a seat on the National Electoral Commission), and a collective of some twenty Muslim associations declared its support for the former prime minister, Ibrahim Boubakar Keita—though on its face, Keita's party, the Rally for Mali (Rassemblement pour le Mali) did not present a particularly Islamic face to the electorate. At the April 26 (Friday) prayers, particularly in Bamako, there were numerous calls from the pulpit to vote for Keita and to demand greater application of Islamic law in Malian life, all of which (according to a French observer on the scene) appeared to have generated some nervousness in government circles (Mayer 2002). Though Ibrahim Keita won only 20.7 percent of the votes in the first (April) round and did not proceed to the second (in May), the marabouts, imams, and almamys declared themselves satisfied with this first, and unprecedented, sally into national politics.

To be sure, the Islamic voice had made itself heard, and there were now doors to the corridors of power that had not existed before, all of which had been accomplished without major violence and more or less within the parameters of the enduring Malian traditions of tolerance and accommodation. However, coming into the new millennium, the overall picture of intra-Islamic and state-Muslim relations had become more complex, shaded, uncertain, and even at several junctures threatening to the general peace to which Malians had become accustomed since the beginning of the colonial era.

The New Malian Picture: Neither Accommodation nor Coexistence?

Arguably, the advent of Malian democracy owes a good deal to the larger contexts in which it occurred: the demonstration effect of the "redemocratization" tide in Africa, led by Benin in 1990; the larger (Huntington's so-called) Third Wave of democracy sweeping over both Africa and Latin America; and the electric calls for democratic change issued by a France celebrating the two-hundredth anniversary of its revolution (see Le Vine 2004:241–270).[26] Be that as it may, it remains that Moussa Traoré may have read the democratic handwriting on the Malian wall when he opened its doors to oppositional politics (and Konare's ADEMA) in 1990, and that the extraordinary surge of associational activity that erupted following the 1991 coup had been building up at least since 1989, if not earlier. Moreover, the collapse of the Traoré regime, followed by the trials of Traoré, his wife, and a number of henchmen, did not unleash general vindictiveness and demands for revenge against the former regime. To put it simply, because both the Modibo Keita and Moussa Traoré regimes had avoided creating widespread intrareligious and interethnic animosities, Mali may have preempted the kind of bloodletting that followed regime changes in neighboring states such as Guinea, Liberia, Sierra Leone, Mauritania, and Burkina Faso. Mali may have been lucky, but it stands to better reason to argue (as does Timothy Docking) that the "success" of Mali's democracy is in considerable measure due to its political culture, in which traditions of tolerance, pragmatic accommodation, and religious syncretism prepared the way for a democratic pluralism nurtured through many years of avoiding zero-sum confrontation. Docking identifies "a rich network of [similar] traditional associations" among Fula (Fulani), Mandinka, and Bambara peoples as undergirding Malian democracy: for example, the groups

> found within Bambara culture form a complex political structure which is infused with two of the key ingredients of all stable democracies: popular participation and political accountability . . . For today, village life among the Bambara and other groups in Mali is still organized by robust associational and political structures. . . . These village institutions still flourish across Mali and help to create an ordered and pluralistic system of local governance. (Docking 1998:205)

Add to this the fact that Islam appears to sit lightly on most village shoulders; recent long-term visitors to Mali report that villagers spend little time on Muslim practices, including the obligatory prayers, and observe important religious holidays or celebrations only when it suits them (O'Brien, interview 2005).[27] Of course, it is possible that outsiders fail to understand the routines of village life and the extent to which Islam has been adapted to indigenous forms of politics, but it does appear that those who are more public in demonstrating their faith may do so because that is appropriate for people of wealth or status or authority. Such people, moreover, would not think of reminding others of their religious obligations.

By and large, then, Islam and democracy have found a relatively frictionless relationship in the post-1991 political environment, due in part to a poliucal culture already accustomed to pragmatic state-religion accommodations and in part to leadership on both sides willing to work within such frameworks. Nor have those traditions found expression only in relation to religious issues: it is a tribute to Mali's democracy, and to its traditions of accommodation, that the Tuareg crisis of 1990–1991, which threatened to undermine, if not destroy, the new democracy, was dealt with by a set of solutions that not only brought the Tuareg into national decisionmaking circles but also gave them a measure of hitherto unreachable autonomy (see Seely 2001).

Given what Malian society brought to the table by way of national identity, traditions of tolerance and religio-political accommodation, and associational pluralism, there was every good reason why the new democratic experiment should succeed, and for the past fourteen years, it has. Yet there is also an obverse to this coin, and it has begun to shred the margins of the state-religious relationships on which, in part, Malian democracy rests. In form, it is the several challenges posed by the stricter forms of Islam, such as the local variant of "Wahhabism," by the growing presence of militant groups like the Groupe Salafiste pour la Prédication et le Combat and Dawa, and by the violence introduced by jihadist groups from the north and east. These challenges and intrusions have been sufficiently worrisome for the Malian government to seek assistance from abroad and for the possibility of activity by terrorist groups to have been raised. A word about each of these issues is in order.

Challenges and Intrusions

The Wahhabis, who briefly operated a school—the Subbanu madrasa—in Bamako in 1949 (shut down by the French authorities in 1951), are part of a broader movement, the Salafiyya, Muslims who promote a return to the original beliefs and practices of the *salaf*—the "founding fathers" of Islam—that is, the Prophet Muhammad and his immediate successors. What worries Malian Sufi religious leaders and the government is not only the extent of Wahhabi conversions (especially among the ranks of educated members of the Malian elite—professionals, civil servants, businessmen) but also the group's history of violence, manifest in conflicts between 1952 and 1957 with traditionalist groups in Bouaké, Kankan, Sikasso, Bamako, and other localities.[28] Even more troubling and of immediate concern is another Salafist organization whose cells have become active in Mali, the transnational Groupe Salafiste pour la Prédication et le Combat (the Salafi Group for Preaching and Combat), usually known by its French acronym, GSPC.

The GSPC broke away from the Algerian Groupe Islamiste Armé (GIA) in 1998, remaining one of the two main fractions of the GIA to continue armed struggle against the Algerian state after the GIA itself was suppressed. "The GSPC . . . were . . . pushed by Algerian security forces into the southern desert [of Algeria], and from there into northern Mali. The GSPC is the only organized, violent Islamic group that can be said to have operated in the four Sahelian countries" (ICG 2005a:7), that is, Mauritania, Mali, Niger, and Chad. Operating in the inhospitable Mauritania-Mali, Mali-Algeria, Mali-Niger, and Niger-Libya-Chad border areas, the GSPC has been involved in violent confrontations with the government forces of the four Sahelian states and Algeria, hostage-taking, attacks on trans-Saharan truck convoys, and the widespread two-way trafficking of cigarettes, fuel, arms, and humans. The GSPC's record for destructive activity is highly varied: notably, in 2004, the GSPC abducted thirty-two Europeans who were touring the desert and border areas of southern Algeria. It eventually released them in Algeria and Mali following reports that ransom had been paid. "In 2003–2004, the GSPC was active in Mali as far south as the region near Lere, by the right-angle of the border with Mauritania, to the extent that the route of the 2004 Paris-Dakar rally had to be changed" (ICG 2005a:28). During the first four months of 2002, some thirteen deaths were registered from clashes on the Niger-Mali border (apparently involving GSPC and allied fighters), "in the course of razzias and kidnappings by armed bands traveling on camel-back," according to an official communiqué (Holzbauer 2002; IRINnews.org 2005a). Some of this activity is carried on solely by GSPC members, and others (such as raids on truck convoys, kidnapping, and smuggling) are in league with other nonreligious and nonpolitical groups (armed gangs and bandits like the mysterious MBM—the initials of its leader, Mokhtar Belmokhtar) operating in the no-man's-lands of the border regions. While the GSPC is not overtly anti-Sufi, were it not for its shadowy links to another Salafist missionary organization, the international Jama'at al-Tablighi and to Osama bin Laden's Al-Qaida, the GSPC's religious challenge to Malian democracy could be dismissed as minimal (which, by itself, it is), and the GSPC, as a criminal enterprise, left to Mali's police and security organizations. In effect, the GSPC operates on the illegal and socially unstable margins of Malian society, recruiting for both its criminal and ideological activities, dangerous both to the Malian polity because of its predatory activities and to the Malian Islamic establishment because it represents itself as an outlier of disaffected, radical Islam. That brings us to the Tablighi and Al-Qaida.

The Tablighi, better known by its iconic motto, Dawa (Call and Preaching), is present in more than 100 countries (including all four Sahelian states) and claims over three million adherents, making it the world's biggest Muslim missionary society. Its roots are in the Deobandi (India-Pakistan) ultraconservative Muslim tradition, becoming, to all intents and purposes, the Taliban version of the faith. It requires its members to travel both around and beyond their own countries, preaching door-to-door, seeking not so much to gain converts from other faiths but to bring endangered souls back to the pure roots of Islam and save them from unbelief, corruption, and the errors of unchecked interpretation of holy texts. Like the Wahhabi, the Tablighi condemn the Sufi reverence for marabouts and saints, the practices associated with local pilgrimages, and the adherence to the *tariqas*' particular—and by Tablighi definition, close to blasphemous—religious texts. Unlike the Wahhabi, however, the Tablighi keep their voices down and seldom enter into doctrinal disputes with non-Tablighi Muslims. In the Sahel, it claims to respect marabouts and local elders and tradition, seeking to blend into the local social landscapes—though that has been difficult, given its missionary zeal and practice of retreats, which (it is claimed) often draws men from other social obligations. Overall, the Tablighi have been law-abiding citizens and, in the opinion of most Malians, good neighbors. However, it is the way they go about their proselytization, as well as their relationship with the GSPC, that has given rise to concern in official circles. Active in the Sahel since 1992, the Tablighi appear lately to have concentrated much of their missionary activity in the Malian north, particularly targeting the Tuareg cadres, the former leadership of the 1990–1991 Tuareg rebellion. According to the International Crisis Group (ICG),

> Western as well as Malian intelligence services are convinced that the Tablighi have specifically targeted former cadres of the rebellion and the political hierarchy of [the town of] Kidal. . . . The [Tuareg] Ifoghas fraction that rules Kidal has almost entirely converted to the Tablighi "way," known locally as the *Da'wa.* Kidal's mayor is Tablighi, as is the traditional leader, Intala. The former head of the Tuareg rebellion, Iyad, has become the spiritual head of Mali's Tablighis and spent six months in 2004 in Pakistan on a Tablighi retreat. (ICG 2005a:17)

It is not unreasonable to surmise that the Malian authorities, who keep a close watch on the Tuareg, wonder why the Dawa would focus on the Tuareg leadership if not to plant the seeds of a new rebellion. So far (by mid-2005) the Tuareg have shown some inclination to start rebelling again, but overall, there is evidence that instead, Tuareg bands have moved increasingly into smuggling, trafficking, and kidnapping activities, reportedly in frequent collaboration with GSPC elements. Kidal is also awash with guns from the local gun running, another good reason for official worry. The ICG states that "as much as 80 percent of the goods for sale in Kidal reportedly come from Algeria. All diesel fuel comes from there and costs between 250 and 400 CFA francs per litre, depending on the season" (ICG 2005a:19).

Finally, there is the Al-Qaida connection, which the Sahelian governments, including Mali's, took seriously enough to accept a US antiterrorist program, the so-called Pan-Sahel Initiative discussed in Chapter 1, by which the United States since 1996 undertook to help train local militaries and security elements in counterterrorist operations, provide logistical assistance to the initiative, and consult with the governments involved about the best measures for their individual and collective security. The Al-Qaida connection, for one, appears in the wider activities of Dawa members arrested for terrorist activity on behalf of Al-Qaida (Richard Reed, the "Shoe Bomber"; Jose Padilla, being held for trying to buy materials for a "dirty bomb"; John Walker Lindh, the "American Taliban"; and the "Lakawanna six," Yemeni-

Americans who participated in Al-Qaida training in Afghanistan and traveled under Tablighi auspices). Then there is the late Malian head of the GSPC, Hassan Hattab, considered a close friend of Osama bin Laden. The GIA probably became an Al-Qaida affiliate in 1992, and it was in 1997 that Al-Qaida, dissatisfied with the GIA, contacted Hattab and convinced him to form a separate organization, which became the GSPC. Hattab was removed as head of the GSPC in 2004 and reportedly killed by his successor, Nabil Sahroui, who has made no secret of his affiliation with Al-Qaida.

Whether all of this amounts to a genuinely serious challenge to the generally manageable state-Islam relationships in Mali—taking into consideration the occasional round of intrareligious violence and intense religious debate in Bamako, Kankan, or Gao—is not clear, but there is and has been certainly enough to have frightened the Malian government into accepting outside help in controlling the new religio-political elements on the scene. What may have also happened is that wary accommodation, the longtime hallmark of state-Islam relations, may have begun to metamorphose into a kind of coexistence. It is still respectful, one hopes, and supportive of both mosque and state. Perhaps neither wary accommodation nor coexistence describes what may be a newer, less stable set of relationships among the several Islamic groups and persuasions. Nor may the relationship between the old Sufic orders and the newer Muslim arrivals on the scene be captured by either term. In the end, it is not inconceivable that both Mali's tradition of mutable Muslim (and ethnic) identities and Mali's new democracy and Malians' strong sense of Malian identity could, perhaps, help forge a newer set of accommodations among the contenders for religious primacy.[29]

Attitudes die hard, as demonstrated by the persistence of domestic slavery, especially among the resident and border Tuareg in the more remote parts of Mali. There may still be somewhere close to 20,000 persons held captive in Mali.[30] Even more difficult to suppress is the barely concealed trafficking of women and children to Mali's neighbors (including Mauritania and Niger) for sexual exploitation, forced mining, and other domestic, agricultural, and commercial labor. Slavery and human trafficking represent not only part of the vulnerable moral underbelly of Malian society, and Malian Islam in particular, but an insidious danger to the country as a whole. Though the Malian government acknowledges the presence of slavery and trafficking, it remains that these are issues usually discussed *sotto voce* in Malian society—when they are discussed at all—and only reluctantly with outsiders; thus kept largely out of public view and discussion, such semi-silence encourages impunity by the slavers and traffickers, not to speak of the official corruption these activities engender. In the end, of course, it will be both Mali's traditions of accommodation and its young democracy that will suffer.

Notes

1. The estimated population of Mali is 13 million. Some 90 percent are Muslims, 1 percent are Christians, and the remainder belong to traditional religious groups (Central Intelligence Agency, *The World Factbook 2004*; US Department of State, *International Religious Freedom Report 2003*, "Mali"; *Jeune Afrique l'intelligent*, "L'Etat d l'Afrique 2005," hors-series #8, Paris: Jeune Afrique, 2005). These percentages are reasonable approximations at best, there being at present no full and reliable religious census for Mali.

2. Article 25 of the constitution adopted by referendum on January 25, 1992. *Laïc* is usually translated as "secular." The formula—of French derivation—appears in the country's earlier constitutions, as it does in other sub-Saharan francophone African constitutions (except Mauritania and the Comoros, both of which proclaim Islam to be the state religion). Although the state is *laïc* by vocation, Islam appears in the Malian constitution by indirect reference (Art. 25 specifies the official motto to be "Un Peuple, Un But, Une Foi"—one people, one goal, one faith), and by reference without being so named on the official coat of arms, which includes the motto and a representation of the great mosque in Djenné. Though the constitution guarantees freedom of religion—a guarantee presently observed in Mali—there is little question that the document and its ancillary symbols also single out and (by implication) defend Islam as the main faith of the country.

3. "Modibo" is how Modibo Keita was popularly mentioned during his tenure as president, and I use that convention here. Malians appear to like contractions, and (according to Jennifer Seely) customarily speak of "IBK" for Ibrahima Keita and "ATT" for Amadou Toumani Touré. Since most readers of this chapter are not familiar with Malian locutions, I use the longer forms.

4. Hazard quotes Modibo's June 30, 1962, speech to the National Assembly. I've taken the liberty throughout this chapter to call Modibo Keita by the familiar "Modibo," by which he was known throughout Mali. To refer to him as "Keita" would only confuse matters: Keita is a Malinké royal line, and literally thousands of Malians have Keita as a family name. For reference to another of Modibo's encomiums on Malian tradition and faith, see Keita (1962).

5. Traoré and his wife had both been condemned to death (Traoré in 1993 on murder charges; he and his wife in 1999 for economic crimes). They were both pardoned "for humanitarian reasons" on May 29, 2002, by Alpha Konaré, as one of his last official acts before leaving office. Though Traoré rejected the pardon, he nevertheless entered into retirement, dallied briefly with an embryonic political party, and in June 2005 made news by refusing to attend a symposium of some fifteen former African heads of state and government, held in Bamako under the auspices of President Adamou Toumani Touré. Though the 1999 trial was badly handled by the prosecution, Traoré was again sentenced to death. The Konaré regime

never really intended to go through with the execution, fearing to offend the regional Islamic dynasties, where Traoré retained considerable sympathy in part because of his relationship with the large Traoré clan, which traces its origins to pre-Sundiata times and even (it is claimed) acquired some royal blood by marriage into the royal Keita lineage. Konaré, Keita, and Traoré are common names in Mali, but they have special resonance socially and politically because of these clans' role in the dynastic history of the western Sudan.

6. Azawad is a Tuareg-populated region in Mali. Tuareg nationalists (e.g., the Tuareg Liberation Front) revived a popular Tuareg dream of creating a Tuareg state ("Azawad") composed of parts of northern Niger, northern Mali, and southern Algeria. From what little information is available on the project, Azawad was to have been an Islamic state. Azawad is mentioned in Keita 1998:9. See also Salifou 1993 and 2002.

7. I have relied on four main sources for my discussion: J. Spencer Trimingham's (1962) classic work; Hunwick (1965); Levtzion (1972); and Hiskett (1984).

8. Niane (1965:85 n3) states that "'Mali' in the Mandingo language means 'a hippopotamus' and it is not impossible that Mali was the name given to one of the capitals of the emperors. So it is not surprising to find villages in old Mali which have 'Mali' for a name." Several of the more recent etymological sources add that "Mali" also means "where the king dwells."

9. For Sundiata's epic tale, see Niane (1965); for the full story on Samory, see Person's (1968) magisterial multivolume work; for a usable list of references to the other precolonial states and iconic figures, see the bibliography in Imperato (1986:256–359).

10. At least one public Malian figure, Adame Ba Konaré, the wife of former president Konaré and a scholar in her own right, condemned the national project of reconstructed history: "The ludicrous nationalism of the colonizer was now substituted by another nationalism. History became a narrative without objectivity, teleological and biased, mixed with civic education as it had been in days of colonialism. Rapidly we fell into the excessive rehabilitation of our heroes, from Sunjata to Babemba . . . and into the exaltation of our pre-colonial states: Ghana, Mali, and Songhay. . . . Our ancestors could be compared to Alexander the Great or Napoleon. . . . We can thus say that historians fell into a trap. . . . This official history, directed from above and without nuance, became a true prison almost everywhere in Africa. It could not be corrected in public, or even in private. When it came to the heroes, a critic ran the risk of offense, or even blasphemy in relation to the warrior heroes" (Konaré 2000:17–18). Konaré has a point, and it is to Mali's credit that she makes it, but neither in Mali nor elsewhere did anyone take much notice of her criticism. The tug, and seduction, of reconstructing history as a national project has been too much to resist for nationalist historians everywhere, not to speak of school textbook writers. It should be added that Sékou Touré, Guinea's president from 1958 to 1971, also claimed heroic descent; in his case, from Samory Touré, a distinction that became part of Guinea's officially reconstructed national past. (Babemba, mentioned by Konaré, was the last king of the Kénédougou monarchy—1893–1898—who committed suicide in his capital Sikasso during the last days of the French siege of the town.)

11. For details of the French conquest, see Vandervort (1998), especially pages 72–84, 119–136; and Crowder (1968:67–115). For the other side of the story, see Crowder (1971), in particular the chapters by A. S. Kanya-Forstner; Oloruntimehin; and Person. See also Boni 1971. *Almamy* is a popular West African version of the Arabic *al-imam*, here referring not to the leader of prayer but most often to whoever has political authority in a community.

12. The higher figure is Crowder's (1969:59) estimate; the lower one is derived from *Les Populations des Territoires d'Outre-Mer* (1956).

13. Most Muslims in North and West Africa are members of one of these Sufi brotherhoods. The most accessible repertory and discussion of the brotherhoods is by Vikør (2000).

14. Translation from the Arabic original by David Robinson (2000) in his authoritative account of Franco-African relations in Senegal and Mauritania.

15. For a summary discussion of French colonial policy and its applications in Francophone Africa, including the Sahelian regions, see chapter 2 ("The Colonial Context") in Le Vine (2004).

16. The misnaming lay in the fact that most of these troops were not from Senegal but from the former French Soudan (now Mali), Niger, Côte d'Ivoire, Guinea, and other African territories. The *Tirailleurs* even included numbers of former slaves. At the end of the war they numbered close to 40,000 men. The most authoritative account of these troops is Echenberg (1991). For the French policy on the recruitment, use, and activities of native levies in West Africa, see Davis (1934/1970).

17. The reference is to Marty (1917 and 1921) and Delafosse 1912. Marty and Delafosse remain basic references to the ethnography of the area, at least as it appeared at the beginning of the twentieth century.

18. Following a June 1962 riot by traders and merchants in Bamako, Modibo had ninety-five of his most prominent opponents, including Fily Dabo Sissoko, Hamadoun Dicko, and Kassoum Touré, arrested and tried for treason and attempting a coup. Sissoko was condemned to death but had his sentence later commuted to life imprisonment. Shortly thereafter, while being transported in the bush, all three were murdered, allegedly (according to a 1964 official statement) in an ambush set by Tuareg rebels. Later evidence firmly established that the order came from Modibo. One destroyed hamlet was the Bambara village of Sokoiba, whose inhabitants were arrested or ordered to leave with such possessions as they could carry, and the village then burned to the ground. For details on these matters, see Imperato (1989:60–62), Diarrah (1986), and Jouve (1974). Soon after the explanation for the death of Sissoko et al. was announced, I was contacted by another opponent of the regime who wished to remain anonymous. I did in fact visit him in 1965, and he and another individual, an official in the presidency, both claimed that the order to kill the prisoners came from Modibo and offered documentary proof. I had, and still have, no reason to question their information, having seen what could only have been an official charge to carry out "*sanction extrême*" on the men.

19. This is Modibo at his most conciliatory: if religion (à la Marx) is the opiate of the people, it wasn't and isn't in Mali.

20. The internal quote in this passage is by an unidentified Malian official, cited by Grundy from *Afrique Nouvelle* No. 754, January 17, 1962, p. 4.

21. The first was the February 1966 coup in Ghana, which removed President Kwame Nkrumah and installed the military National Liberation Council (NLC). The NLC stepped down in 1969 to make way for the civilian Second Republic headed by Prime Minister Kofi Busia. Arguably, the military palace coup of June 1998, which put Gen. Abdulsalam Abubakar at the head of a Nigerian transitional ("provisional") government until May 1999, when the elected president, Olesegun Obasanjo was inaugurated, should be included.

22. For a discussion of the SNCs in Francophone Africa, including Mali's, see chapter 8 ("Redemocratization") in Le Vine (2004:241–269). The Malian SNC is highlighted in Nzouankeu (1993).

23. Correspondence with Malik Suleiman (pseud.), a religious leader, in June 1983. Suleiman asked not be identified by name and suggested I use "Malik Suleiman" in any reference to our correspondence.

24. CARE (1997) reports that nearly 6,000 associations—village-level coops, school/parents' associations, community health organizations, professional organizations, advocacy groups, religious associations, civic bodies, and other NGOs—had been registered under two separate laws between 1992 and 1997.

25. The latter figure is from Salih (2002). ICG (2005a:11) indicates that in 2000 "there were 106 Islamic NGOs in Mali, compared to six before the political opening in 1991. Of these, eleven were international NGOs, including the major ones also operating in Niger and Chad." I assume that the ninety-five noninternational NGOs fall within Salih's tally of associations, and that Salih and the ICG report use the terms interchangeably.

26. The Malian situation has been discussed in detail in ICG (2005a), one of the ICG's eight excellent 2004–2005 reports on Islamist activity throughout the world. The Sahel report, the result of four months of extensive interviews and onsite observations in Mauritania, Mali, Niger, and Chad during 2004–2005, is highly detailed, analytically sophisticated, and objective, though its policy recommendations (to the US government, the Sahelian governments, donors, NATO, and the EU), consonant with the ICG's mandate, lean toward peaceful resolution of the several crises in the area.

27. My field notes from a visit to Mali contain an interview with a Malian agronomist (Sy, interview 1965) who bewailed the casual attitudes toward Islam, sometimes bordering on irreverence, that he had observed in many of the Malian villages in which he worked.

28. For details and an excellent study of the Wahhabi movement itself, see Kaba (1974).

29. I take the point from Louis Brenner's fascinating discussion about the mutability of Malian Muslim identities. As Brenner (1993a:59) puts it, "Identities are constantly being constructed and reconstructed, by self and/or others, through continuing actions and discourse in a political context. Identities, both Muslim and non-Muslim, are formulated through the appropriation and reassortment of various elements and building blocks which may be religiously significant, but are also socially, politically, and economically motivated." For the Algerian picture, see ICG (2004), which suggests that the GSPC may be prepared to give up the armed strug-

gle in Algeria and accept the government's reconciliation initiative. The mutability of ethnic identities in Mali is explored by Amselle (1998:43–57).

30. Mali's government has never denied the existence of slavery within its borders. My conversation with Sheikh (interview 2005) is the source of the numerical estimate. It may include the number of individuals being trafficked north or southward.

5

Mauritania: Clash of Authoritarianism and Ethnicity

CÉDRIC JOURDE

THE ISLAMIC REPUBLIC OF MAURITANIA STANDS AS AN AMBIGUOUS COUNTRY in West Africa. Straddling northern and sub-Saharan Africa, it was never considered as a "real" North African country, but neither was it considered to be a "real" sub-Saharan country. It is the only country in West Africa with a demographically dominant portion of its population that speaks Arabic (a dialect of Arabic, to be more precise, called Hassaniyya). But its large Haalpulaar, Sooninke, and Wolof communities, together called Futanke ("the people of Futa," the Senegal River Valley region), definitely anchor Mauritania to its immediate West African environment as well.[1] It is the only country of West Africa in which the entire population defines itself as Muslim, yet its ethnic diversity has been violently politicized in the postcolonial era. What is certain, however, is that Mauritania has always been a central region for the diffusion of Islam throughout West Africa. *Bidhan* (or "Moor") and Haalpulaar religious figures have, since the seventeenth century, contributed to the dissemination of Islam across West Africa. Given its historical background, it is not surprising that the most recent wave of Islamic reform, Islamism, has also played a significant role in Mauritania. In this chapter, I will argue that two major political dynamics have shaped the course of political Islam in Mauritania: the authoritarian nature of its political regime, and the politicization of ethnic relations.

First, the authoritarian nature of all its postcolonial regimes, including the latest "neoauthoritarian" regime of the 1991–2005 period, has affected dramatically the evolution of Mauritania's Islamism. Despite the adoption of formal democratic institutions in 1991, the regime's attempt to preserve its authoritarian core led it to a direct confrontation with various opposition movements and parties. The Islamists were no exception. To counter the Islamists, the regime engaged in a process of identity construction, by which it sought to define the Islamists as inherently foreign to Mauritania's own vision of Islam, as the propagators of a deceptive religious message, and as a source of civil strife (*fitna*). In contrast, the regime defined itself as the only political force capable of both defending the true values of Islam and protecting the country against instability. Hence, Mauritania's various Islamist figures and movements, like all other opposition forces, evolved in a context of growing repression.

Second, Islamism in Mauritania has been deeply influenced by the politics of ethnicity. The number of Futanke leaders and followers in these Islamist movements is extremely small; Islamism is almost exclusively a Moorish phenomenon. A brief analysis of the evolution of ethnic identities since the colonial period sheds some light on this peculiar characteristic of Mauritanian Islamism. Whereas Islamist movements in other West African countries have pushed, among other things, for the introduction of Arabic in the education system and for the development of closer ties between their states and Middle Eastern countries, such demands have almost never been heard among the Futanke communities of Mauritania (with a few exceptions to be discussed in this chapter). In addition, the Islamists' relative silence about the tragic massacres and expulsions perpetrated by the regime against its Futanke ethnic minorities in 1989–1991 also explains the movement's failure to mobilize Futanke followers. Finally, the influence of Sufi *tariqa* (brotherhoods) over the Futanke communities constitutes another significant obstacle for the Islamists. Sufism is an integral aspect of Futanke identities, and the Islamists' discursive attacks against Sufism are perceived as an assault against what it means to be a Futanke.

Between Authoritarianism . . .

Islamism and the First Civilian and Military Authoritarian Regimes

Like too many other aspects of Mauritania's political history, very little is known about the historical trajectory of Islamism in Mauritania. Furthermore, what actually constitutes "Islamism" and "Islamist" is highly contentious. In this volume, the working definition for *Islamism* is "organized activity and/or a systematic thought process that forcefully (but not necessarily violently) strives to bring politics into line with Islamic precepts. Such activity and/or thought process self-consciously positions itself within a wider, transnational movement of similarly inspired political change." But like many social sciences concepts, the definitions observers use do not always coincide with those of political actors engaged in political struggles. As we shall see, the Mauritanian state has offered its very own definition of what Islamism is and who the Islamists are. This was a politically charged definition, opposed by those being so labeled.

We owe to the Mauritanian political scientist Zekeria Ould Ahmed Salem (1996; 2001) the only systematic (and brilliant) study of an Islamist leader and his political discourses, Mohamed Ould Sidi Yahya. According to Ould Ahmed Salem (2001:7), the emergence of the first Islamic movements on the Mauritanian political scene occurred when Mauritania's first military regime was established at the end of the 1970s. At that time, a few activists founded the Harakat al-Islamiyyat fi Muritaniyya (The Islamic Movement of Mauritania, or Hasim). The Mauritanian government claims that Hasim first appeared to the public during a youth conference in 1977 and that it convened its own conference in 1978 (Radio-Mauritanie 1994a). Why did Hasim arise during that period? Ould Ahmed Salem (2001:7) explains the foundation of Hasim by the rise of a global Islamist discourse throughout the Muslim world in the mid-1970s, which influenced young Mauritanian activists. For Yahya Ould El-Bara (2004:231), another key factor is the rapid urbanization that took place at the end of the 1970s, following the devastating droughts that decimated the livestock, wells, and oasis culture upon which many Mauritanians relied. This humanitarian crisis opened the door to various nongovernmental organizations (NGOs) and humanitarian state-sponsored initiatives from the Gulf countries, which brought with them not only aid but also a new vision of Islam.

But regardless of the exact date of its foundation in the 1970s, it seems clear for Ould Ahmed Salem (2001:7) that this movement failed to gain any significant popular support at that time. Like many other political movements in Mauritania, including Haratin movements and Maoist and Marxist factions, the Islamists were rapidly divided among themselves, partly due to individual factors (quarrels among leaders) and to the diversity of international influences, thereby making it difficult to form a coherent movement. Ould Ahmed Salem (2001:8) explains that the various splinter groups included three loosely defined strands: the local version of Al-Ikhwan al-Muslimin (Muslim Brothers); the Salafists; and the Mauritania version of Jama'at ad-dawat wa tabligh (Dawa, or Call and Preach). Among each of these groups, the leaders' discourses are also very diverse, ranging from global Islamist themes to very local and popular issues. Though this threefold classification is interesting, it still needs to be confirmed and improved by systematic fieldwork research, as yet not undertaken.

At the end of the 1970s and during most of the 1980s, the authoritarian regime, under its military guise, did not seem to pay great attention to the Islamists, whose internal divisions and lack of popular appeal rendered them relatively inoffensive. Furthermore, the authoritarian nature of the regime made it difficult for opposition movements to make their voice heard. The legal, political, and security apparatus quickly repressed any antiregime activities (even if, as often, the real threat against the ruling clique came from within the regime, i.e., from rival military officers). In addition, the state never failed to define itself as a strong defender of Islam, thereby neutralizing (if only in part) the Islamist discourse. In effect, since the coup that brought Mohamed Khouna Ould Haidallah to power in 1980, the state reasserted the unique status of Islam in Mauritania, thereby eliminating the "dual legal system" (Muslim and French) that characterized the first twenty years of the postcolonial era. The dual system meant that both legal codes coexisted. But a new unified system "under the banner of the Muslim law" was established in 1983 (Marchesin 1990:262). In 1985, a few months after Maaouya Ould Sid Ahmed Taya successfully staged his coup against Ould Haidallah, the new constitutional charter confirmed that Islam was the religion of the state and its people; it also stated that "the only source of law is the Islamic Sharia" (quoted in Marchesin 1990:263). However, many legal experts explain that the French legal legacy was, and still is, greatly influential in Mauritania's legal texts (Ould Bouboutt 1989; Marchesin 1990; Ly 1993); the Islamization of Mauritania's legal system was more symbolic and political than truly legal (Marchesin 1990:263).

An Adapting Authoritarian Regime: The Discursive Repression of Islamism Under the "Democratic Era"

In 1991 the Mauritanian political landscape changed significantly, though perhaps not as much as expected. Officially, the military junta opted for a complete democratization of the political regime, with the adoption of a democratic constitution that provided for a multiparty system, free and fair elections, and the protection of human rights. However, beyond the formal legal texts, ruling elites sought to preserve their power and embarked upon a different path, which Bayart (1993) called the "authoritarian restoration." This process consisted of replacing formal authoritarian institutions with formal democratic ones, yet without changing the authoritarian nature of political relations between ruling elites and the masses. The hybrid, or "neoauthoritarian," regime that emerged out of that process in Mauritania shares striking similarities with other regimes in Africa and elsewhere (Schatzberg 1998; Brownlee 2002; Carothers 2002; Ottaway 2003; Levitsky and Way 2005). The military junta and its civilian allies had no intention of implementing reforms that could force them out of office; politically and financially profitable positions were at stake.

Therefore, the "hijacking" of formal democratic institutions, as Michael Schatzberg (1998) nicely puts it, required a continual adaptation to the evolving political reality. Ruling elites had to deploy much financial, military, and symbolic capital to repress, co-opt, and weaken domestic opposition forces that hoped to use the formal democratic institutions to change the regime. And because antiauthoritarian pressures were both internal and external, ruling elites invested both the domestic and international political stages to deflect and minimize such pressures.

On the domestic stage, the regime targeted specifically the individuals and sociopolitical groups who demanded the actual implementation and respect of the reforms of 1991, be they secular political parties, musicians and *griots*, small-town youth organizations, journalists, civil society organizations or, of course, personalities and movements who denounced the regimes through a religious discourse. Physical coercion, symbolic exclusion, co-optation, or economic marginalization constituted key options for the regime. It is in this larger context of an adapting authoritarian regime, or neoauthoritarian regime, that the recent trajectory of Islamism in Mauritania must be understood.

Defining the Other (Threatening Islamists) and the Self (the Protective Regime)

Although repression and co-optation were the regime's universal options (i.e., applicable to all opponents), ruling elites had to adapt to each particular opponent and its discourse. Consequently, the regime set up a specific strategy to respond to those opponents who expressly referred to Islamic precepts to contest the regime and who put forward alternative political paths based on Islam. The analysis of the 1991–2005 period suggests that only a few Islamists were co-opted by the regime; for the others, the Mauritanian government opted for a strategy seen in most other North African states: categorizing them as foreign to the legitimate political arena, and taking the necessary measures to deal with illegitimate actors. Like most of its neighbors to the north, the Mauritanian state could not tolerate being criticized from a religious viewpoint, possibly knowing the potential that such a discourse could have on its legitimacy. Furthermore, as some have suggested, the Islamist movements' egalitarian rhetoric has been specifically appealing to many Haratin (the low-ranking status group of the Bidhan society), the mobilization of whom was seen as particularly threatening for the regime (Stone 1994). The anti-Islamist strategy was thus based on the discursive construction of dichotomous "self-other" identities. Through various physical and symbolic performances, which I will analyze in this chapter, the regime defined the "other"—the "Islamists"—in contrast with the "self"—the regime—along three main axes:

First, the Islamists are inherently foreign to the Mauritanian nation. Their "foreignness" thus requires that they be extracted from Mauritania's body politic. By contrast, the regime defines itself as truly representative of Mauritania.

Second, and in relation to the previous point, their foreign nature makes them the carrier of a deceptive and false religious discourse. In contrast, the regime represents, protects, and promotes the Mauritanian vision of Islam against foreign and deceptive threats.

Before elaborating on the third point, it is worth mentioning that these first two characteristics of the "self" and "other" identities reveal an interesting discursive tension for the regime. Arab states have always been coping with two often contradictory goals: promoting "raison d'état" as individual sovereign states *and* "raison de la nation," that is, the *Arab* nation (from the Atlantic Ocean to the Gulf, regardless of state borders and sovereignty). In other words, the interests of each individual sovereign Arab state do not always match those of the Arab nation at large (Barnett 1998). In very similar terms, the issue of Islam and Islamism raises the tension between the "reason of the state" and the "reason of the nation," here the Muslim nation, or *umma* in Arabic: how can the Mauritanian state defend its unique and distinctive Mauritanian Islam (its "sovereign" Islam, we could say) against "foreign" influences while at the same time defending Islam as a global religion? Surprisingly, then, this "nationalist religious" discourse trumps the universal aspiration of the Islamic *umma* and instead pegs Islam to the national territory (a territory, we should recall, that was crafted by French colonial administrators).

Third, the Mauritanian regime defines the Islamists as inherently driven by a thirst for *fitna* (disorder and sedition), which they subversively attempt to import in "orderly" Mauritania. By contrast, the regime depicts itself as an ultimate source of stability and security. As we shall see, the regime's discourse constantly advances a depiction of the Islamists, and most political opponents in general, as political agents whose thirst for power is a potential source of disorder. As Ould Ahmed Salem (2000) suggests, this discourse is predicated upon a larger conception of power in Mauritanian political culture: political opposition is characterized as a source of instability; accommodation with incumbent power-holders, with whom people are accustomed to dealing, is preferable to political change. Although we can only speculate about the actual magnitude and salience of this political conception among the Mauritanian population, it is nonetheless apparent that the regime's construction of the self and the other did tap into that conception, as it constantly set the image of Islamists as a source of *fitna* against the image of itself as the bastion of stability. Whether the regime's discourse successfully resonated (and resonates) among the population cannot be proven here; but the regime's intention to do so, indeed, is clear, as the empirical analysis indicates.

Before pursuing the argument further, it is important to reassert the dual dimension of the regime's adaptation strategy under the new "democratic institutions": targeting both domestic and international audiences. Though this chapter concentrates mainly on the *domestic* front, it must be said that the regime simultaneously deployed great effort toward the regional and international arena. Indeed, the regime's definition of the Islamists and of itself was partly built on *international* discourses on Islamism and terrorism (Jourde, forthcoming). Following the first attack against the World Trade Center in 1993, the bombings of various Parisian sites in the mid-1990s, and the (failed) Millennium Plot against Los Angeles International Airport in 1999, which all involved individuals from North Africa (Egypt and Algeria), Western governments became very receptive to "Islamic threat" discourses held by West African and North African regimes. Even if Mauritania was seen as relatively peripheral to North Africa's core countries, its shared borders with Algeria and Morocco became an asset for the regime when it sought to define itself as a bastion against the "Islamist threat."

More recently, in 2003, the Sahelian faction of what is described as a splinter group of the Algerian Groupe Islamique Armé (GIA)—the Groupe Salafiste pour la Prédication et le Combat (GSPC)—helped the Mauritanian regime in its attempt to communicate the idea of an Islamist threat to its Western audiences. An alleged attack of the GSPC against a remote Mauritanian military garrison in June 2005, which according to official media led to the death of fifteen Mauritanian soldiers, nurtured this public relations image. For sure, some observers have correctly stated that the Mauritanian government did not present clear evidence about what really happened in that garrison (CRIDEM 2005; ICG 2006); and Keenan (2006) has argued that the GSPC is more or less a creation of the Algerian services rather than a genuine Islamist armed group. In any event, the regime's domestic policy of discursive and physical harassment of Islamists both tapped into and nurtured a regional and international context in which Islamism was replacing communism as the new great "threat." Like their predecessors during the Cold War, small Third World authoritarian regimes like Mauritania quickly managed to use these global simplistic dichotomies

(Free World vs. Communism; Democracy vs. Islamofascism) for domestic politics purposes. It is in this context that, as Miles points out in Chapter 1, the US government provided Mauritania (along with Mali, Niger, and Chad) with substantive military aid in 2003–2004 through its Pan Sahel Initiative military program and then in 2005–2006 through its Trans-Saharan Counterterrorism Initiative program (which expanded the list of beneficiary countries to Nigeria, Senegal, Morocco, Algeria, and Tunisia) (Jourde, forthcoming).

The Anti-Islamist Campaign (1991–2006)

With these analytical elements in mind, we can better understand how the evolution of Mauritania's neoauthoritarian regime affected the politics of Islamism. The representation of the self and the Islamists was indeed constructed over more than fifteen years, from 1990 to the mid-2000s, through a series of public performances. The regime's first action against the Islamists came in the weeks following the formal adoption of the new constitution, in the fall of 1991. This was a period of uncertainty, as both the government and the opposition were still not clear about how and to what extent the new rules of the game defined by the constitution would shape relations among them. Various organizations and networks of political activists applied for the status of political party in this newly instituted multiparty system. Among them was an organization that sought to create a new party, called the Ummah party. This organization included well-known religious figures such as Shaykh Mohamed Ould Sidi Yahya, a popular imam in the district of Sebkha, one of Nouakchott's poorest and most populous districts. As a Mauritanian observer explained, the would-be Ummah party recruited its followers precisely among the "marginalized strata of the capital's poor neighborhood" (Fall 1991:4).

Though the government had authorized the creation of various political parties, it decided not to grant the status of legal political party to the Ummah party. The Interior Ministry referred to Articles 4 and 6 of the *ordonnance relative au partis politiques*, which state that "Islam cannot be the exclusive monopoly of a political party" and "no political party can identify itself with a race, ethnic group, region, tribe, gender, or brotherhood." The minister argued that because of that party's overt religious ideology, as seen in the preamble of the party's program, which began with a Quranic *surat*, it violated Article 4 of the constitution (Fall 1991:4).

This refusal instantly generated anger among Ummah's members, and demonstrations were organized to denounce the decision. In what was to become a recurrent strategy, the regime called on members of the religious establishment to counter the discourse of these emerging religious opponents. Accordingly, the religious figure with the closest and firmest ties to the regime, Bouddah Ould Bousseyri, made an important sermon during the Friday prayer.[2] We see in his lecture the foundations of the dichotomous "self-other" identities, as the moderate, official Islam was set against the disorderly vision of Islam put forward by organizations such as Ummah. Ould Bousseyri stated that "we cannot call for disorder [just] because the creation of a party was denied by the government. The authorization to create a party must be made in a serene climate; if the government accepts, this is good, and if it doesn't, then no Islamic law justifies the use of force or of threat [as a reaction to this refusal]" (cited in Baduel 1992:923; see also *Éveil-Hebdo,* November 25, 1991).

Despite demands from other political parties to authorize the creation of the Ummah party, the Interior Ministry maintained its decision. This decision echoed similar policies adopted by North African governments in the early 1990s in Algeria (against the FIS), Tunisia (against an-Nahda), and Morocco (Hizb at-Tajdid al-Watani). In Mauritania, Ummah activists denounced the regime's authoritarian decision, arguing that their party would have always played by the rules of the game and they were not radicals as the regime portrayed them. As leaders of the party argued,

> Islam is against this infidel, unjust and corrupt government; Islam is founded upon the idea of *shura* (consultation) and the free will of leaders, and for that reason, it is against all putschist and monarchist governments, those decadent governments that dominate Muslim countries today. . . . The Ummah party has no foreign connections, and it has no tribal, racial or ethnic basis. The fact that we want to create an Islamic party does not mean that we consider other parties to be infidel. The refusal to authorize our party underscores that the government has no sense of democracy and freedom. (quoted in Hamès 1994:50)

Leaders of the Ummah party also pointed out that other parties, such as the Arab nationalist Alliance populaire pour le progrès (APP), made stronger references to Islam, even calling for the strict application of sharia, yet had been authorized by the government (Baduel 1992:923, quoting *Mauritanie-Demain*).

Yet the regime's decision was final. As a consequence, some members of this organization decided to keep the party alive for some time, even if it was illegal to do so, while at the same time becoming members of other authorized opposition parties, such as the Union des forces démocratiques-ère nouvelle (UFD/en), whose leader had supported Ummah in its campaign for official recognition in December 1991. Other members, however, were co-opted by the regime. Aboubecrine Ould Ahmed, for example, was appointed minister of culture and Islamic orientation in the first post-1991 government (Clausen 1994:652). Finally, others instead decided not to join organized political groups and retreated in a less publicized sphere, such as Shaykh Mohamed Ould Sidi Yahya, whose Friday sermons attracted an increasing number of followers (Ould Ahmed Salem 1996; 2001).

International contexts also provided the regime with the opportunity to elaborate on its definition of Mauritanian Islamists as a threatening force. In November 1992, Nouakchott was the host of the fifth annual summit of the Arab Maghrib Union (Ittihaad al-Maghrib al-Arabyy, referred to herewith as UMA), North Africa's regional organization that includes Algeria, Libya, Mauritania, Morocco, and Tunisia. This regional meeting constituted a significant occasion for Mauritania to inscribe its anti-Islamist stance in a regional context: the Algerian government was just experiencing the first wave of violence following the army's cancellation of legislative elections and dismantling of the Islamic Salvation Front (FIS), the Moroccan government was denying "moderate" Islamist organizations access to the official political party arena, and the Tunisian government was harshly repressing the moderate Islamic party an-Nahda and its leadership. In these countries, the authoritarian regimes skillfully subverted the political liberalization process through an anti-Islamist terrorism campaign. The Mauritanian government thus inscribed its policy vis-à-vis its domestic opposition in this context, aligning its position with those of its UMA partners: as representatives of the five governments took the stage, they declared that they would cooperate to "contain terrorism, this dangerous phenomenon which is foreign to our Muslim society" (quoted in "Le cinquième sommet de l'UMA" 1992:3129). Though national audiences were targeted by this joint proclamation, Yann Le Troquer (1992:509) rightfully reminds us that this statement was also aimed at "reassuring [UMA's] European partners" who were concerned by the emergence of political Islam on the southern shore of the Mediterranean.

Following its refusal to authorize the creation of an Islamic party, the regime moved forward in its construction of dichotomous identities. In 1993 it launched what was to become a long series of arrests of "Islamists" while also shutting down associations or groups also labeled as Islamist. That summer, the government shut down social associations, called Naadi Aicha (Aicha Club), arguing that they were exploited "by the Islamists to communicate their messages" (*Éveil-Hebdo,* December 6, 1993). Following an assassination attempt against the minister of culture and Islamic orientation by an alleged Islamist, security forces arrested for the very first time in the new "democratic" period individuals it considered to be Islamists. They were eventually released without charges (Clausen 1994:650).

A year later, in the fall of 1994, the degree of repression increased as the government launched a more systematic campaign of arrests. On September 25, 1994, about sixty individuals were arrested on the basis of their alleged ties to Islamist organizations. The interior minister stated that the government had uncovered a subversive plot by Hasim, the Islamist movement founded at the end of the 1970s, and the "Jihad Group."[3] Among the sixty people arrested were the imam and leader of the illegal party Ummah, Shaykh Mohamed Ould Sidi Yahya; the former minister of culture and Islamic orientation in the first post-1991 government, Aboube crine Ould Ahmed (Clausen 1994:652); members of the opposition party UFD and municipal councilors, Jamil Ould Mansour and Hassan Ould Moulay Ely; and a madrasa teacher, Mohamed Sidiya Ould Jdoud, also known as "Nawawi" ("Nuclear") (Radio-Mauritanie 1994b).

These arrests enabled the regime to consolidate its threatening narrative about the "Islamists" and their organizations. Through government officials' press conferences, state-owned media editorials, sermons by "official" imams, and public confessions of prisoners on television and radio, the regime defined the typical Islamist enemy and, by opposition, defined the typical state-promoted Islam.

These dichotomous identities were clearly exposed in the government's first public announcement, on September 25, 1994. The interior minister, Mohamed Selim Ould Dah, explained,

> Recently secret and alien organizations were established in our country, carrying out their activities under the slogan of a call for Islam. It should be known to you that a pretext such as this is no more than a means of disturbing security and stability in this country and of harming its sovereignty. . . . These organizations have found a new method for the spreading of their malicious propaganda: they have resorted to the exploitation of the houses of God [mosques] during prayer times and transforming these places into provocative political forums. (BBC Summary of World Broadcast, September 27, 1994)

Two weeks later, the interior minister held another press conference, in which he provided the details of security forces' investigations:

> The investigation which was carried out recently regarding the Islamic Movement in Mauritania . . . revealed that the movement was engaged in political activities covertly. . . . By this behaviour it was following in the footsteps of the other extremist movements in the world. This covert movement's ties with circles abroad have been proved beyond any shadow of doubt. . . . The goals and objectives of this movement include the following: using religious propaganda and deceiving all those who did not adopt its ideas or style . . . spying on our society by planting

> agents in every district and home to learn about the weaknesses of the Muslims and [to] send information to their masters abroad. . . . At this point there began the operation aimed at shaking the country's stability and security and sowing fear in the hearts of the citizens, and from there seizing power. (BBC Summary of World Broadcast, October 11, 1994)

The notion of Mauritanian Islamists' foreign ties and influences, their deceptive nature, and their attempt to instill disorder in orderly Mauritania were strongly reasserted. To add to the veracity of these claims, the government organized public confessions of prisoners on national television and radio. Ten of the sixty prisoners made very similar confessions, all of which claimed that they held misled religious beliefs, provided details about their foreign patrons, and promised not to carry out similar activities in the future. Among those who made public confessions were No'emane Ould Ahmed Ould Bellahi, who allegedly died in 2001 in Afghanistan; Mohamed Sidiya Ould Jdoud (also known as Nawawi), who would be arrested again in 2005; and Mohamed Ould Ahmed Ould Sid'Ahmed Ould Zerrough (also known as Sha'er, the poet), whom the government accused in 2005 of being a member of the GSPC.[4] In addition, the government sought to substantiate further its claim by shutting down various domestic and foreign associations, including the Cultural Islamic Association, founded in 1980; the Bin Mas'ud Institute; and the Higher Institute for Islamic Philosophy (Radio Africa No. 1, 1994). It also prohibited the organization of political conferences in mosques, and expelled Moroccan and Sudanese citizens (Clausen 1994:672).

However, following these public confessions the government declared, through the voice of the Ministry of Culture and Islamic Orientation, that it had decided to grant "a general amnesty for the Islamic group. . . . They have repented and they will not be the object of any legal proceedings. . . . Islam and its preservation have always been and will remain an important objective for the government" (Deutsche Presse Agentur 1994). A few days earlier the regime's most collaborative imam, Bouddah Ould Bousseyiri, had made a public call for clemency toward the prisoners (Boubrik 1998:139). In response, the regime decided to end this episode with a "presidential grace." It is worth noticing that the decision to opt for this "grace" meant that the regime would not have to organize a comprehensive trial, and thus would not have to publicly debate the role of the Islamists and to disclose to the population concrete proof of the Islamists' "criminal" activities.

In 1999 and 2000 the regime undertook another, yet minor, wave of arrests. This time, however, it barely publicized it. Epitomizing once again the close interrelation between the domestic and international scenes, the reemergence of Islamism on Mauritania's domestic political agenda could be tied to two international events that took place a few months earlier. First, the US government became more interested in the issue of Islamism in Africa following the bombings of two of its embassies, in Kenya and Tanzania, in 1998. Second, the Mauritanian government was involved in a process of rapprochement with Israel, and by extension with the United States. The process culminated in October 1999, when Mauritania and Israel instituted full diplomatic relations. After Egypt and Jordan, Mauritania became the third country of the Arab League to hold such diplomatic ties with Israel. The timing was not fortunate for the Mauritanian government, however, because less than a year later, the second intifada broke out in Palestine, which increased anti-Israeli feelings among Arab and Muslim countries and put great pressures on those governments, such as Mauritania, that maintained diplomatic ties with Israel.

These international events helped some individual Islamists to gain an unprecedented publicity and to attract more followers. Among them were Jamil Ould Mansour and Mohamed al-Hassan Ould Deddew. The former was among those arrested in the wave of 1994. As Mauritania accelerated its rapprochement with Israel, Ould Mansour, a member of the leading opposition party (UFD), was appointed general secretary of the association Ribat, which fought for the complete diplomatic rupture with Israel. The anti-Israeli demonstrations of 1999 and 2000 thus provided Ould Mansour with a very valuable public stage, which he skillfully exploited (Sud Quotidien 2000; Clausen 1999:282). For his part, Ould Deddew, a brilliant Muslim scholar and imam, also gained a new status during the anti-Israeli demonstrations, when he wrote and made public a fatwa that declared the establishment of diplomatic relations with Israel a violation of Islam (*Calame,* October 20, 2004).

This is the context in which security forces arrested five or six individuals in March 1999, most of whom were small businessmen, on the basis of their alleged ties with Afghanistan and with Osama bin Laden's brother (*Éveil-Hebdo*, March 7, 1999). A year later, in February 2000, state officials said little more concerning the arrest of a Mauritanian citizen, Mohamed Ould Sellahi, who was believed to have close ties with bin Laden's Al-Qaida network. According to news reports, Ould Sellahi, who belongs to a well-known *zawiya* tribe ('Idablehsen) from southwest Mauritania, is married to a Palestinian woman whose sister is married to a high-ranking member of Al-Qaida (*Calame,* February 12, 1999; *La Tribune,* February 16, 2000; *Éveil-Hebdo,* February 15, 2000). Overall, these arrests concerned only a few individuals, not the "Islamist movement" in Mauritania.

However, the scope of state repression changed drastically in the aftermath of the September 11, 2001, attacks against the United States and the US military invasion of Iraq in March 2003. In such a context, the regime's relation with the United States and Israel became a significant liability on the domestic political front. In effect, the protracted conflict in Palestine and the US invasion of Iraq served to reconcile former adversaries, the various Mauritanian factions of Islamists and of Arab nationalists. The two world events could be simultaneously interpreted as an aggression against either the Arab world or the Islamic world, and thus helped the Islamists and the Arab nationalists to find a common source for mobilization: the United States, Israel, and their common ally, the Mauritanian government. Islamist figures, including Ould Mansour and Ould Deddew, again used the public stages set up during the antiwar demonstrations to denounce the government and its Western allies. Ould Deddew read out another fatwa that defined the invasion of Iraq as an aggression against all Muslims, while Ould Mansour reminded his audiences that Iraq had always supported Mauritania in the past (*Nouakchott Info,* April 6, 2003). None of these activists, however, used violent means in their condemnations of the government. In this general context, several leaders of an Arab nationalist organization who were trying to have their political party authorized by the government were arrested on May 1, 2003, and dozens of Islamists were arrested three days later. The arrests of Islamists continued for almost a full month, and several schools, newspapers, colleges, and cultural centers were shut down by the government on the basis of their Islamist orientation.

Through this new wave of arrests, the regime consolidated the dichotomous "self-other" identities. Hence, if the invasion of Iraq and the repression in the occupied territories constituted international events that fed into Mauritanian opponents' antiregime discourses, the Islamist violence in other countries (e.g., terrorist attacks in Riyadh and Casablanca, the endemic violence in Algeria) nurtured the regime's politics of identity construction. A good illustration of this process was the prime minister's rhetorically violent accusation launched at those who dared use religion to denounce the regime. Here again the main elements of the "us vs. them" definition can be found. While visiting a public library, Prime Minister Cheikh Al Avia Ould Mohamed Khouna declared to the media:

> Our country has recently faced behaviours that are foreign to our people, which is known for its tolerance and its concern for the preservation of moderate values, far from any form of extremism. . . . These behaviours are the work of extremist movements who claïm to speak on behalf of Islam but who in reality follow the orders that come from abroad. . . . You

> know that they have propagated disorder, anarchy, terror, and death in numerous other Arab and Muslim countries that were much stronger than ours. Our country faced attempts by these extremist movements to carry out terrorist plots, more precisely in 1994 and 2000. But these plots have failed thanks to the vigilance of our people and the support it gave to our government. (Agence Mauritanienne d'Information, May 19, 2003)

Meanwhile, most of those who were arrested were officially charged of "inciting violence and using mosques to recruit youngsters for subversive purposes" (*Nouakchott Info,* May 29, 2003; Agence France Presse, May 14, 2003) and "plotting against the domestic and external security of the state; plotting against the constitutional order; and membership in an illegal organization" (*Nouakchott Info,* June 5, 2003).

In addition to the arrests of Islamists, the regime sought to assert its control over mosques and its religious leaders. This assertion of power was made through legal and rhetorical means. The government designed a new "Mosque Law," four weeks after the first arrests of Islamists, by which it defined mosques as public spaces subject to the control of the state. As the minister of communication stated, this law "specifies the supreme objectives of the Mosque, which is a sacred space devoted to worshipping and knowledge, and a public space devoted to the diffusion of knowledge, fraternity, and tolerance among members of the Islamic society, far from the deeds prohibited by the Malikite rite, be they political, or related to a faction, a group or a person" (Agence Mauritanienne d'Information, June 30, 2003). A few weeks after the adoption of this law, the Ministry of Culture and Islamic Orientation organized a seminar to educate about 120 imams on how to conform to the law, in order to ensure that they understand that "mosques are exclusively dedicated to worshipping, far from the incompatible activities that violate their noble mission" (Agence Mauritanienne d'Information, September 16, 2003).

Meanwhile, the regime's top officials engaged the rhetorical battlefield, launching "demonization" campaigns against imams and mosques that "deviated" from the right religious path. For instance, a few weeks before the arrests of Islamists, the minister of culture and Islamic orientation met with various imams and warned them not to use mosques for political purposes. He denounced the politically motivated actions of "parasites operating in Mosques" and reminded them that the Prophet once demolished the mosques of imams who divided the community (*Nouakchott Info,* April 30, 2003). Later on, during another state-sponsored religious ritual, the Colloque Scientifique Islamique, attended by religious scholars from around the world, he declared that the government would "guarantee the security of honest *ulama* against provocations, destructive ideas and demonstrations of extremism in mosques, and would ensure that mosques regain their sacred status" (Agence Mauritanienne d'Information, May 13, 2003).

Finally, the regime used the religious establishment in its process of identity construction. Religious figures were called upon to support the regime and denounce the deceptive message of dangerous preachers. Amidst the wave of arrests, about a hundred imams and religious scholars (*fuqaha*) wrote a public letter in which they denounced violence and extremism, calling the public to support the president: "We pledge to support the government and to stop all forms of extremism and terrorism, which are prohibited by our holy religion. [We call upon Mauritanians] to oppose any attempt against the security and stability of our country" (Agence France Presse, May 22, 2003). Interestingly, the third presidential election of the country's history took place a few months after the massive arrests of Islamists, in November 2003. During the campaign, a very important member of the ulama from southwest Mauritania, Mohamed Salem Ould Addoud, organized in his small village a big electoral meeting in favor of President Ould Taya. To underline the significance of the meeting, President Ould Taya sent his national campaign director and his party's general-secretary. During the meeting, the clergyman explained the "religious foundations of his support [to President Taya], which [he] saw as an obligation. . . . It is therefore imperative that all the ulama preach the good, that they support their Emir, and that they not be deceived by some preachers" (*Nouakchott-Info,* October 1, 2003).

It must be said here that the repression of Islamists in the spring and summer of 2003 coincided with two other important events that revealed the weakness of the regime. First, the regime was confronted with a coup attempt by young military officers in June 2003. The regime eventually thwarted the attempt after a two-day gun battle in the streets of Nouakchott. Though the arrests of Islamists a few weeks before the attempt were not the cause of it, President Ould Taya represented the Islamists and the military coup-makers as members of a single group of opponents. As he was making an official visit to the mining city of Zouerate, in the northern region of Tirris-Zemmour, he told his audience that he saw a "synchronicity" between the "calls for jihad" (which justified the arrests of Islamist leaders in early May) and the coup attempt, and that "we can only wonder if the leaders of these two campaigns were involved in a race for power or whether there was a coordination between them" (Agence Mauritanienne d'Information, July 12, 2003). Second, the presidential election of November also revealed the inherent weakness of the regime. Presumably troubled by the unexpected candidacy of former head of state Ould Haidallah, and by the growing popularity of this candidate, the regime resorted to its usual tactic of repression, arbitrary arrests, and accusations of threats against the security of the state (*Éveil-Quotidien,* November 5, 2003). It is worth noting that many Islamist leaders, including Jamil Ould Mansour and Mohamed al-Hassan Ould Deddew, gave their support to Ould Haidallah (*Éveil-Quotidien*, November 26, 2003; *Nouakchott Info,* August 31, 2003). Thus, whereas the regime made important concessions to the opposition for the 2001 legislative and municipal elections, holding the fairest elections since 1991, it rather fell back on its older habits in 2003 and decided not to take the risk of organizing a free and fair contest for the presidential election.

The 2003 repression of Islamist activists nurtured and accelerated the cycle of popular frustration and state repression in the following months and years. The regime continued to categorize Islamists as the local allies of foreign forces and as a source of disorder. As a new alleged plot was uncovered in September 2004, Islamist leaders were arrested once again; security forces argued that some of their "young followers were sent [by coup plotters] to northern Côte d'Ivoire, in the rebel zone, to be trained for terrorist actions in Mauritania" (*Nouakchott Info,* October 11, 2004). The regime emphasized again both the foreign and violent characteristics of the Islamists. This cycle reached a peak exactly two years after the 2003 arrests, as another major wave of arrests was launched, as well as a renewed attempt to reassert state control over mosques. At the end of April 2005, and in the following weeks, numerous imams, scholars, activists, professors, students, and journalists were taken into custody. Security forces claimed that their investigation had "revealed that a group of twenty people were sent to the Algerian camps of the Salafist Group for Preaching and Combat (GSPC) to get military training; seven of them came back to Mauritania, and were arrested. The rest of the group is still in the GSPC camps" (Agence Mauritanienne d'Information, April 25, 2005). As in 1994, the government claimed that Mauritanian Islamists were directly tied to Algerian Islamists. But the accusations moved further ten days later, as the government eventually claimed that Mauritania was hosting a local cell of Al-Qaida. A government spokesman told journalists that the massive wave of arrests allowed security forces to uncover "the existence of a dangerous secret organization, which takes the form of a local jihadist salafist cell directly connected to Al Qaida, and which receives its order from that organization. . . . We now know the story of this sleeping cell which has been here for a long time, which took various forms, and which seeks to undertake operations of destabilization in our country" (*Nouakchott Info,* May 7, 2005).

The state also aimed at reasserting its control over mosques as it did in the aftermath of the 2003 events. On the ground, police forces investigated dozens of mosques as well as their surrounding buildings (learning centers and houses of religious personnel), searching for weapons and documents (*Eveil-Hebdo,* May 17, 2005). The interior minister justified this policy, arguing that "we need to be vigilant in the face of such a danger. We will implement the [June 2003] Law on Mosques with firmness to get rid of those lawless criminals who inhabit these mosques and seek to disseminate death and disorder among Muslims" (Agence France Presse, May 18, 2005). Meanwhile, the regime again resorted to members of the religious establishment, who appeared on national television to denounce and condemn the "political use of mosques" (*Nouakchott Info,* May 12, 2005).

This campaign of repression against the Islamists was later reignited by the attack on the very remote military garrison of al-Megheyti, close to the Malian and Algerian borders, in June 2005. The attack, which allegedly caused the death of fifteen Mauritanian soldiers, was attributed to the GSPC and its Mauritanian associates. Some opposition groups claimed that this attack was, at best, a fight among networks of traffickers who operate in this border area and include local military officers, and at worst a plot staged by the government to substantiate the Islamic threat in Mauritania (CRIDEM 2005). But for the Mauritanian government, this latest event once again served to dichotomize the identities of the regime and the Islamists. The foreign, deceptive, and anarchical nature of the Islamists was emphasized by the interior minister, as he declared that the perpetrators of the attack were part of a group of

> deceivers who do not have their place in an Islamic country such as Mauritania, *Bilad Chinguitt,* a truly Muslim country both in its spirit and its habits; they try to eliminate the true Islam which left its mark on this country for more than fourteen centuries. . . . This group is using certain mosques in Nouakchott and Nouadhibou to encourage subversion, violence, and quarrels among Muslims, using the fatwa of jihadist salafist leaders in Mauritania. (*Nouakchott Info,* June 27, 2005)

Repression of Islamists slowed with the coup d'état of August 3, 2005. It is too early to speculate on the type of relationship that the new leaders will build with the various individuals and organizations who base their political discourses on Islam. It is worth noting that the new regime has released almost all of the Islamists who had been jailed since April 2005, with the exception of about twenty individuals. However, the government is still not putting them on trial, which means evidence against them is still not known to the public. In addition, in a context of forthcoming elections, the head of state, Col. Ely Ould Mohamed Vall, who led the country's National

Security forces for twenty years, has forcefully refused to authorize the creation of an Islamist party, as his predecessor did. During his visit to the town of Rosso, as part of his tour of the country's administrative regions, he made a speech in both Arabic and French during which he repeated the representations of the previous regime (though with an unusual animation, as I myself witnessed on national television), arguing that the form of Islam called "Salafist Jihadist, or Takfir, or Kalachnikov, or whatever it is called, are foreign to our culture" (Nouakchott *Horizon*, June 5, 2006). As the state-owned newspaper's main headline (in Arabic) announced with force: "No partisanship in the name of Islam in a Muslim country!" (*Chaab,* June 5, 2006). A few days before that speech, in what was then a usual routine, the government had announced the arrest of "Salafist terrorists" who were allegedly preparing a terrorist attack in Nouakchott (*La Tribune,* June 1, 2006).

Two general conclusions come to mind at this point. On the one hand, the new military junta in power may at least attempt to improve its relations with the Islamists, as it seeks to diffuse the opposition that has built up since the mid-1990s. For instance, though it does not authorize the creation of Islamist parties, it may allow independent candidates, known for their Islamist "credentials," to run in municipal and legislative elections. In effect, those who prefer to call themselves the "centrist reformists," defining themselves as "moderate Islamists," acknowledge that the regime will never allow them to have their own electoral list but nonetheless frequently voice their opinions and make no secrets about their intention to run as independent candidates. Some of their leaders are even allowed to speak on national television, something previously unthinkable. (I have personally seen a debate with Jamil Ould Mansour on national television, a man who was arrested on many occasions under the previous regime.) On the other hand, all the current military leaders (and many civilian leaders as well) were major pillars of the previous regime. This raises the question as to what extent the change of a few men can actually change a whole political system. How can high-ranking military officers who have designed the policy of repression against the Islamists quickly shift gears? Will the few concessions to the "moderate Islamists" positively balance with the continuing refusal to authorize Islamist political parties? When (and if) a new elected government comes to power after the transition period, the crucial question will be whether the new civilian leaders enjoy complete freedom from the military, or whether the latter will continue to rule indirectly, as in Algeria. The answer to this question will undoubtedly impact the fate of political Islam in Mauritania.

To sum, Islamism in Mauritania was affected to a significant extent by the process of authoritarian restoration. Like most opponents who sought to use the new democratic institutions designed in the early 1990s to peacefully advance their cause, the Islamists were quickly confronted with the regime's strategy of survival, which was translated into a policy of political, financial, and symbolic repression. In this later case, the politics of identity construction became a major strategy by which the regime hoped to counter and weaken the Islamists. It sought to "demonize" the Islamists, defining them as inherently foreign to Mauritania's religious culture, as carriers of a deceptive vision of Islam, and aspiring to import anarchy in the country. In the absence of any systematic fieldwork research on the evolution of Islamism, it would be difficult to measure the precise impact of the regime's policy. Discussions with average Mauritanians reveal ambiguous opinions. On the one hand, many people saw that the former regime was repressing the Islamists in the absence of any concrete proof of their intention to destabilize the country. On the other hand, the government's language of *fitna* and foreign manipulation may also strike a chord among various segments of Mauritanian communities. How the new regime will deal with this issue will tell us more about the actual impact of the previous regime's construction of dichotomous identities.

. . . And Ethnicity

Though strongly affected by authoritarianism, the evolution of Islamism in Mauritania is also significantly tied to a second defining feature of Mauritania's political scene: the politics of ethnicity. In effect, a simple fact strikes the analyst as he or she looks, for instance, at the names of Islamist leaders mentioned in the media and in informal discussion or at lists of Islamist prisoners: there are very few of Haalpulaar, Wolof, or Sooninke origin. Islamism is essentially a Moorish/Bidhan phenomenon. A few exceptions can be mentioned; they include the Futanke leaders and followers of the Al-Falaah movement (Harakat al-Falaah), whose Senegalese branch is generally labeled as Islamist. This organization has its roots in a movement created in the 1940s by a Mauritanian Haalpulaar, al-Hajj Mahmud Ba. Though Ba was Mauritanian and ended his career in the Mauritanian administration in the 1960s and 1970s (as an adviser to President Ould Daddah), he spent most of his time and resources in Senegal (and partly in Mali, too). Al-Falaah is mostly educational and social, structured around a network of schools where much time is spent teaching Arabic and Islamic culture (Kane 1997; Loimeier 2000:181–183; Piga 2002:46–49). In today's Mauritania, the Al-Falaah movement is relatively small, attracting a few Haalpulaar, most of whom come from the Fulbe Aynaabe subcommunity,[5] that is, the seminomadic herders of the socially complex Haalpulaar community.[6] It is worth noting that it was precisely among the Fulbe Aynaabe that in the mid-1990s the government of Ould Taya officially encouraged, and probably financed, the creation of a sociopolitical association called the Association for Friendship and Return to the Origins (L'Association pour l'amitié et le retour aux origines). The main goal of this state-sponsored association was to publicize and promote the Arabic roots of the Fulbe community (Fulbe's Arabness, or *arabité*). According to Sall (1999), the government's objective was to divide the Haalpulaar community at a time (mid-1990s) in which the regime was trying to weaken opposition parties' quasi-monopoly over the Haalpulaar electorate. The regime sought (but eventually failed) to co-opt part of the Haalpulaar by manipulating historical status distinctions among the sedentary, farming Toorobe (also the ruling caste of the Haalpulaar community) and the seminomadic Fulbe. The small size of the Al-Falaah movement in Mauritania, when compared to its large Senegalese branch, epitomizes very well our main research question here: how to explain that in a country where the entire population is Muslim, a significant share of that population, the Futanke, is left out, or keeps itself out, of the Islamist movement?[7] William Miles (2004) provides a fruitful theoretical basis to understand this phenomenon: despite its transnational and increasingly globalized feature, Islamism is "mediated" and "inflected" by each state's political and social history. Though we may be witnessing the development of a global "virtual Umma," made possible by the globalization of communication technologies, financial transactions, and diaspora movements (Roy 2004b; Kepel 2004), Miles reminds us that researchers should not discard the significance of the state, both as a specific political arena and as an actor. In the specific case of Mauritania, the country's unique ethno-linguistic fabric and its distinctive history of state-society relations and interethnic relations have undoubtedly inflected the global Islamist discourse. This could explain differences between the configuration of Islamism in Mauritania and that of its North African and West African neighbors. In sum, if the authoritarian policies of the regime have molded Mauritanian Islamism to a significant degree, the country's specific ethnic configuration also played a major role. Accordingly, this final section's task is to explain the "ethnicization" of Islamism in Mauritania. It does so by highlighting three interrelated causal factors: the close ties between ethnicity and language; the ethnic violence of the 1989–1991 period; and the influence of Sufi *tariqa* in the Senegal River valley.

For want of space, this chapter cannot provide an exhaustive background on the politics of ethnicity in Mauritania. However, a few key points can be raised to understand this important sociopolitical characteristic of Islamism in Mauritania. Since the colonial period, ethnic identities have become major issues in Mauritania's political system. In effect, it is mostly during the colonial period that ethnic labels became politically meaningful. Although it is commonsensical today to talk about Mauritania's four ethnic groups (Moors, Haalpulaaren, Sooninke, and Wolof), in the precolonial era other forms of solidarity were much better predictors of political conflict and cooperation than these broad ethnic terms, such as lineages, occupation, status, and locality. However, as the French began to interfere in what Robinson (2000:12) calls the "Senegalo-Mauritanian zone," ethnicity began to acquire new meanings (Jourde 2004). One of the most important decisions made by the colonial power was to "territorialize" the political space. The creation of two distinct territorial entities at the very end of the nineteenth century, the colony of Senegal and the colony of Mauritania, and of various territorial subdivisions within each colony (*cercle*; *canton*; *villages*; *campement*), combined with the creation of new political institutions, such as the *chefferies* (chieftaincies) and the various elected assemblies, impacted significantly on local political games. In addition, the implementation of new administrative, social, and economic structures (agricultural schemes, health centers, French schools, public investment funds, and so many others) altered the sociopolitical stakes and thus changed the significance and saliency of identities.

Language, Ethnicity, and Religion: Is Arabic the Language of All Muslims, or the Language of the Ethnic Moors?

The issue of languages illustrates this process quite well. Before the creation of the colonies of Senegal and Mauritania, language as a form of identity was infused with a specific political meaning in what was to become Mauritania. As elsewhere in the region, knowledge of classical Arabic, the language of the Quran, represented a useful social capital for its speakers. But with the creation and institutionalization of a territorial and political entity called the "colony of Mauritania," language suddenly became invested with a new political dimension. The language of the colonial state triggered both opposition and attraction, being the language of power and oppression. But it also raised the question of the language(s) that "native" civil servants should speak. When the departure of the French became imminent, these questions became even more important, as the knowledge of specific language(s) would determine one's appointment in the civil service, and consequently one's access to significant financial and political resources. As the colonial era neared its end, the debates became more intense, notably those about the future independent state's official language(s).

It is important to note that throughout the colonial period, the Haalpulaar, Sooninke, and Wolof populations of the Senegal River valley, or Futanke, had a greater access to the colonial schools and, consequently, learned French in greater numbers than did the Moors. This can be explained by the fact that they were sedentary populations, established along the Senegal River, and were thus more easily controlled by the colonial administration. Military conscription, head-tax collection, and compulsory European-style education were implemented with more ease in these communities. Moorish communities, in contrast, thanks to their nomadic and seminomadic lifestyles, could not be easily reached by the colonial administration. The bulk of native civil servants therefore came from Futanke communities, and much less from Moorish communities. The colony's native political leaders, however, were mostly drawn from ruling Moorish *qaba'il* (singular *qabila*; tribe), whom the French considered to be the dominant group in the colony (as the name of the colony itself suggests).[8] Tensions about the importance of Arabic in the administration had already broken out during the colonial era, but it was mainly a few years after Mauritania gained its independence that serious conflicts erupted. After they had made Arabic the only official language of Mauritania, political leaders decided to increase the share of Arabic in the education system. A series of reforms were adopted, each of which increased the importance of Arabic at the expense of French; meanwhile, the three other native languages of Mauritania—Pulaar, Sooninke, and Wolof—were completely excluded from the education system until 1979. Even then, the small programs devoted to these three languages were never given enough resources to fulfill their role.

At stake in this whole process was not only the ethnic and/or national identity of Mauritania (an Arab country? An Afro-Arab country? A Francophone country?); it was also about access to the state apparatus and its bureaucracy. By making Arabic the official language of the bureaucracy and by increasing the time allocated to Arabic in schools, at the expense of French, Moors could get a more significant share of the state apparatus than individuals from the three minority groups. For the Futanke, however, this meant a drastic decline in their share of administrative positions. In fact, the most violent cases of political violence that erupted between the year of independence (1960) and 1989 all related to language (Taine-Cheikh 1994). In sum, the process of "Arabization," as Futanke leaders called it, accelerated over the years, and was perceived by the latter as a policy of exclusion. This process culminated between 1989 and 1991. At that time, Arab nationalist factions (of Ba'athist and Nasserist obedience) enjoyed a powerful influence over the presidency, the military, and the intelligence services. Following local clashes between farmers and herders in the Senegal River valley, security forces and paramilitary troops launched a violent wave of repression against Futanke communities, forcing about 80,000 of them to take refuge on the Senegalese shore of the river, and killing hundreds of them. In 1990 and 1991, about five hundred Futanke military officers were executed, and hundreds were fired from the army (Fleischman 1994).

This brief historical account helps to explain why Islamism in Mauritania is largely mediated by the politics of ethnicity. Whereas the growth of Islamism in other West African countries was translated on the political field by the growing demand for Arabic schools and for the increase of Arabic in the official education system, this dynamic has taken a completely different meaning in the Mauritanian context, where debates and policies about the role and space devoted to Arabic have nurtured violent ethnic tensions. Hence, I hypothesize that given the prominent role of Arabic in the social and political conceptions of Islamist activists, their movement has faced, and will continue to face, a strong resistance among Futanke. The very meaning of Arabic for the average Mauritanian Futanke differs significantly from that of, say, his Senegalese or Malian counterparts. I argue that the meaning of this language comprises a sense of state violence and political exclusion in Mauritania that it does not have in neighboring countries.

The 1989–1991 Massacre of Futanke: The Unforgotten Silence of Islamists

Closely connected to this last point, a second factor that explains the ethnic character of Islamism in Mauritania relates specifically to the violence of the 1989–1991 era. The Islamists were not involved in this violence. However, their otherwise violent discourse against the regime had nothing to say about the violence on Futanke. It must be remembered that in the years following the massacres, the regime has purposefully attempted to obscure what happened between 1989 and 1991. Not only was an Amnesty Law adopted in 1993, thereby prohibiting any investigation and sanction against those who committed human rights violations, but debates about this era were banned from public discourse. In the common language, this violence was euphemistically called "the national question." And this silence reached some other opposition movements and parties, including the Islamists, who were either incapable or unwilling to publicly and strongly criticize the regime about this violent era. No research has been carried out yet to explain that silence, but we can expect to find a partial answer in the contentious point discussed previously. Given that language policies, and more specifically the role and status of Arabic in the Mauritanian polity, were a major factor leading to the 1989–1991 violence, and given the peculiar importance of Arabic for the Islamists, their understanding and representation of that violent period must differ with that of Futanke Muslims. More generally, then, the Islamist movements' antiregime discourse may have gained a growing appeal among Arabic-speaking populations, but their silence concerning the 1989–1991 period and their decision to spare the regime about its terrible role during those years greatly limited their capacity to attract Futanke followers. Perhaps Islamists' silence regarding the 1989–1991 attacks can simply be explained by the fact that they did not have the opportunity to forcefully condemn them, being persecuted by the regime and excluded from most political stages. Yet other opposition forces who were also repressed by the regime did voice their condemnation. Interestingly, since the coup of 2005, "moderate" Islamist leaders (the vast majority of whom are of Moorish background) have strongly criticized the previous regime for its human rights violations against Futanke and have asked that the regime's actions be the subject of investigation and prosecution. One of them, Jamil Ould Mansour, called for the systematic repatriation of Mauritanian Futanke refugees who were forced to leave their country in 1989–1991 (*Nouakchott Info,* August 2, 2006). Whether Futanke populations will perceive this new Islamist position as being "too little too late," or whether it will strike a positive chord among them, should be an interesting question to explore.

A third factor contributed to the formation of an "ethnic obstacle" for Mauritania's Islamist movement: the continuing strength of Sufi orders among Futanke believers. Generally speaking, a defining feature of West African Islamist movements' discourse, in addition to their demand for the Arabization of the education system, is their critical position vis-à-vis traditional Sufi orders. In effect, Islamists define themselves partly in contrast with the Sufi orders, denouncing the non-Islamic role played by the shaikh and marabouts as well as the numerous non-Islamic rituals and habits they practice. The tensions between, on the one hand, the Qadiriyya and the Tijaniyya, and on the other hand the Izala (Jama'at Izalat al-bid'a wa Iqamat as-Sunna) in northern Nigeria epitomize very well this defining feature of Islamist movements (Miles 2003; Mahmud 2004; Loimeier, this volume). However, it is important to keep in mind, as some have noted, that the boundary between Islamism and Sufism may be more porous than what is often assumed (Kane 2000; Schmitz 2000; Villalón 2004).

In Mauritania, as in other West African countries, Islamists have also sought to differentiate themselves from the Sufi *tariqa*. As Al Hassan Wuld Moulaye Ely, a leading Islamic figure, explains, "This Muslim society ignores Islam. Its interpretation of Islam is incorrect, because it follows the teachings of marabouts, or the tradition of its ancestors, or that of the Imam Malick. But the only source of Islam is the Qur'an and the Sunna of the Prophet" (Boubrik 1998:143, citing *Mauritanie-Nouvelle,* January 9, 1995). But this critical perspective on Sufi *tariqa,* which constitutes a discursive mechanism by which Islamists define themselves, can explain (in part) the ethnic containment or "ethnicization" of Mauritanian Islamists. In effect, since the great jihad of Al Hajj Umar Tall in the mid-1800s, the Tijaniyya *tariqa* has gained a hegemonic position in the Senegal River valley. Though more research is again needed to elaborate that argument, it seems that the Tijaniyya has become an integral part of Futanke identity. To take the example of the Haalpulaar (or Tukulor) community, the largest Futanke community in Mauritania, being Haalpulaar is, in part, being Tijani. Hence, as I. A. Sall (2000:389) argues, the Haalpulaar identity is a "triple L" identity: it is made of the Tijaniyya "way" (*laawol* in Pulaar/Fulani), its cultural lineages (*lenol*), and its territory (*leydi*), the Futa. Altogether, this "triple L" identity (*laawol—lenol—leydi*) forms a kind of "ethno-religious nationalism" that defines the Haalpulaar community. If, as Sall hypothesizes, the Tijani way is one of the three major pillars of the Haalpulaar identity, then it comes as no surprise that the Islamists' anti-Sufi discourse has impacted negatively on their capacity to recruit followers outside of the Moorish communities.

Conclusion

The main argument of this chapter is that Islamism in Mauritania has been caught between two interrelated dynamics: authoritarianism and ethnicity. On the one hand, the Mauritanian Islamist movement has faced an adaptive authoritarian regime that has sought to preserve its political foundations while excluding opposition voices from the political arena, and which has seen no place for a political movement that talks in the name of Islam in what is officially an "Islamic Republic." Fearful that this movement could eventually mobilize an increasing number of disfranchised people with a religious discourse that strikes a sensitive chord among them, the regime deployed symbolic and physical violence to weaken this movement. It did so in an international context defined by North American and West European states' (mis)conceptions of Islam and that provided the Mauritanian regime with substantive support to fight its local "war on terror." On the other hand, Islamist leaders and activists have been confronted with an increasingly polarized ethnic arena, in which core pillars of their ideology, namely the central, sacred role of Arabic and their anti-Sufi position, have been interpreted by the Futanke ethnic minorities as an attack on their very identity. The ethnicization of Islamism has certainly weakened the movement and limited the possibility for expansion as it cut itself from about 30 percent of the population. The 2005 coup d'état, if it fulfils its promise of truly democratizing political institutions and rectifying ethnic inequalities, might produce some drastic changes in the trajectory of Islamism in this intriguing, multiculturally Muslim nation.

Notes

1. I use the term *Futanke* to refer to those who originate from the three non-Arabic-speaking communities of Mauritania: Haalpulaaren (often called Toucouleur, or Peul), Sooninke, and Wolof. *Futanke* means "inhabitants of the *Futa*," which is the name of the Senegal River valley, where these three communities were originally located.

2. His sermons were broadcast weekly on the state-owned radio. See Boubrik (1998:139).

3. The interior minister belongs to a *qabila* (Tajakant) that has strong ties with the Middle East (ICG 2005). It is worth noting also that he is a well-known member of the Nasserist network (a pan-Arabism nationalist faction that was accused of being an architect of the massacres against Mauritania's Haalpulaar, Wolof, and Sooninke communities in 1989–1991).

4. Excerpts of these "confessions" can be read in Radio-Mauritania (1994a; 1994b).

5. This information was confirmed to me through various discussions with Haalpulaar informants in Nouakchott, May–June 2006.

6. The constitution of the Haalpulaar community is complex. Though they all share the same languages, the "speakers of Pulaar" are internally differentiated along caste and occupational lines. One of these differences is that between the herders (Fulbe Aynaabe) and farmers, the latter being also divided along caste lines (from the ruling Toorobe to the former slave Maccube).

7. I am currently carrying out a research project in Mauritania and Senegal in which I try to explain the striking contrast between Senegalese and Mauritanian Haalpulaar participation in Islamist movements.

8. *Mauritania* means "land of the Moors" (in French, *Maures*).

6

The Gambia: Islam and Politics

Momodou N. Darboe

Man is my secret and I am his. The inner knowledge of the spiritual essence is a secret of my secrets. Only I placed this in the heart of my true servant, and no one can know his state but I.

—*A Hadith of the Prophet*

Religious leaders and politicians often use the emotions of the faithful for their specific agenda of political gain or survival, reorganizing society to conform to religious doctrine. A notable example of this is seen in The Gambia, where since the early 1990s the practice of Islam has undergone a perceptible change from a tolerant and accommodating type of Qadiriyya-inspired Islam to a more radical form. This transformation has coincided with changes in the leadership of The Gambia and use of religion within the political arena. Politicians have used Islamic symbols or rationale to gain or maintain political power. In their aspirations to modify society, Islamists have used politics in furthering the interest of their religion and its followers. The co-optation of Muslim clerics by political powers, especially those who have significant influence and following, takes different forms: legislation, bribery, extortion, and force or the threat of force in the form of arrest, detention, and imprisonment. With the tacit approval of the state, radical Islamists have also often resorted to violence in the form of assaults, arson, intimidation, and harassment to impose and enforce their radical ideas, practices, and reforms. Consequently, the Gambian Muslim population and civil society are caught between the often oppressive forces of politicians on the one hand, and radical Islamists on the other. The violence and intolerance often associated with this new brand of Islamic fundamentalism and radicalism have raised questions regarding the potential for a freer, more open society for The Gambia as a whole.

Conceptual Framework

Islamism is generally understood as the organized efforts by believers in the Islamic faith to influence national politics along Islamic precepts (Butterworth and Zartman 1992). Islamism aspires to organize or reorganize, by means of the political institution, the social structure of a particular society in accordance with the dictates of Islamic values, law, and principles. This definition of Islamism is limited in scope because it does not include the reciprocal relationship between the religion and politics. Instead, it implies that the relationship between Islam and politics is *unidirectional* in effect; that is, in the interaction of the two, politics do not have a modifying influence on the organization, activities, and values of Islam and Islamists. On this point, Jeff Haynes observes that "the relationship between religion and politics is both dialectical and interactive: each shapes and influences the other" (Haynes 1998:5). A narrow definition of Islamism ignores the fact that although Islamists strive to influence the course of politics, politics and political leaders also attempt to influence the activities and/or thought processes of the Islamists.

Additionally, the accepted definition tends to ignore the use of Islam by national politicians for their own political gain. Within the context of differentiating between genuine and nongenuine religious leaders and activities, William Miles acknowledges the use by clerics and lay leaders (politicians) of "religious rationale primarily to gain or maintain power" (Miles 1996:526). Islamists, in their aspirations to modify society, use politics in the interest of their religion and its followers, and politicians use Islamic symbols or rationale to gain or maintain political power.

In light of this argument, a more comprehensive definition of Islamism should reflect both the reciprocal influence between Islam and politics and the use of Islamic symbols and doctrine by Islamists on behalf of Muslim and Islamic interests and by politicians to gain and/or maintain political power. It is within the context of this more comprehensive definition of Islamism that I discuss Islam and politics in The Gambia.

Ethnoreligious Backdrop

The Gambian population consists of several ethnic groups, the largest of which are Mandinka, Fula, and Wolof, in that order. Although relatively small, the other significant ethnic groups include Jola, Serahule, and Aku. Until the 1970s, English Creoles (Aku) constituted about 2 percent of the population but had the most influence in national politics because they had relatively more Western education than the rest of the population (Gailey 1965:9–17).

Historians estimate that the influence of Islam spread to the west coast of Africa around the twelfth century. However, it has been documented that initial contact between Islamic culture and traditional African culture may date as far back as the eighth century (Nyang 1984:20). The success of the dissemination of Islam relative to Christianity in Africa was due to the inherent flexibility and accommodative nature of early Islam. This tolerant nature allowed Africans to adapt Islam to their own indigenous cultures. Thus, the West African or Gambian brand of (Sunni) Islam is perceptibly different in practice compared to the (also Sunni) one practiced in Saudi Arabia and in other Sunni and Shi'ite societies in the Middle East. The average Gambian Muslim is not disturbed by these differences. This accepting aspect of Gambian culture may also explain the receptive attitudes toward the introduction of Ahmadiyya and other sects of Islam later in the country's history. This is not to say, however, that Islamic tolerance, either in the past or today, has insulated the religion from politics.

A relevant colonial example of the political-religious nexus in The Gambia allied the British with non-Muslim Soninkes against the marabouts, the traditional Islamic clerics and traders. As the ruling and aristocratic class of the Mandinka kingdoms, the Soninkes often excluded marabouts from land ownership and holding of state offices, heavily taxing them. In the 1840s, this tense relationship between marabouts and Soninkes led to a civil war in the marabout-dominated town of Sabiji (modern Sukuta) when the marabouts rebelled against the Mansa Kombo (Quinn 1972:86–87).

During this period, both the British colonial authorities and merchants were concerned about any political instability that would threaten the production of the colony's main and only cash crop, groundnuts, and also feared that their interests in Upper British Kombo would be adversely affected in the event of an insurrection. It was believed that Mansa Kombo would cede more land to the British colony if he prevailed in the conflict with the marabouts. These were sufficient reasons for Governor O'Connor to ally with the Soninke king to crush the marabout revolt (Quinn 1972:85–91; Gray 1966:367–368; Napier Hewett 1969:239–242).

Today, at least 85–90 percent of the population (1.5 million) is Sunni Muslim. The smaller religious groups consist of Roman Catholics, Anglicans, Wesleyans, and animists. Of those who follow the Islamic faith, a relatively small number include members of the Ahmadiyya sect. Of the non-Muslim populations, the largest are the Irish Catholics, whose missionaries are the most influential.

Irish Catholic missionaries have been in the country since 1849 (Cleary, interview 2005[1]). Like the other Christian faiths, Catholicism was established in the country around the inception of British colonization of The Gambia. Irish Catholic headquarters are in the capital city of Banjul and its suburbs of Kanifing and Cape Point. Their satellite missions are strategically located throughout the country in the Fula and Jola districts, the relatively larger proportion of which ethnic groups are animist. Since its introduction, the Catholic missions' primary instrument of proselytizing has been through Western education. The influence of the Catholic mission remains significant because of its impact on educational opportunity. Until relatively recently, the Catholic mission maintained one of the two high schools in the country. Neither the Catholic missionaries nor the parents of the students have problems with this seeming contradiction of Muslim students attending Catholic schools. Reading the Scriptures, both the New and Old Testaments, were optional rather than a condition of admission to these Catholic schools. A significant number of today's Gambian educated elite attended the Catholic mission high school.

Historically, the majority of Gambian Muslims practiced a brand of Islam that was accommodating to many indigenous African customs and beliefs. This changed over time as Saudi influence increased in The Gambia. During the First Republic, the government received technical assistance from the Kingdom of Saudi Arabia in the form of scholarships to train Gambians to become teachers of religious studies in the established schools providing Western education. By the late 1970s and early 1980s, Islamic studies were taught in most of the schools in the metropolitan areas of the capital and its suburbs by Gambians educated in Saudi Arabia who spoke fluent Arabic, instructed in Arabic, and taught Islamic values that were perceptibly different from those traditionally practiced in The Gambia. By this time, Gambians were exposed to competing religious values of various sects as well as to different versions of Islam. For example, the Catholic missions taught Christianity in ways strange to Anglicans and Wesleyans. The Ahmadiyya perspective of Islam was quite different from that of the Saudi-favored practice of Islam, and both differed from the traditional Gambian Muslim practices.

The factors that unite all Gambian Muslims, like the rest of the Islamic community (*umma*), are the Quran, Sunna, Hadith, and sharia. However, as in the whole of the Islamic civilization and among all Muslims, Gambian Muslims interpret these unifying factors differently (Nasr 2002:57–59). Such differences in interpretation have not only led to the diversity of the Gambian Muslim community but also often caused tensions and crises within it. Worldwide, about 87 percent of all Muslims are Sunnis and 13 percent are Shi'ite (Nasr 2002:65–68). In The Gambia almost all Muslims are Sunnis except for a few Shiites who are relatively recent immigrants from Syria and Lebanon.

The four schools of Islamic jurisprudence that constitute the main body of traditional Sunnism are Hanafi, Maliki, Shafii, and Hanbali. Thus the followers of Sunnism are divided according to the schools of law they follow. Most of the Gambian Sunni community follows the Maliki school of thought as a consequence of the spread of Malikiism from North to West Africa (Nasr 2002:67–68). In The Gambia the school's followers may be categorized into the Ahmadiyya, Traditionalists, and Modernists. The latter are also known as Wahhabis or Subbanu (followers of Sunna). The Modernists include the subcategories of formally educated Wahhabis, Ma'shala, and Salaf.[2] Both Traditionalists and the Wahhabis belong to the Sufi orders of Qadiriyya, Tijaniyya, and Muridiyya. The Qadiriyya forms the majority among them, whereas the followers of Muridiyya are very few, consisting primarily of Senegalese immigrants.

The Ahmadiyya movement was founded by Ghulam Amad from Pakistan. In a sense, he was a modernist and a reformer "who claimed for himself a new Divine dispensation" (Nasr 2002:79). The Ahmadiyya Jama'at, or the Ahmadis, claimed to be Muslims and follow Islamic practices. However, they further claim that "the name Ahmadiyyad is the name of a reinterpretation or restatement of the Religion of the Holy Quran." Such a restatement, the followers believe, was presented under the divine guidance of the founder of the movement (Mahmud Ahmad 2002:3; Ahmad 1992). The mainstream Islamic community's views of the Ahmadiyya, particularly its implicit challenge to the finality of the Prophet of Islam, ranged from Ahmadiyya being considered as an Islamic sect, although deviant in some ways, to outright declaration that they are not Muslims. The Ahmadiyya Muslims began to make their impact at the beginning of the First Republic (1965–1994). They built schools and medical clinics throughout the country but were primarily located in the urban areas of Banjul, Kanifing, and Brikama.

The beginnings of fundamentalism in Islam, in terms of the more orthodox interpretation of the religion, can be traced to the impact of European colonialism in the Islamic world. One clear example of this is the rise of the Ahmadiyya movement as a reaction to English missionary activity in India. The prevailing belief then was that as a consequence of the intrusion of European civilization, Muslims had strayed from the original message of Islam and had become corrupted by luxury and deviations (Nasr 2002:80, 100–102).

In West Africa the reform movement gained much strength in the 1950s after the return of graduates from Al-Azahar University in Cairo and other schools in the Middle East. These graduates, based on their newly acquired interpretation of the faith, sought to purify the practice of Islam (Kaba 2000:190). Thus, the major difference between the Traditionalists and the Modernists in The Gambia lies in their perception of each other with respect to Islamic orthodoxy. The Wahhabis' basis for the need for Islamic reform in The Gambia lies in their belief that current practices of the religion depart from orthodoxy due to either a misunderstanding of Islamic doctrine or the community's refusal to conform to the true principles of the Quran and Sunna.

The Traditionalists, in comparison, insist on conserving what they believe to be true and sacred practices of Islam. These conflicting views and beliefs have given rise to the reform movement to eliminate syncretic practices and to introduce new educational methods (Kaba 1974:21; Janson 2004; Janson 2006). The conflict centered on issues and practices such as posture and prayers in performing the ritual of prayer; attitudes about family and marriage; naming and wedding ceremonies; saint worship; and the proper mode of dress both for men and women. Examples are whether the proper posture for the ritual of prayer is with the arms along the sides of the body or hands crossed on the chest, and whether music and dancing, as opposed to prayer and the reading and recitation of the Quran, should be used to celebrate the naming of a newborn. The Wahhabis (Subbanu) even question whether the common practice of polygamy is consistent with Islamic doctrine. According to them, any deviation from the strict practice of the Sunna is considered a wrongful innovation and thus *bid'a* (Kaba 1974; Kaba 2000:190; Janson 2004).[3]

Another important difference between the Traditionalists and the reform-oriented Wahhabis is the source and background of Islam and Quranic education. The Traditionalists are home-grown Islamists whose education was from the indigenous *majilis* or Quranic schools. (*Majilis* is derived from the Arabic word *djalasa,* "to sit.") It refers to students sitting in a circle around their teacher, who is often a marabout (religious leader) (Janson 2004). Their mode of instruction is less formal and less structured. Since their teachers were originally themselves products of these local *majilis,* their pronunciation of the classical Arabic words in which the Quran is written is significantly influenced by the local languages. It is a difference that has added to the reasons for condescension toward them by the Modernist Wahhabis. The Wahhabis, in contrast, are graduates of universities from such renowned institutions as Al-Azahar in Cairo, Egypt; and universities in Sudan, Saudi Arabia, and other Middle East institutions. The instruction in these universities is formal, well structured, and in classical Arabic.

These differences in views and characteristics clearly distinguish the Traditionalists from the Modernist Wahhabis. However, in The Gambia the Wahhabis are not a monolithic group. They can instead be subdivided into three categories: the older, more formally educated Wahhabis; the Ma'shala; and the followers of Salafiyya. In general, the three subcategories share the views of strict adherence to the Sunna, including the mode of dress. However, their methods and target population for Islamic reform are significantly different from one another.

Unlike their younger and less-educated colleagues, the older university-educated Wahhabis have almost exclusive access to the government-controlled media of television and radio for the dissemination of their more orthodox Islam. Friday mosque sermons are televised, and during weekly talk shows Islamic scholars are invited to answer questions concerning matters of Islamic doctrine, specifically the Sunna, with regard to rituals of prayer, marriage, divorce, inheritance, and other aspects of Muslim life. Imported television programs from the Arab world, for example, programs about the life of the Prophet Mohammed, radio broadcasts, and the distribution of sermons on radio tapes, writing columns in the local newspapers, religious pamphlets, Islamic journals, and the building of madrasas are all used as effective tools for the orthodox Islamic reform movement (Darboe 2004:73–82; Janson 2004). The younger and less-educated Wahhabis, known as Ma'shala or Tabligh Jamma'at, use less sophisticated methods for dissemination of their orthodox Islamic methodology. (*Ma'shala* is derived from the Arabic expression Ma Sha Allah—"what God wishes." *Tabligh Jamma'at* means "organization for proselytization" [Janson 2006].) Based on their belief that the Prophet's teachings were done in mosques as opposed to the classroom, and that profound or advanced knowledge of the Quran is not a prerequisite for teaching about the faith, the Tabligh Jamma'at relies primarily on lay preaching, traveling from village to village and mosque to mosque to disseminate their theological views. They clearly explain that their target population is not non-Muslims but instead fellow Muslims whose practice of the faith has strayed or deviated from the path of proper Sunna and Islamic doctrine. Central to their preaching is the emphasis on the rewards and benefits of prayer and following the path of the Prophet as opposed to the consequent punishment for the deviations. This strategy is important because it clearly distinguishes them from the followers of Salafiyya. "It is important that people understand that we are different from the followers of Salafiyya in important ways even though we dress alike and share the same theological views. Their strategy is to direct people on the right path by instilling the fear of hell and its horrors. We disagree with that method. It is more effective if people follow the path of Allah and his Prophet out of love and not fear" (Ceesay, interview 2006; Kabir, interview 2006).

Most of the university-educated Wahhabis are either Mandinka or Wolof. However, many Sarahule businessmen have also been instrumental in introducing this form of orthodox Islam in The Gambia. They have used their own money to build mosques and madrasas in the greater Banjul area and in predominately Sarahule communities. The majority of the provincial Mandinka, Wolof, Fula, and other ethnic groups received their Islamic education from the local *majilis* or from similar institutions in other West African countries.

Religion and Partisan Politics

The Gambia became a separate colony of Great Britain in 1888, but it was not until the election of 1951 that real political parties began to develop, putting organized pressure on the Colonial Office to revise the governmental system in the country. This pressure, coupled with political advances elsewhere in Africa, caused the Colonial Office to respond with a constitutional revision in The Gambia in 1953. It was not, however, until 1960 that political parties began to serve the function of pressure groups to force an increase in the rate of constitutional revision (Gailey 1965:184–193). At their outset the political parties were not initially based on any particular religious or ethnic groupings. When the first of these parties, the Democratic Party, was formed by the Reverend John C. Fye, political success largely depended on the personality of the leader. This was still true when in January of 1952, I. M. Garba Jahumpa formed the Muslim Congress Party, the second political party in the country. The formation of the Muslim Congress Party was followed by that of the United Party, led by Pierre Sarr Njie; in 1960, the Progressive People's Party, the centrum of which was David Kairaba Jawara, was formed (Gailey 1965:194–199). It was not until 1967 that Noah Sanyanga formed the National Convention Party. As a consequence of an internal leadership fissure within the Progressive People's Party, as of 1975 it was led by Sheiff Dibba (Hughes and Perfect 2005:232–299).

Between 1975 and 1994, several political parties were formed, but only two made any significant impact in the political arena—The Gambia's People's Party (GPP), established in 1982; and the People's Democratic Organization for Independence and Socialism (PDOIS), established in 1986. Andrew Camera founded the GPP; Halifa Sallah, Sam Sarr, and Sidia Jatta cofounded the PDOIS (Hughes and Perfect 2005:300–302).

An early manifestation of the use of Islam as a partisan political tool in The Gambia was the formation of The Gambia Muslim Congress Party, which developed from the Bathurst Young Muslim Society (BYMS). As the name implies, the BYMS was intended to appeal to Muslims on sectarian grounds (Nyang 1979:101–109). The formation of the society in 1946 was not politically motivated; the primary objective was to promote Islamic culture and religion in The Gambia. Interestingly, the society had a specific agenda and target population. In an interview, a founding member revealed that one of the society's goals was to indoctrinate young Gambian Muslims into the Islamic way of life after their return from their studies in the West. The idea was to spiritually reclaim them by cleansing their hearts of the spiritually corrupting influences of Western culture (Badji, interview 2005[4]). Although politics in The Gambia historically depended much on the personality of a party leader, whose religion was rather irrelevant, this was no longer the case by the end of the 1960s and the beginning of the 1970s.

Even though the overwhelming majority of the Gambian population is Muslim, this had not historically been reflected politically. The Muslim Congress Party could not capitalize on Muslim support, whereas the United Party and the Progressive People's Party, both led by Christians, have had significant success in elections since their inception (Gailey 1965: 200–201). Harry A. Gailey explains this by the following observations: First, politics was personality-oriented, making the popularity of political leaders more important than their religion or even political platform; second, the extended family system, which was core to the Gambian social structure and organizational system, superseded religious differences. A person's change of religion did not affect his popularity or prestige within the group. Third, there was little or no connection at the time between Gambian Muslims and any pan-Islamic movement that equates Islam with political goals (Gailey 1965:201).

In 1994, when the First Republic was overthrown by a group of military officers led by Lt. Yahya Jammeh, the political landscape in The Gambia was radically transformed. The military junta, in an effort to civilianize itself, changed itself into a political party from the Armed Forces Provisional Ruling Council (AFPRC) to the Alliance for Patriotic Reorientation and Construction (APRC) to contest the staged presidential elections in 1996. The unbanning of political activity and parties by the junta in 1996 led to the emergence of the United Democratic Party (UDP) and the National Reconciliation Party (NRP). The former's leader is Ousainu Darboe, commonly known as Lawyer Darboe. The NRP is led by Hamat Bah. The UDP and NRP formed a coalition with Darboe as the flag bearer to contest—unsuccessfully—the September 2006 presidential elections.

The End of Tolerance in a Culture of Religious Diversity

The cordial and harmonious coexistence of the various religious denominations and sects in The Gambia almost ended with the overthrow of the

First Republic in July 1994 by Yahya Jammeh. Unlike his predecessor, who was democratically elected, Jammeh's rise to power necessitated urgent and radical measures to entrench himself politically. The new president began his campaign for legitimacy and acceptance by a methodical manipulation of Islam and Islamic symbols. Examples of such manipulation included a change of his personal dress code from a military uniform to what he perceived as Islamic; the building of mosques in various public places, including the State House; the creation of a new cabinet position of religious affairs; the politicization of the Supreme Islamic Council by adding it to the portfolio of the Ministry of Religious Affairs; and the cooptation or intimidation of Islamic religious leaders, especially imams. These measures were calculatingly factored into his adopted policies, state actions, and changes in his public lifestyle.

Until recently, Libyan president Mu'ammar Qaddafi, a master of manipulation of Islamic symbols and imagery, was President Jammeh's closest ally and mentor in the Arab world. Qaddafi guided Jammeh in establishing himself politically. The political successes President Jammeh gained by the manipulation of Islam and co-optation of Muslim leaders had and continues to have an adverse effect on the Gambian culture, where adherents of diverse faiths have historically enjoyed a relationship of mutual respect and acceptance.

It has become increasingly important in politics whether a Gambian is a Muslim or a non-Muslim and how Islam is practiced. Muslims, cognizant of the fact that they form the majority, wear their faith on their sleeves. As the social pressures to conform to precepts of Islam increase, the insensitivity toward the religious minorities' civil and constitutional rights also increases. Consequently, the general comfort that historically characterized the relationship between Muslims and non-Muslim friends and colleagues was gradually but perceptibly replaced with uneasiness and tension. Undoubtedly, these consequent social relations have profound sociological implications. The emergence of Muslim fervor has resulted in the Catholic Church modifying its recruitment. Ironically, the Catholic Church has benefited from the prevailing social conditions by appealing to the socially and politically marginalized ethnic minorities such as the Manjagos and Ballantas.

Gambian Politics and Religion: The Jawara Era

In a society where over 85 percent of the population is Muslim, personal success in national politics is likely to be linked to religious faith. It is, therefore, hardly surprising that Islam has been used as an instrument or vehicle of achieving political success at the national level in The Gambia.

The phenomenon of success in national politics being linked to religious faith is clearly seen by the strategies of the first president of the republic: a Muslim named Dawda Kairaba Jawara who had converted to Christianity and thereby become David Kairaba Jawara. When he entered national politics in the late 1950s, he reconverted to Islam and retook his birth name. Jawara was further pressured by leading figures in his party (the Progressive People's Party, or PPP), some of whom were members of the Bathurst Young Muslim Society, to divorce his Christian wife and marry a Muslim woman (Nyang 1979:183–185). He eventually succumbed under the pressure, becoming legally permitted to marry a Muslim after the passage of the Marriage (special circumstances) Act, which allowed for automatic divorce if one partner converted to another religion (Senghor 1979:388). Much of Jawara's political success was due to his reconversion. His primary opponent, Pierre Sarr Njie, was a Catholic, and Jawara was able to enlist the support of the Muslim population through the Muslim clerics, an advantage his opponent lacked. The reverse was the case historically, when the Muslim Congress lost elections to the UP and the PPP, both led by Christians.

During the period of the first election, Gambian politics had neither the various patterns nor forms of violence or civil rights violations now characteristic of the political arena; neither did it have the current pattern of use of Islam by both politicians and Islamists. Even though Jawara may have owed his political success to his Muslim brethren, he was very sensitive to the secular nature of the government and was thus a keen observer of the separation of church and state. He sought advice from all the various religious sectors of the society without giving the impression to any religious leaders that he depended on them or would be guided by any particular religious values for constructing public policy. Using the constitution as the basis of his reasoning, by which the separation of religion and state was unambiguously articulated, his administration rejected the suggestion of putting the Imam Ratib on the government payroll and the ratification of the newly formed Supreme Islamic Council.

This strict adherence to secularism was further clearly demonstrated in the 1970s in the severance of relations with the Libyan government. As part of Qaddafi's campaign for Islamic solidarity by means of petro-dollar diplomacy, the Libyan government offered to assist the Gambian government to develop and improve its much-needed transportation infrastructure. Both governments signed the agreement, and Libya started supplying the Gambian government with well-equipped luxury buses as part of the agreement.

However, the Gambian government was simultaneously in the process of developing the manufacturing sector of its economy. One of the ideas of the government was to start a beverage—including alcoholic beer—factory. Since the production and/or the consumption of alcohol is a violation of Islamic values, the Libyan government threatened to withdraw its assistance if the Gambian government went ahead with the development of a *haram* (Islamically prohibited) factory. President Jawara made clear that though his government was in need of Libyan assistance, his public policy would not be dictated by a foreign power or any particular religious values. He therefore terminated all relations, including diplomatic relations, with the Libyan government. The government of Libya then started a campaign to overthrow the Jawara government. For the same reasons, President Jawara equally declined assistance from the governments of Saudi Arabia and Pakistan when their aid was linked to the expulsion of the Ahmadiyya Muslim missionaries. (Saudi Arabia and Pakistan were among the Islamic communities who consider the Ahmadiyya as not Muslim or, at best, deviant.) This example confirms S. S. Nyang's assertion that "Islam could [continue to] be used to legitimate or gain [political] authority without any effort being made at creating an Islamic state" (Nyang 1984:23).

A Call for the Reformation of Traditional Islamic Practice and the Emergence of Anti-American Rhetoric

In the early 1980s, Libya was implicated in an attempted bloody overthrow of the government of President Jawara. Although this effort failed, he was deposed in 1994 in a bloodless coup d'état led by Yahya Jammeh, a young military officer in the national army. The Libyan government was among the first to give both diplomatic recognition and material assistance to the new military government formed by Jammeh.

After assuming the office of the presidency, Jammeh had to immediately contend with several daunting problems, the resolution of which would determine the success or failure of his political career. These problems included the following:

- The means of assuming power, unprecedented in the history of The Gambia, by overthrowing a democratically elected government
- Being under thirty years of age
- Having only a high school education
- Being from one of the smallest ethnic groups (unlike the larger ethnic groups, the Jolas, the new president's ethnic group, is geograph-

ically confined to a fraction of the southwestern region of The Gambia)
- Most important, Jammeh's questionable religious background as a Muslim in a predominantly Islamic society

These obstacles were not lost on the new president, for he quickly summoned his comrades to a strategy session (Bojang, interview 2005[5]). The new government quickly launched a vigorous campaign to discredit the old regime as justification for the coup and to legitimize their actions. Since, as evidenced by more recent history, Islam is critical to any successful ascendancy in national politics in The Gambia, Jammeh used the politics of religion to entrench his position in the office of the presidency. It quickly became obvious that the president would employ any feasible means to co-opt Muslim clerics, especially those who commanded significant influence and following, even if such means included legislation, bribery, extortion, force, or the threat of force in the form of arrest, detention, and imprisonment. However, President Jammeh also realized that he must undergo dramatic outward transformation of his public demeanor and mode of dress to lend credibility to his strategies. For example, he exchanged his military uniform for expensive traditional garb conforming to the proper Islamic dress code. In public appearances he carried a lengthy string of prayer beads in one hand and a sword in another, manifest symbols of his religiosity. Both rumor and some evidence suggested that he was raised a Christian and had scanty and shallow knowledge of Islam. Nonetheless, his approval rating increased significantly following these outward displays of piety.

The employment of this particular mode of manipulating Islamic symbols for political legitimacy was not unique to President Jammeh or to The Gambia. For example, in Sudan, when Ja'far al-Numeri, a military officer, took over power, he adopted the *jellabiya* (robe) and *amima* (turban) for many public appearances in place of his favored military uniform (Haynes 1998:112).

Following this reinvention of himself as a religious Muslim, Jammeh began intimidating and discrediting the traditional religious leaders who were loyal to the Jawara regime and its secular approach to governance. An example of his approach can be seen in his public treatment of religious leaders. He summoned all the religious leaders in The Gambia, including the imam Ratib of Banjul and the bishop of the Catholic Church, to the State House. On national television, at prime time, he chastised, insulted, embarrassed, and humiliated them and accused them of being part of, and sponsors of, the corrupt old regime. His coercive tactics are exemplified by the Brikama mosque incident involving Imam Karamo Touray, a cleric of significant following and influence.

Brikama is one of the largest constituencies in the Kombo Municipal Council (KMC) area and a stronghold of the opposition. The incident started with a D10,000 (ten thousand dalasies) donation from the then first lady Tuti Jammeh (the president's first wife) to the Brikama mosque committee for repairs on the central mosque of the community where Imam Touray led prayers. It was obvious that the first lady was trying to win political support for her husband. The sum of money was handed to the July 22nd Youth Organization, a militant wing of the APRC party and the regime. The youth organization gave the money to Dembo Bojang, the *seyfo* (chief) of Brikama and a strong supporter of the president, who vowed to deliver the Brikama constituency to the president. The *seyfo* delivered the donation to Imam Touray, who accepted it on behalf of the mosque committee. However, in accepting the assistance, he added clear and firm instructions that a specified area of the mosque must remain undisturbed. It turned out that the specified area was viewed by the chief and the members of the militant organization as a political meeting place for the mosque elders, whom they believed to be supporters of the United Democratic Party, the major opposition political party. When the imam was away on a short trip, repairs on the mosque began, and, against his instructions, the restricted area was demolished and rebuilt differently. Upon discovery, a relative of the imam and a congregant of the mosque demanded the demolition of the new structure. When the imam returned, he was arrested along with other suspects and charged with malicious destruction of property.

The imam was first detained at the Brikama police station, but as tensions rose in the community because of the arrest, he and his alleged co-conspirators were transferred to the central prison that night. They were denied legal representation, and their whereabouts were hidden from family members. However, on the second day of their detention, Major Momodou Bojang, the minister for the interior, went on national television and on air with the British Broadcasting Corporation and publicly announced that the imam and the other defendants would remain in detention for two weeks.

Since the whereabouts of the defendants were unknown to the families, their lawyers filed a writ of habeas corpus application with the high court (Supreme Court). Late on the day of the habeas corpus application, the defendants were taken before a magistrate in the Kanifing Municipal Magistrate Court, after all government offices were closed, in an attempt to legitimize the detention of the imam and his fellow defendants. This action suggests that the government was conspiring with certain components of the judiciary to advance the president's political agenda. The defendants appeared before Magistrate Inyang, an expatriate civil servant who was lobbying for renewal of his soon-to-expire contract. Conforming to the pronouncement by Interior Minister Bojang that the defendants would be detained for two weeks, Magistrate Inyang ordered the imam and his colleagues to be detained for two weeks. The order, however, was contrary to the provision of the criminal procedure code that imposes duty on magistrates to remand for a period not exceeding seven days at a given time (Darboe, interview 2005[6]). Based on this provision of the criminal procedure code, the high court judge ordered the release of the defendants on bail.

While in detention, the *alkalo* (community head) removed Imam Touray as imam of the central mosque. The dismissal was sanctioned by the *seyfo* of Brikama, Dembo Kara Bojang, and approved by Lamin Kaba Bajo, the minister for religious affairs. Imam Touray's lawyers filed a suit with the high court challenging his removal and also asked for an injunction to restrain the purported successor from performing the duties of imam. The state raised objection and submitted that matters of customary law were involved and, as such, the suit should be transferred to the district tribunal. The plaintiffs noted that the president of the tribunal, Dembo Bojang, was also among those who sanctioned the imam's dismissal. The case was a demonstration of the president's elaborate and extensive network being used for political agendas.

Attendance in the central mosque drastically dwindled while Imam Touray's removal was being legally argued in the courts. In response, a significant number of the congregation boycotted the mosque and instead chose to pray behind Imam Touray in his compound. Realizing the apparent failure of his strategy to get the imam's political support, President Jammeh held a political rally in Brikama and publicly demanded the cessation of all hostilities and the immediate reinstallation of Imam Touray to the imamship of the central mosque (Touray, interview 2005).

A few days after the political rally in Brikama, Imam Touray and other imams of the Banjul metropolis were invited to the State House for another session of propaganda for political support. When Imam Touray realized the agenda of the meeting, he walked out. He was later arrested and detained for a few hours before being released (Touray, interview 2005). The Brikama incident, like some of the president's other strong-arm tactics, backfired. Not only was his political agenda unaccomplished, but his actions alienated the older traditional religious leaders, making it necessary for him to find new allies to consolidate and increase his power. He capitalized on a newly emerging source of religious support: returning Gambian graduates of Arabic Islamic studies.

During the First Republic, a significant number of Gambians traveled to Saudi Arabia, Egypt, Pakistan, and Sudan to pursue a university education in Islamic studies. There were two categories of Gambian students of Islam: those who had a relatively advanced schooling in the Gambian *majilis* (institutions for Quranic and Islamic education), and those whose background in Quranic and Islamic studies was marginal at best. The distinction is noteworthy because their attitude toward Islamic clerics and practice in The Gambia, upon their return, was significantly different. Unlike the students who had a more solid foundation in Islamic education before pursuing further studies, those without this training demonstrated an attitude of condescension and intolerance toward local Gambian Islamic scholars and practice. Such attitudes gave birth to the agenda of Islamic reformation.

Many of the Gambian graduates, particularly those educated in Saudi Arabia, had been indoctrinated into the strictly orthodox Sunni Muslim sect of Wahhabism during their studies in the Saudi Kingdom and other Middle East Islamic institutions. They grew their beards long and followed the more rigid practices of Islam rather than the more flexible and accommodating traditional practices followed by the majority of Gambian Muslims. This newly emerged fundamentalist sect was very critical and disapproving of the traditional practice of Islam in The Gambia. With time, as their numbers grew, they became more distinctive from other Gambian Muslims. They set up institutes where they recruited more followers. They attended funerals, naming ceremonies, or any social gathering to preach Islam according to the doctrines of Wahhabism. Their primary objective was to reform the practices of Islam in The Gambia along the principles of their fundamentalist orthodox sect (Bojang, interview 2005). Initially, they lacked the backing of the official government authority to facilitate their campaign to reform Islamic practice in The Gambia. However, President Jammeh seized the opportunity to form an alliance with the Wahhabis for their mutual interest and benefit. He provided the necessary official authority and platform to foster the Wahhabis' agenda of Islamic reform and personal enrichment, and the fundamentalist sect provided him the political resource he needed following his loss of support from the older and more traditional religious leaders.

It should be pointed out that beyond religious reform, the new fundamentalist sect had an agenda of a more personal nature. Since the time of the First Republic, under the guise of spreading and strengthening Islam in black Africa, many of the graduates in Islamic Studies solicited funding and sponsorship of various projects from the countries of their alma mater, particularly Saudi Arabia and Pakistan. Because of the support of the Gambian government, many of the grant proposals were successful and generous. The funds generated led to the building and administration of several private madrasas, including the Talinding and the Brikama Islamic Institute, headed by Alhaji Saja Fatty and Alhaji Banding Drammeh, respectively. In addition to the establishment of madrasas, the recipients prospered personally from the donated funds, as evidenced by the acquisition of new houses and expensive automobiles. Thus with the external aid, the fundamentalist sect was able to create economic prosperity for its leaders facilitated by the support and sanction of the Gambian government.

As mentioned earlier, the president of the First Republic, Sir Dawda Kairaba Jawara, was quite cognizant of and sensitive to the clear line of separation between the state and the religious institutions of the country. This line of separation between the secular state and the Islamic institutions became quickly blurred when the president of the Second Republic, Yahya Jammeh, took the unprecedented action of building a mosque on State House grounds for the purpose of Islamic services and worship. He appointed one of the Wahhabis, Imam Fatty, as his personal spiritual adviser and also allowed him to lead nationally televised Friday sermons and prayers at the mosque. Further, the imam was given additional broadcast time on both national radio and television. It was exactly the kind of platform—one backed by the power and authority of the president's office and thus the state—that the fundamentalist Wahhabis yearned for. They saw it as an opportunity to enable them to fulfill their ambition of reforming Islamic practices in The Gambia while at the same time protecting their personal economic interests.

The building of a mosque on State House grounds was followed by a proliferation of mosque-building on other public grounds of various government departments. The government also ordered that the Arabic words *walahu yassimuka minalnas* ("Save us from evil men") be inscribed above the entrance of main government offices. The State House mosque was built by funds from the Saudi government; the funds for the construction of the other mosques were provided by the Africa Muslim Agency (AMA), founded by Abdul Rahman Smith, a Kuwaiti business tycoon. The AMA is in general funded by Muslim individuals, institutions, and governments based in the Gulf region—Kuwait, Qatar, Saudi Arabia, and the United Arab Emirates—along with the United States and Europe.[7] The agency has offices and projects in east and southern Africa, and it expanded into West Africa in 1988. The Gambia was the first country to host the agency. However, during the First Republic, the agency's mosque-construction activity was restricted by the government to private grounds. Most of its earlier mosques were built by invitation from individual village or town communities, which was an indication of the former regime's strict adherence to the policy of separation of religion and the secular state.

Prior to the building of the State House mosque, the president worshiped at the Grand Mosque of Banjul (donated by Saudi Arabia during Jawara's regime), where Imam Ratib Jobe led the prayers. Imam Jobe and his followers, represented, in the eyes of President Jammeh, the old order from which he had to disassociate himself in order to lend legitimacy for his presidency and political tenure. These feelings were shared by his new allies—the fundamentalist Wahhabis—who viewed them as part of the old political order and also as the source of a corrupt and incompetent religious establishment that needed urgent reform.

The Wahhabis believed that in order to reform Islamic practices in The Gambia and put it on the right path, Gambian Islam must be rid of all the corrupting Western influences. The West was viewed as the enemy of Islam. The Friday televised sermons and other radio and television programs often clearly relayed these views. These radical fundamentalist ideas were an extension of the philosophy and ideologies of Osama bin Laden and his disciples. This period became the beginning of open and harsh anti-American rhetoric by the fundamentalist group. It was not unusual to hear anti-American sentiments and criticisms of US foreign policy and its relationship with Islam at funerals, naming ceremonies, weddings, or any social gatherings at which the Wahhabis were present. In fact, when the United States was attacked on September 11, 2001, the comments made by Imam Fatty and his followers were very similar to the reactions of the bin Laden followers.

Also, in his address to the nation on July 21, 2006, the eve of the celebration of the twelfth anniversary of his overthrow of the democratically elected Jawara government, President Jammeh's attack on the United States was unprecedented but unmistakable. Remarking on the Israel-Hezbollah conflict in Lebanon, the president expressed his "unflinching support to and solidarity with our brothers and sisters in Lebanon and Palestine, who as we speak are being subjected to the most inhumane, degrading and unprecedented cruel treatment by the state of Israel whose sole objective is to annihilate the Lebanese and Palestinian people not only with impunity but with the tacit approval and logistic support of the anti-Islamic forces." He further implored all Muslim nations "to stand together in defense of Islam—and the new forces of domination and recolonization" (*Gambia Daily Observer*, July 22, 2006). In addition, perhaps in response to The Gambia's disqualification on June 6, 2006, for the Millennium Challenge Account assistance because of civil and human rights abuses and undemocratic governance, an account set by the United States, President Jammeh invited the Iranian president, Mahmoud Ahmadinejad, and the Venezuelan president, Hugo

Chavez—clear American adversaries—to the African Union Annual Summit held in The Gambia that July. As a consequence of these political motivations and sentiments toward the United States, which are consistent with the Wahhabi movement, the new Islamic sect's position became so well entrenched in the Jammeh government that it could influence public policy.

Further Manipulation of Islam to Control the Political Machinery of the Provinces

The influence of the fundamentalist Wahhabis has been greatest in the Banjul and Kombo metropolitan areas of the country. The rest of the country practices Islam in the traditional and less orthodox fashion. In order for the president to extend his political control to the provinces, he has had to reconcile his differences with the traditionalists he had offended at the onset of his presidency, without alienating the Wahhabis. It should be noted again that religious leaders in The Gambia often have a significant political influence. The marabouts usually dictate the political allegiance of their disciples or followers, which can sometimes constitute large communities or whole villages or towns.

During the Jawara era, there was an independent nonpolitical, but influential, body consisting of the traditional Muslims, called the Supreme Islamic Council. In his efforts to politically co-opt this segment of the Gambian Muslim population, the president created a portfolio for religious affairs in the Ministry of the Interior. He then used the same portfolio not only to politicize the Supreme Islamic Council but also to determine its leadership structure. The council was empowered by the Ministry of the Interior to oversee all Muslim religious affairs in the country except those of the orthodox Sunni Wahhabis. The council consequently became the president's political tool to extend and exert his political control in the provinces of the country.

The Politicization of the Supreme Islamic Council

The roots of the Supreme Islamic Council may be traced to one Alhaji Soriba Jabi, a private citizen. Alhaji Jabi's intention was to form an organization whose purpose would be to strengthen Islam by facilitating Quranic education and Islamic studies and coordinating the uniformity of Islamic practice in The Gambia. He traveled throughout the country, using his personal funds, to campaign for the new idea among Islamic scholars, Islamic communities, and marabouts. As mentioned earlier, when the council was first formed, he tried to get it ratified by the Jawara administration but failed. The government, however, informally acknowledged and approved of the new organization's activities. It is noteworthy that Alhaji Soriba Jabi was educated in the local *majilis* and was a traditional Muslim. Dissatisfied with the level of education of the newly formed Supreme Islamic Council, Gambians educated in Arab universities decided to form their own organization—the Arabic League. The primary objective of the Arabic League was to foster Islamic Arabic education in The Gambia.

When the Jawara regime was overthrown, the new regime sought to integrate the Arabic League and the Supreme Islamic Council as part of the strategy to entrench itself politically in a predominantly Islamic society. The leadership of the Arabic League, for reasons previously discussed, was already a staunch supporter of the regime. The Supreme Islamic Council, which enjoyed much broader support and membership, either did not support the new regime or remained politically neutral. Integration of the Arabic League and the Supreme Islamic Council entailed a new executive board consisting of members from the original organizations. This changed in early 1995, when the proregime executive members suggested the idea of soliciting funds from the Libyan government for their first congress, at which they would elect a new council president. Such solicitation of funds occurred through the influence of Baba Jobe, the architect of President Jammeh's political machinery and the most influential and powerful non–civil servant in the administration. Baba Jobe had long and strong ties with the Libyan government. Sensing the political implications of the suggestions, the nonpartisan executive members skillfully argued against the idea and suggested instead that the necessary funds be raised by membership contributions.

Candidates for the presidency of the Supreme Islamic Council were Alhaji Soriba Jabi, who was publicly nonpartisan and politically neutral; Alhaji Abdoulie Fatty, who was publicly partisan and a strong supporter of the regime; and Alhaji Banding Drammeh, who was politically moderate and a more moderate supporter of the regime. In order to prevent the election of Imam Abdoulie Fatty, an Islamist radical who flaunted his ties with the regime, the politically neutral members of the council maneuvered to get politically moderate Banding Drammeh as their new president.

The constitution of the council was approved on December 13, 1998. Chapter 9, Article 36, clearly states that "the President of the Republic of The Gambia where [*sic*] shall be the chief patron of the council by virtue of his position as the Head of State." The regime's influence on the Supreme Islamic Council became so extensive that many of the original members and officials resigned from it. Since the inception of its new politicized form, the council intervened as arbitrator, backed by the power and authority of the state, in almost all religious or even quasi-religious disputes throughout The Gambia. Noticeable examples include the dispute over the annual *gammo* (prayer meeting) in the village of Banni in Baddibu, the conflict over the separation of madrasas in Kiang Keneba, and the mosque disputes in Brikama, Bansang, and Gambissara.

The incident in Kiang Keneba is an example of the assumed exaggerated power and influence of Jammeh's Islamic supporters. Emboldened by the belief that he had the automatic personal support of the president, the backing of the APRC influence and machinery, and the president's controlled Supreme Islamic Council, during the academic year 1997–1998 the director of the madrasas in Kiang Keneba single-handedly declared the independence of the Arabic school from the Islamic Union under the jurisdictional control under which the institution had been for over twenty-two years. A faction of the school community, alleged to be supporters of the opposition party UDP by the director, argued that the director's declaration of the school's independence from the Islamic Union was an effort to cover up administrative corruption and malfeasance. Consequently, the faction opposed the severance and insisted that the madrasas remain under the jurisdiction of the Islamic Union, threatening otherwise to build a separate school for their children. When the director and his supporters refused to back down, the opposing faction carried out their threat and built and opened a new madrasa. The idea of two schools in the village being unacceptable to the director, he appealed for remedy from the *alkalo* (village head) and the secretary of state for local government and lands, Yankuba Touray, who later spearheaded the president's bid for reelection in the September 22, 2006, elections. He was confident he would get the support of these offices based on his allegations that the builders of the new school were anti-APRC and members of the opposition. Based on the allegation that the new school was propagating improper Islamic religious teaching, the Ministry of Local Government, with the instigation of the director and the *alkalo*—and, most important, the tacit approval of the president—forced the school to close down. The community became bitterly divided and rife with tension and the potential for violence. The Supreme Islamic Council was summoned to arbitrate the dispute. The council ruled in favor of the opening of the new school, but because of underlying political tensions and implications it could not enforce its decision. In June 2000, Jankonding Minteh, on behalf of the new school, filed a lawsuit in the Supreme Court of The Gambia against the secretary of state for local government for violation of their constitutional right to have a separate school. A month later, the Supreme Court ruled in favor of the applicants and ordered the reopening of the new madrasa.

However, in violation of the court order that all interference with the administration of the applicant's running of the Arabic school cease and desist immediately, in May 2001 the school was destroyed, and in the process the teachers and students were assaulted. Of the many who sustained injuries, two died. Interestingly, even after the solicitors for the applicants had filed several complaints with the officer commanding the police in Mansa Konko (the nearest police depot) about threats of violence against their clients, the police did not intervene, nor did they investigate the incident that led to the two deaths (Court Document 2000; also, Bensouda, interview 2005; and Minteh, interview 2005).

The best illustration of the effectiveness of the council as a political tool was evidenced by its intervention in the religious disputes in Gambissara and Bansang, two fairly large Muslim communities in the hinterland of the country. In Gambissara, a dispute arose between the relatively small group of orthodox Sunni Wahhabis and the much larger traditionalists over the practice of Islam. The source of the dispute was the difference in the rituals of prayer as performed by the Traditionalists and the orthodox Wahhabis. The grand marabout of the community, Alhaji Bakineh, insisted that all congregants must follow the rituals as dictated by him; he even had enforcers to assure compliance in the mosque during prayers. The Wahhabis, led by Alhaji Alfusaine Dukureh, who is assumed to have founded the radically conservative Islamist Ma'shala group, found the dictates of the grand marabout unacceptable. Unhappy with the ways of the traditional practice, the Wahhabis decided to build their own mosque in the village. Whether by reason of custom or as dictated by edicts of Islam, the Traditionalists argued that it was improper to have two mosques in the same community, regardless of the community's size. The president dispatched the vice president, Sana Sabally, a fellow soldier who was widely feared for his violent temper and acts that had terrorized the entire population since the overthrow of the Jawara regime. Sabally visited Gambissara and quickly, without much consultation and to the displeasure of most members of the community, resolved the dispute by imposing the decision that the orthodox Sunni sect could build its separate mosque. It was a judgment that would later facilitate the president's efforts to get the political support of the grand marabout of the village and his significant number of the less orthodox Traditionalist followers. Not long after the incident, the vice president was arrested and imprisoned for allegedly trying to overthrow the Jammeh government (US Department of State 1996).

When he decided to contest the 1996 presidential elections, President Jammeh sent his personal emissary from the Supreme Islamic Council to Gambissara to apologize for and reverse the actions of his former vice president. Not only were the Wahhabis asked to demolish their mosque, but also their leader, Alhaji Dukureh, was arrested, and an administrative decision was made to detain him without judicial process. He was detained for six months. After his release, he sued the government for wrongful imprisonment. While the case was in court, his lawyer miraculously escaped an assassination attempt after he was shot several times one evening on his way home from his office.[8] The case suggests that under President Jammeh, political expediency takes precedence over religious reform. In this case, he willingly and readily ignored the agenda of his Wahhabi allies for the grand marabout of Gambissara, who had significant political influence and following. The strategy worked, at least for a period, to win the support of the grand marabout and his followers.

The dispute over the imamship of the Bansang mosque, after the death of the imam, was more complicated than the situation at Gambissara (Bojang, interview 2005). Bansang was the birthplace of the leader of the main opposition political party in the country, and the opposition leader's family had built the village and the mosque. Furthermore, appointment of the successor imam, who led prayers at the mosque, was traditionally made by the Darboe family; that is, the family of the opposition leader. The dispute over the succession was between the children of the former imam and one of his favorite disciples. The community, which is ethnically diverse, became split mostly along ethnic lines with regard to their support of the potential successor. The Supreme Islamic Council intervened on behalf of the president. Jammeh received the political backing of one of the groups, and thus made some political gains because of the dispute. In this instance, however, it was not clear whether the gains arose from his actions or from the controversy and resulting competition between the two groups in the community. According to the president of the council, the recommendations of the government were ignored, and thus intervention to resolve the dispute as suggested by the council failed. One of the sons of the deceased imams now leads prayers in Bansang (Bojang, interview 2005).

In the metropolitan area of the capital city of Banjul, the president employed a different strategy to win the political support of the imam Ratib and his large following. As a gesture of an apology and reconciliation, he personally offered the imam, who was then seriously ill, an all-expense-paid overseas trip for medical treatment. The strategy worked as expected. Even though the imam himself did not openly or actively endorse the president, a significant number of his followers did.

It should be noted, however, that like the imam himself, some of his followers were not comfortable with the relationship the president wished to build between the state, the mosque, and the Islamic institutions of the country. The imam was at the time weakened by old age and illness. In the event of his death, the successor was likely to be one of his deputies, First Deputy Imam Kah or Second Deputy Tafsir Gaye. It was assumed that the successful candidate must have the support of the Supreme Islamic Council and thus the endorsement of the president. At the time, the odds seemed to favor Tafsir Gaye, who was more open and active in his support of the president and his political party. Jammeh, however, did not show a preference and continued to keep the supporters of the two deputies guessing as to the ultimate successor.

The Banjul Mosque Imamship

Tafsir Gaye's political maneuvering for the imamship of Banjul began when Imam Ratib became ill and started to show signs of senility. Gaye was said to have taken advantage of the imam's condition to win his support as his successor. Although Imam Kah was the first deputy and had held this position for ten years prior to Gaye's entrée into the inner circle of the mosque elders of Banjul, the older imam had on several occasions allowed him to perform duties that were supposed to be executed by the first deputy.

Realizing that President Jammeh needed the political support of Imam Ratib and his followers, and also that support from the president would eventually strengthen his bid for the imamship, Tafsir Gaye began to endear himself to Jammeh and the APRC. He wore green, the color of the president's party, and made frequent social visits to the State House. It was rumored that he made an attempt to court the president's mother for marriage, but the attempt failed because of the president's disapproval.

Imam Kah, in the meanwhile, was relying on his position as the duly appointed first deputy and the rule that the first deputy was the rightful successor. He assumed that the Banjul elders would enforce the rule at the appropriate time. However, rather than automatic appointment of Imam Kah to the imamship after the death of Imam Ratib, Gaye's skillful political manipulation forced an election to determine succession. Imam Kah received the support of the majority of the Banjul elders; these elders had much political influence in the Banjul constituency. The president chose political expediency and immediately sanctioned the election of Imam Kah as the new Imam Ratib after his political tool, the Supreme Islamic Council, did the same. The controversy has alienated Tafsir Gaye both from the president and the majority of the Banjul community.

Other Uses of Islamic Symbols to Gain and Control Political Power

President Jammeh employed various other less subtle strategies of using Islam to fortify and/or add to his political legitimacy and strength. In the minds of the Gambian Muslims, there is no distinction between Arabic and Islamic cultures (Darboe 1982:169–177). The "perfect" Muslim (Nyang 1984:21) is thus the one whose culture is inextricably interwoven with Islamic culture; that is, with the Arabs of the Middle East and North Africa. Accordingly, it is firmly believed that a non-Arab African cannot attain a perfect or complete acculturation into Islamic culture. It was this belief that formed the basis of President Jammeh's strategy when he divorced his "imperfect" Gambian Muslim *acculturate* and replaced her with a Moroccan Muslim. This exchange of wives was undoubtedly designed not only to enhance his piety as a Muslim but also to gain the friendship of the leadership in Morocco and thus a meaningful place in the Islamic world and among Islamic leaders.

Another common technique of co-opting African Muslims is the all-expenses-paid trip to Mecca to perform the *hajj*. It is a technique that was employed by European rulers during the colonial period (Nyang 1984:21). President Jammeh used the same strategy with some modifications. Since the First Republic, the Kingdom of Saudi Arabia has annually given The Gambia a number of all-expenses-paid trips to the holy city of Mecca. During the Jawara regime, these free tickets were given to health officers, security officers, and officials from the Ministry of Communication to enable them to accompany the Gambian pilgrims. However, President Jammeh distributes these gifts from the Saudi government to his political patrons as personal favors.

The invocation of the *fatiha* at the opening and at the end of political rallies and meetings is another Islamic symbol employed by most political parties in The Gambia as a prayer and for legitimacy (Nyang 1984:21). More recently, in a public meeting, President Jammeh chastised opposition parties' leaders as infidels because they do not recite the *fatiha* in their meetings.

In Islam, the consumption of alcohol is condemned and is therefore perceived as a serious offense. In a society such as The Gambia where the majority of the population and electorate are Muslims, the offense can have a detrimental effect on a political career. It is thus not surprising that during the past two presidential campaigns, President Jammeh and his supporters, during most of their political rallies, publicly accused the leader of the largest opposition party of being a drunkard. In fact, it was not unusual to hear the young militants of the party rhythmically shouting, "Lawyer Darboe *dolo bula*" (Lawyer Darboe stop drinking alcohol). Even though Lawyer Darboe is a devout Muslim and the allegation was untrue, it confirms the perception that the charge of alcohol consumption is an effective political tool.

Backlash of the President's Strategy: A Political Dilemma

Jammeh assumed another five-year term of office when he won the presidential elections in 2001, a month after the attack on the United States by members of Al-Qaida. During the campaign the opposition party made several condemnations of the attack whereas the president and his office were noticeably silent. However, the imam of the State House mosque publicly, on both television and radio, praised the attack as befitting all enemies of Islam. This is another example of the power and influence the orthodox Sunni Wahhabis have on the regime and the president. It was clear to both the orthodox sect and the Gambian public that the Sunni Wahhabis' influence and authority extended to making public policies, including foreign policy toward the United States, as well as domestic policies affecting non-Islamic religions and religious institutions. The controversy over the Ahmadiyya presence in The Gambia and practice of Islam is yet another example of the influence of the Wahhabis in national affairs and the president's political calculations in responding to religious pressure.

The amir of the Ahmadiyya movement in The Gambia was the first religious leader to meet with and wish President Jammeh well when he overthrew the Jawara regime. His gifts to the new president included a copy of the Quran and literature on Islam and the Ahmadiyya movement. President Jammeh acknowledged and commended the amir and his Muslim sect for the many years of service to the Gambian people and society. He also confessed that the little he knew about Islam had come from the literature on the religion and the sect shared by the son of the amir, with whom he sat in school. However, political expediency and economic circumstances soon forced the president to have a change of heart about the Ahmadiyya.

As indicated earlier, Pakistan and Saudi Arabia held strong anti-Ahmadiyya sentiments. At the start of his presidency, President Jammeh needed the support of the Arab world for both economic reasons and the enhancement of his personal image. Saudi Arabia and Pakistan promised the much-needed support on condition that Jammeh rid The Gambia of the Ahmadiyya movement. Whereas the Jawara administration had rejected a similar offer from these same countries, President Jammeh accepted the offer and began to develop a plan to expel the Ahmadiyya. Instead of a presidential decree for the expulsion of the sect, he devised a more subtle strategy of frustration and harassment to be carried out by some of the executive members of the Supreme Islamic Council. The choice of the council to perform the task was deliberate because it was controlled by Alhaji Banding Drammeh and Alhaji Imam Abdoulie Fatty. The two executive members of SIC were openly staunch supporters of the president, and their

Arabian academic alma mater vehemently disapproved of the Ahmadiyya movement. Imam Fatty, the imam of the State House mosque, led the attack on the Ahmadiyya by making condemnations of their alleged distortions of Islam part of his Friday sermons.

The mission demanded from the authorities an opportunity to respond to Imam Fatty's nationally televised attack on the authenticity of their version of Islamic practice. Their demand resulted in the Ahmadiyya being forced to cease all activities and halt all missionary-related projects—despite years of missionary work in The Gambia and their profound impact on the social and economic welfare of its people in terms of schools, hospitals, and health clinics

According to the amir, the attack on the movement and the order to have their non-Gambian officials pack and leave the country coincided with the decision from London headquarters to transfer responsibilities of the movement's institutions from resident Pakistani and other non-Gambian citizens to Gambian nationals. The president's objective to remove the Ahmadiyya was partially realized without a direct confrontation with the movement. In an effort to convince his benefactors of his sincerity, President Jammeh made a public statement to the effect that he had rid The Gambia of the Ahmadiyya and included as evidence the government's takeover of the Mohammedan School and the closing down of the movement's other educational institutions. The amir, however, pointed out that Ahmadiyya educational institutions, including Nustrat High School, were not affected and continued to function as always. Furthermore, he stated, the Mohammedan School had never been an Ahmadiyya institution but rather a Gambia government school since the colonial period.

During the heat of the controversy, the leadership of Ahmadiyya threatened to completely shut down all its institutions and other activities if attacks on their sect persisted. Recognizing the potential impact of the curtailment of these services, especially in the area of health care, the president had no choice but to rein in the Wahhabis and asked them to refrain from further attacks. At the time of this research the government was working to appease and make amends with the Ahmadiyya, as evidenced by the new expansion of the movement's activities and services and the huge acreage of land donated by the government to facilitate the expansion (Tarawale, interview 2005).

This incident is but one illustration of the influence of the orthodox Sunni sect on the national government, even when such intervention was not in the national interest or welfare of the Gambian people. Combined with the president's political calculations, similar religious interference subsequently created an even more complicated dilemma, one that was politically costly to his regime.

The situation arose when the president fell into disfavor with the Libyan government. All the projects being financed by Libya came to an abrupt halt, followed by several rather undiplomatic and unfriendly exchanges between the two governments. At the same time, the Gambian economy took a downward spiral: the rate of unemployment jumped; the cost of living sharply increased while wages remained stagnant; the production of peanuts, the only cash crop, fell, and the government could not raise the capital to buy what was produced; tourism, the only other industry, was in steep decline; the high rate of inflation was unprecedented; and the government could not meet the conditions of accountability and transparency that were the prerequisites for a bailout by both the World Bank and the International Monetary Fund. Discontent among the Gambian electorate became as apparent as the physical deterioration of the nation's infrastructure. In light of these desperate times, it became apparent to the government that the only hope for a bailout lay with the United States, which was now engaged in fighting terrorism perpetrated by Islamic extremists. It was this alternative search for foreign assistance that led to the tension and eventual confrontation between the president and his politically powerful Wahhabi allies.

As a way to impress the US government, Jammeh began, ostensibly, to tone down his own anti-American rhetoric and also to distance himself from such sentiments and rhetoric from the Wahhabis. The government, through its police force and immigration offices, started a campaign of harassment of Middle Eastern "look-alikes" and those who bore the orthodox Sunni sect characteristics of long white robes and a long beard. These efforts increased the tension between the Wahhabis and President Jammeh.

The most dramatic public showdown between the president and the imam of the State House and his followers (particularly the Federation of Gambian Muslim Student Organization, FEGAMSO) was prompted by the veil controversy. Imam Fatty, the imam of the State House and the leader of the Wahhabi sect, proved to have commanded considerable influence and following in the Gambian society as a consequence of his weekly radio and television programs and the authority vested upon him by the president. This influence was clearly evident by the change in the dress code of a significant number of young persons, including the wearing of the veil by many schoolgirls. As mentioned earlier, the majority of the students in the Christian schools are Muslims. From the time of the establishment of the mission schools, all students have been required to wear uniforms as designated by the individual schools, and this requirement has been enforced without exception. The specific incident that sparked the controversy involved St. Theresa's, a coeducational junior high school established by the

Catholic mission. The school was situated directly across the street from a supermarket, on top of which was the Masjid Bilal, a mosque built by a Gambian businessman of Wahhabi orientation. The supermarket was owned and operated by the Gamlush family of Syrian origin. The bishop of the Catholic mission was convinced that the family had affiliations with Hezbollah, an extremist Islamic political organization with significant political influence in Lebanon and Syria. It has been alleged that the Gamlush brothers who operated the supermarket gave money and free veils to the girls when they visited the market during their lunch break or after school. The St. Theresa School authorities became concerned when a significant number of the girls began wearing veils over their uniforms (Grey-Johnson, interview 2005). The controversy began when the schools sent the veiled students home for not adhering to the school code of wearing the proper uniform. The government's immediate reaction, with the tacit approval of the president, was a threat to close down these mission schools if the students were not allowed to wear the veil.

However, on July 22, 2003, in his speech to commemorate the overthrow of the Jawara regime, the president waged a public attack on the Wahhabis and their way of practicing Islam. He reversed the government threat to close the Christian schools and instead threatened to prosecute and imprison any schoolgirl wearing a veil to school. The response from Imam Fatty and the Muslim student organization was immediate and harsh. The imam charged the president with blasphemy and warned him that on Judgment Day, he would be judged for his sins, including this attack on God's way (i.e., the orthodox Sunni way of life and practice of Islam), and his soldiers will not be there to protect him. The imam also noted that the president had missed several consecutive Friday prayers and that if he missed one more, he would be declared a *kaffir,* a nonbeliever and an enemy of Islam. These sermons were usually televised. However, on this particular day the president ordered the sermon not to be televised and had authorities confiscate all video and audiotapes of it.

Apparently the strain between the orthodox Muslims and President Jammeh had undesirable consequences for both parties' agendas. However, as indicated by the radically diminished influence of Imam Abdoulie Fatty, the Wahhabis' loss was relatively more than the president's. Imam Fatty now only occasionally leads prayers in the State House, and his fiery Friday sermons, which were an open attack on the traditional practice of Islam in The Gambia and on the West, especially the United States, have come to a halt. The imam is seldom invited to the State House or Kanilai, the president's private residence, in contrast to the time before the veil controversy, when he frequently shuttled between the president's two residences. The president's loss of political support is more apparent among the younger following of the radical Islamists. It is a loss much compensated by the president's success in establishing himself as a good Muslim leader and a champion of Islam in a predominantly Islamic society. The only current threat to these political gains of the president are the severe economic conditions of The Gambia, exacerbated by the current potentially explosive strained relations with its neighbors, Senegal and Guinea Bissau.

Interestingly, during the height of this rift between President Jammeh and the orthodox Muslim sect, the newly appointed deputy chief of missions at the US Embassy, Bruce Knotts, a Muslim, made an unprecedented courtesy call on Imam Ratib Jobe, the leader of the Traditionalist Muslims of the greater Banjul area. It was a manifestation of the times since the September 11 attack on the United States and the dawn of the bin Laden phenomenon: an interplay of diplomacy, politics, and Islam.

Conclusion

Not unlike other African Muslim societies, the spread of Islam to The Gambia was mainly peaceful, involving the incorporation of local customs and traditions. This process has led to the development of a Gambian brand of Islam characterized by syncretic Sufi practices, tolerant and moderate. The Islam of the traditional Muslim Gambian is a manifestation of the overlay of the religion on local belief systems without wholly eliminating the latter. The resultant Islam is not a rigid understanding and observance of the Quran and the Sunna but rather a less doctrinal observance that is more accommodating. However, the emergence of Wahhabi Islam and the advocacy for reform has had significant influence on local customs, values, and other aspects of daily life in The Gambia. The introduction of Islamism with its intent to reorganize Gambian society and the state in conformity with the orthodox and stricter interpretations of the religion has been immensely facilitated by the country's large Muslim population, a weak economy, and the quasi-military and undemocratic government. Consequently, the radical reform movement has corroded the moderate and tolerant Islamic and secular traditions.

Although Islam and Western politics are both foreign to sub-Saharan African civilizations, Gambians, like other West Africans, have in general adapted these elements of foreign civilizations to their own indigenous conditions. Shortly after the development of party politics in The Gambia, the politicians accordingly became adept at using one element to manipulate the other so as to enhance their political careers and to consolidate political power. With the introduction of Islamism, the Islamists quickly learned from the prevailing political strategy to foster their Islamic agenda of reorganizing the Muslim society and reforming Islamic practice.

The Western societies' war on terrorism, with the United States at the forefront, has had profound implications for the Islamic reform movement and an unintended consequence for domestic politics in general and the economic and foreign policies in The Gambia. Internationally, the country is caught between the forces of Western economic and political powers and the forces of Islamic radicalism of the oil-rich Islamic countries. In terms of domestic politics, the society is caught in the grips of democracy and secularism, on the one hand, and the pressures of the Wahhabis' reform movement, on the other. Consequently, a career in Gambian politics necessarily involves balancing allegiance to radical or orthodox Islam with the realities of increasingly desperate economic conditions. This study of The Gambia clearly illustrates just how delicate such a balancing act can be.

Notes

I wish to extend my thanks and utmost gratitude to William F.S. Miles, a committed Africanist, without whose initiative and inspiration this contribution to the social science literature on the African continent would not have come to fruition. I am also indebted to Eve Powell-Griner, who read an earlier version of this chapter and made valuable suggestions with respect to the coherence of the text. Many thanks to Sherry Clem for the typing of the manuscript and many useful editorial suggestions. Finally, I wish to acknowledge the Shepherd University Professional Development Committee for funding part of the research for this work.

1. Bishop Michael Cleary is Irish by birth. He came to The Gambia in 1951 as a young priest in his early twenties. He taught and served as principal of St. Augustine's High School for many years before being appointed the first bishop of the Catholic mission in The Gambia.

2. The Salafis (from Salafiyya) are those who emulate early predecessors seeking to imitate the tradition of the fathers of the faith, that is, the companions of the Prophet and the Muslims of the first century (AD seventh century) (Nasr 2002:102; Kaba 1974:22; Miles 2000:214).

3. *Bid'a* refers to some view, thing, or mode of action the likes of which has not formally existed or been practiced; also, an innovation or novelty (Kaba 1974:4).

4. Alhaji Alieu Kama Badji was one of the founding members of the Bathurst Young Muslim Society, which eventually became The Gambia Muslim Congress. He held several cabinet positions during the Jawara administration and remained active in politics until the overthrow of the First Republic in 1994.

5. Maj. Momodou Bojang was a senior military officer when Lt. Yahya Jammeh staged a coup d'état in July 1994. He served first as commissioner of the Central River Division, during which time he played a vital role in the 1996 election of President Jammeh. He was later appointed secretary of state for the interior until after the 2001 presidential elections. In 2003 he was suspected of plotting against the regime, but managed to flee to the United States before he could be arrested. He is currently living in Atlanta, Georgia, while he seeks political asylum.

6. Ousainou Darboe, legal representative for the imam, June 2005. Alhaji Ousainou Darboe was the lead counsel in the defense of Imam Karamo Touray.

7. Staff members complained that the agency, since the events of September 11, 2001, has been experiencing funding problems because of the strict financial transfer regulations imposed by the United States and Great Britain.

8. Alhaji Dukureh is deceased, and his lawyer, who came to the United States for medical treatment, is currently seeking political asylum. The case remains pending in the courts.

7

Senegal: Shades of Islamism on a Sufi Landscape

LEONARDO A. VILLALÓN

IN THE WEST AFRICAN CONTEXT OF ITS FIRST THREE DECADES OR SO OF INDEpendence, Senegal distinguished itself as exceptional in two crucial domains: the religious, and the political. On the religious front the country was unique in the extent and degree of organization of an overwhelmingly dominant system of Muslim Sufi orders (*turuq*) under the authority of a class of religious leaders commonly known as marabouts. Whereas many of Senegal's Sahelian neighbors discussed in this volume—including Mali, Niger, and Mauritania—largely share Senegal's religious demography, only in Senegal has the Sufi maraboutic system been so deeply and widely institutionalized. In the political realm, Senegal remained a postcolonial oasis of stability, and even a quasi-democracy, in a region where such phenomena were rare indeed. These two factors, I have argued elsewhere, are closely linked: the Senegalese religious system has been an integral element of Senegal's political successes (Villalón 1995).

By the early 1990s, however, questions could be raised about the long-term sustainability of this exceptionalism in the context of the dramatic political changes occurring across the world. Even in those rare stable and putatively democratic African countries such as Senegal, political systems across the continent came under intense pressure for liberalization and reform in the early years of the decade. In Senegal this took the form of demands for institutional changes in the electoral system, intended to give substance to the label of "democracy," and of intense pressure for regime change or *alternance* (*soppi,* in the Wolof rallying cry of the streets), after decades of uninterrupted rule by the dominant Parti Socialiste (Villalón 1994b). Much of the 1990s was thus marked by a deepening crisis of the Senegalese regime in the face of its eroding legitimacy and mass popular protests that were further driven by economic downturn and the growing impoverishment of much of the population.

Within the context of the Muslim world, other transnational trends also had their echo in Senegal. The persistence and even intensification of the Islamic "revival" that had begun with the Iranian revolution of the late 1970s was now frequently read by both supporters and critics of Islamic movements as a question of the "compatibility" of Islam with democratic reform in the post–Cold War order. In the early 1990s Algeria's tragic and bloody war between religious and secular fundamentalists ushered in the debate, and this North African case seemed to many to exemplify the limits of the so-called Third Wave. Echoing Samuel Huntington's (1984) cavalier dismissals of Islam as a religion not "hospitable to democracy," scholars and practitioners alike predicted the extreme unlikelihood or even impossibility of building democratic political orders on Muslim societies.

In Africa in general, and in Senegal in particular, the question of the compatibility of Islam and democracy was often nuanced by invoking the long-standing academic and political distinction between variants of Islam: Sufism on the one hand, and reformism or "Islamism" on the other.[1] In the common depiction, the reputed tolerant and peaceful nature of Sufism, and especially its Black African forms (*l'islam noir* of the French colonialists), was seen as more or less compatible with a democratic regime. "Islamism" by contrast, understood as a political ideology proposing the alignment of political structures with religious strictures (with consequent actions undertaken in its name), was understood as inherently incompatible with—and indeed a hostile alternative to—democracy.[2]

These questions loomed in the background as the Senegalese political crisis deepened during the 1990s. They were further exacerbated as the internal dynamics of religious families fueled an apparent new dynamism among the younger generation of heirs to religious standing (Villalón 1999; Villalón 2000). Yet, strikingly, the doubts and fears suggested by these developments seemed to lose their salience following the country's historic elections of April 2000. The long-awaited change brought about by the victory of perennial opposition leader Abdoulaye Wade and his Parti Démocratique Sénégalais (PDS) served for many, both within and outside the country, as a dramatic confirmation that the "land of the marabouts" was indeed (or finally) a full political democracy.[3]

This very *alternance*, however, also called into question virtually all aspects of the established sociopolitical patterns and systems. In its aftermath, Senegalese politics and society were left very much in flux, amid questions and doubts about the precise future contours of the system. Yet precisely because Senegal today is unquestionably a democracy, it is also a political system in which politics has increasingly found itself closely intertwined with debates and issues of concern to the socioreligious sensibilities of its overwhelmingly Muslim, and highly religious, population. In the significant public debates about what changes should be made in the institutions and substantive content of Senegalese democracy, various groups have organized and mobilized at least partly along religious lines, and many have staked out positions inspired by religious convictions. This process in turn appears to be feeding evolutionary changes in the nature of Senegalese religious society.

Senegalese Sufism remains the dominant form of religious devotion in the country, but its dynamic forms and manifestations are also adapting in ways that have heavily blurred, if not completely erased, the distinction between "traditional" Sufi and Islamist groups. In the significant public discussion about what it means to be Muslim in a world of apparent civilizational clashes, in non-Arab Africa, and in a vibrant democracy, many Senegalese intellectuals—both the long-dominant francophone elites and the *arabisants* intellectuals who have been historically marginalized—are building on the rich Sufi traditions while reinterpreting several of its important elements and borrowing from other Muslim traditions, including those labeled "Islamist."

Does this signal the rise of Islamism as an incipient threat to Senegal's democracy and to its historical accommodation to Muslim institutions? This is not at all clear. Close consideration of the Senegalese case suggests, on the contrary, the limitations of the Sufi-Islamist dichotomy and the need to nuance our analyses. In what follows, I first provide a brief discussion of the evolution of the historically dominant Sufi model and then examine the challenges to the system brought about by the changes of the 1990s. I then consider the issues raised following the election of Abdoulaye Wade, which simultaneously (and somewhat paradoxically) confirmed the full democratization of the system while also calling many of its key elements into question. A final section will consider the intellectual transformations in the understanding of religious identity that appear to be underway in Senegal, in the context of the broader globalized debate on Islam following the events of September 11, 2001, in the United States, and the subsequent US-led wars in Afghanistan and Iraq.

The Senegalese Sufi System and Its Critics

Senegal's highly organized religious society, comprising some 90 percent of the population, is structured hierarchically around several religious lineages, affiliated with two major—and several smaller—Sufi orders.[4] The demographically dominant Tijaniyya order is divided among several branches owing allegiance to different religious families. The indigenous Mouride order, founded at the turn of the previous century by the Senegalese religious leader Amadou Bamba Mbacké, counts more disciples than any one of the Tijani branches, though it does not comprise a majority. Other Sufi orders include the Qadiriyya, widespread and with deep roots across much of West Africa and beyond but rather small in Senegal, and the indigenous Layène order concentrated on the Cap Vert peninsula.

The distinctive Senegalese institutionalization of these religious traditions is an artifact of the colonial period, but was to be continued—and indeed reinforced—in the postcolonial setting (Triaud and Robinson 1997; Robinson 2000; Babou 2002). The system is founded on the classic relationship at the core of Sufism: the attachment of a disciple to his or her religious guide (ashaikh, or more commonly "marabout" in francophone Africa). For the vast majority of Senegalese, this relationship to a marabout is a centrally important aspect of an individual's identity and social life. Marabouts, in turn, must carefully cultivate these relationships so as to maintain the followings that ensure their status. In theory the status of marabout is earned by piety and mastery of the esoteric knowledge of the different orders, but in the realities of contemporary Senegal maraboutic status is based largely on inheritance. Most of the major marabouts in the country today are the direct descendents of the founders of the country's main religious centers early in the colonial period.

Starting under the colonial system and continuing throughout the postcolonial period, the system has been institutionalized by the organization of disciples into increasingly formal associations. These associations are linked to the religious centers led by the family dynasties that developed after the deaths of the generation of "founding fathers" in the first quarter of the twentieth century. The distinctive Senegalese associational form, known as the *daaira*, that links followers to each other and to the leadership is reinforced and celebrated in an extensive symbolic system of ritual ceremonies and pilgrimages (Villalón 1994a).

This level of religiously based social organization led naturally to a significant potential for political influence, a fact that was recognized early in the colonial period. The initial French reaction was one of fear in the face of such massive mobilization—as evidenced by the deportations and long exiles of Shaikh Amadou Bamba, founder of the Mouride order, in the early years of the movement. Yet the colonial powers and religious movements were ultimately to find "paths of accommodation," in David Robinson's (2000) phrase, and indeed much of the later colonial political and economic regime was built on symbiotic collaboration with the orders.

Beginning with the advent of party politics in the 1950s, the (Catholic) politician Leopold Sédar Senghor built the political bases of what was to be his independent regime on these same ties. At the elite level this involved mutually beneficial relations, based on state concessions to religious authorities in exchange for their political support—most famously in the form of maraboutic religious injunctions known in Wolof as *ndigals*, and frequently invoked as voting instructions. Centrally important, at the popular level the orders also provided a mode of organization and vehicles for transmitting popular sentiment that allowed for a more productive engagement with the state than was possible in much of Africa. Thus from the 1970s one of the keenest observers of the Mouride order could describe the marabouts as "spokesmen and organizers of rural interests" and famously argue that "the Mouride order was well on the way to become Africa's first independent peasant trade union" (Cruise O'Brien 2003, 37–38).[5]

The merits of the system were much debated—both by academic analysts and by Senegalese intellectuals—but it was in any case to serve Senghor well throughout his two decades of rule, and to be inherited by his dauphin, Abdou Diouf, at least for the first decade or so of his own rule. Though religious authorities in Senegal were thus central to political structures, and despite the fact that they were occasionally to mobilize support in an effort to shape political decisions to their religious preferences, they also maintained an overt accommodation with an explicitly secular state. Sufi orders have thus been politically central Islamic organizations in Senegal, but they have not been "Islamist" groups.

If the Sufi model has been dominant in Senegal, however, it has not been unopposed. There is a long presence of small but persistent anti-Sufi reformist movements in the country, which since the 1950s have wanted "to replace the existing secular state by an ideal 'Islamic State' based on the *sharia* (Islamic Law) and want to resolve all existing social problems by the recourse to Islam" (Loimeier 1996, 183; see also Gomez-Perez 1991; Sambe 2003). While these groups have historically had only a very modest impact on society or politics, there appear to be signs that both the long crisis of the 1990s and the post-*alternance* changes since April 2000 have provided a more hospitable climate for the development of Islamist ideologies and the strengthening of such groups.

Historically, reformist associations were concentrated among urban intellectuals and, like other urban groups, regularly enmeshed in political maneuvering for resources from the state. At times they have seemed simply opportunistic, "prepared to suspend their principles or give them up entirely" in pursuit of material gains, with some state officials even accusing some of having been "set up purely for the purpose of being co-opted sooner or later . . . thereby gaining access to resources" (Loimeier 1996, 195; see also Fall 1993).

Reformists' ideological arguments have at times had an impact on the leadership of the Sufi orders, and various marabouts have occasionally borrowed parts of their rhetoric or joined such groups in staking a political or social position on such key issues as family law. But when reformists have attempted to expand their influence to the more popular level, they have regularly failed, tending instead to be captured by the maraboutic system, and even incorporated into it (Villalón 1995, 232–243). Other formal and officially sanctioned religious organizations that have existed in Senegal have likewise tended to either originate in or be quickly dominated by the maraboutic families. Thus, for example, the umbrella organization known as the Fédération des Associations Islamiques du Sénégal (FAIS), which originated in the 1960s as a reformist effort distinct from the Sufi model, quickly found itself dominated by the representatives of the major maraboutic families. While it has received some criticism and there have been efforts to challenge it, from its inception in the colonial period and throughout the period of independence the dominance of the Sufi system has never seriously been threatened in Senegal.

The System in Question

While remaining dominant, however, by the late 1980s the system was under significant stress as persistent economic decline and a sense of political frustration produced wide dissatisfaction with the established sociopolitical order in Senegal, like elsewhere across Africa, and particularly among youth and urban dwellers.[6] In this context the 1988 elections in Senegal were marked by what was to prove to be the last major electoral *ndigal* by one of the caliphs of the orders, the Mouride Abdoul Ahat Mbacké, and by violence and a political crisis following the official declaration of President Abdou Diouf's reelection. The resulting crisis was fed by two major factors:

- A widespread sense of political stagnation after three decades of rule by the Parti Socialiste (PS), built on a consensus that only a change of leadership could hope to reverse the economic decline, but that the system long touted as "democratic" was in fact incapable of producing such a change.
- Generational shifts brought about by the maturation of a new generation of urban citizen-disciples, born after independence, as well as generational tensions *within* maraboutic families as the leadership transition to the third generation from the founding fathers neared.

In the years following the explosion of postelectoral violence in the summer of 1988, and continuing through the early 1990s, then, the legitimacy of *both* political and religious authority in Senegal eroded significantly and consistently.

The high levels of popular frustration and dissatisfaction that had built up by the time of the 1988 elections, and opposition confidence that this would translate into victory, had raised expectations of change in the country, particularly among urban youth. When the official results declaring the reelection of President Abdou Diouf and the ruling Parti Socialiste were quickly announced, mass social mobilization in major urban areas of Senegal produced the most significant violence in the country since independence. Unable to control the situation, the government declared a curfew and a state of emergency. In the context of ongoing contestation, various opposition leaders were arrested, tried, and convicted, although they were eventually to be granted amnesty and released. The opposition, however, refused to back down on its demands for fundamental changes in the institutional rules of Senegalese democracy, notably the electoral system.

The following year a border incident in the context of tense relations with Mauritania, Senegal's northern neighbor, triggered waves of ethnic violence in both countries and a significant displacement of populations in both directions. By the beginning of the 1990s, Senegal's reputation for stability and democracy was seriously tarnished, and to many observers Senegal's politics seemed instead to be paralleling the difficult political histories of many of its West African neighbors. Thus, when various neighbors took significant steps toward reforming or overthrowing authoritarian regimes and experimenting with democratic transitions in the early years of the decade, the pressures on the Senegalese regime to make concessions to opposition demands and reform the democratic and electoral system were magnified.

In 1992 Abdou Diouf's government, in negotiation with the opposition, in fact promulgated a series of significant reforms, notably the passage of a new and consensual electoral code, widely extolled by all parties for its democratic nature. The extent of these reforms, and the fact that they were largely based on concessions to opposition demands, again raised major expectations of an impending sea-change in Senegalese politics. Proclaiming the inevitability of its victory in the next election given the new electoral rules, the opposition further raised the expectations of *alternance*. In this context, the presidential elections of February 1993, followed by legislative elections in May, proved again to be a major disappointment for the opposition and the partisans of change. The new electoral system itself, with its many safeguards and checks on power, proved so cumbersome that it took weeks for the official results—declaring Diouf and the Parti Socialiste again the winners—to be announced. Although there were fears of renewed violence and protests, in fact the results produced instead a widespread cynicism and disenchantment with both the entire political elite and with the promises of democracy as a vehicle for change. This political mood was to mark much of the decade of the 1990s.

The declining legitimacy and public questioning of the established political order had, in turn, various effects on religious organization in Senegal. We thus witnessed both the expansion of the anti-Sufi, reformist, or "Islamist" movements explicitly critical of the prevailing patterns and the rise of new movements *within* the Sufi orders but that nevertheless borrowed from Islamist critiques to push for changes in leadership and in organization.

As elsewhere in the Muslim world, the main locus of the Islamist movement was within the universities. As I have noted, in Senegal such groups had a long history, but they had also long been small and with only marginal popular appeal. Over the course of the 1980s, however, Islamist groups such as the Jamatou Ibadou Rahmane grew in importance, eventually winning the symbolic victory of building a mosque on the Dakar campus (see Bathily et al. 1995; Loimeier 1996). The unprecedented adoption of a form of veiling by a significant minority of young university women was the most visible manifestation of the dynamism of these movements in the 1990s.[7] In 2002 a formal Islamist student organization, the Mouvement des Etudiants et Elèves Jamaatou Ibadou Rahmane (MEEJIR), was founded and quickly established branches at both state universities and in many high schools around the country.

These movements were important, to be sure, but they also had a very limited popular appeal outside the class of young intellectuals. More significant was the development of new religious movements growing out of the maraboutic system itself. These were most frequently led by young marabouts of the third and fourth generations after the founding fathers. At times these younger figures came from lineages not directly in the lines of inheritance for leadership of the orders, but in all cases they arose in a context of a large number of potential heirs to the legitimacy of the older generation of leadership. In the highly polygamous contexts of maraboutic families, over many years the number of direct descendants of the founders increases exponentially with each generation, and the ambitious younger figures must find ways to distinguish and call attention to themselves. Coming of age in the context of widespread popular disenchantment with the established order, the more entrepreneurial of them found fertile terrain for mobilizing followers around innovative structures and ideologies.

Perhaps the most visible of these was the Dahiratoul Moustarchidine wal Moustarchidaty. Led by Moustapha Sy, a young marabout from the important Tijani lineage founded by El Hajj Malik Sy in the town of Tivaouane, the Moustarchidine movement was built on the *daaira* model but consciously portrayed itself as more "rationalized" and modern. The movement developed a highly structured and centralized organization, with local "cells" throughout the country. In the 1980s it began organizing a series of highly visible national ritual ceremonies and sponsored frequent local activities designed to encourage its youthful clientele to adopt more "Islamic" moral behaviors, frequently portrayed in opposition to the corruption brought on by the adoption of Western mores.

In 1993, at the height of the presidential campaign, Moustapha Sy flexed his new political muscles for the first time in a dramatic and surprising public attack on President Abdou Diouf in a public speech before a large crowd of disciples (Kane and Villalón 1995). Tellingly, he also issued strong criticisms of several of his uncles, themselves major marabouts in the family, creating a serious rift in the lineage. When Moustapha and his followers became involved in violence as protests continued in 1994, the Moustarchidine seemed to emerge as the first serious contestatory political movement built on a religious basis in Senegal. In some Western media and elsewhere this was described as the arrival of "fundamentalism" in Senegal (Da Costa 1994).

These reports, however, proved unduly alarmist, and by the mid-1990s Moustapha Sy had reconciled with Abdou Diouf and the Parti Socialiste in a shift that might (perhaps somewhat cynically) be read as a purely pragmatic realignment so as to reposition himself as an intermediary between his youthful followers and the resources of the regime. As the 2000 elections approached, however, this alliance bore high risks, given the widespread disenchantment with Diouf and the Parti Socialiste. Moustapha Sy's response was to take the unprecedented step of founding his own party, the Parti de l'Unité et du Rassemblement (PUR). This new party undertook a broad campaign of mobilization of young people to register them on the electoral lists, feeding intense speculation about Moustapha's intentions and whether he would stand for election himself. In the end, and despite his father's endorsement of Abdou Diouf between the two rounds of the presidential elections, Moustapha stood cautiously on the sidelines and instructed his followers to "vote their conscience."

The development and politicization of the Moustarchidine movement signaled a substantial variation from the established relations between maraboutic authorities and the political elite, while it nevertheless built on the historical role of marabouts as intermediaries and on the organizational bases of Senegalese Sufism. Borrowing at the same time rhetorical and ideological postures as well as organizational tactics from the critics of the Sufi model, the movement was particularly noteworthy in that it blurred the distinction between "Sufis" and "Islamists" or "reformists," a fact clearly evident in the rhetoric of Moustapha's 1993 speech (see Kane and Villalón 1995).

A major parallel development within the Mouride order was the movement of the Hizb at-Tarqiyyah, which started as a Mouride students' association at the University of Dakar (see Sène 2003). As with the Moustarchidine, this movement billed itself as an effort to "modernize" and "rationalize" the *daaira* model. Its leadership, however, was drawn from educated younger disciples rather than from the holy family itself. Although it was initially blessed by the caliph, and built on a very strong allegiance to the founder Amadou Bamba Mbacké and to the Mouride order itself, the movement grew to eventually challenge the order's hierarchy by critiquing the idea of hereditary leadership.

Apparently emboldened by the growth of the movement in schools across the country, the Hizb at-Tarqiyyah leadership's critique of inherited authority was to provoke a bitter confrontation with younger marabouts from the Mbacké family. A series of dramatic events in Touba in 1997, widely covered in the press, required the intervention of the caliph and, in the end, largely discredited the Hizb at-Tarqiyyah's young leaders. The resulting intense controversy and conflict within the order caused the Hizb at-Tarqiyyah to splinter and decline. It has not disappeared, however, and in addition, various successor groups maintain significant followings among Mouride students at universities and in high schools, and they continue to espouse much of the Hizb at-Tarqiyyah ideology and emulate its organizational practices. These movements thus integrate various Islamist themes, including a strong anti-Westernization stance, in the name of "modernizing" and "rationalizing" the order, while maintaining a loyal devotion to the figure of the founder and the idea of the Mouride way.

While the Hizb at-Tarqiyyah thus weakened in the late 1990s, another movement from within the Mouride order—one that like the Moustarchidine is organized by and around a young marabout from a branch lineage of the family—increased in visibility and strength (see Audrain 2004). The putatively purely religious Mouvement Mondial pour l'Unicité de Dieu (MMUD, World Movement for the Oneness of God), founded by Shaikh Modou Kara Mbacké Noreyni, must clearly be understood as another expression of the effort by an entrepreneurial young marabout to distinguish himself from his peers in the search to build a following that might translate into political clout. Drawing in particular from marginalized and even delinquent urban youth, Modou Kara intentionally cultivated a highly original and rather idiosyncratic image, simultaneously playing on his Mouride genealogy and breaking the expected norms of Mouride maraboutic behavior. He often speaks of himself as a "general" in charge of his troops, whom he "saves" via membership in his disciplined and rigorous movement.

Having built a large following among these youth in the dispirited climate of the 1990s, Modou Kara stumbled when he attempted to translate this following into political influence. On the last day of 1999, at the huge annual religious rally that the marabout regularly organized on new year's eve in a major football stadium in Dakar, the young marabout directed his disciples to vote for Abdou Diouf in the upcoming elections. With Diouf's closest ally and presumed heir, Ousmane Tanor Dieng, sitting at his side, the youthful crowd publicly and vocally rejected their shaikh's appeal. Unable to control the jeering of the thousands of assembled disciples, Modou Kara was obliged to abort his sermon, and Tanor Dieng to leave the stage.

The incident, and Diouf's subsequent defeat, would seemingly have dealt a major blow to the marabout's ambitions, and indeed he subsequently maintained a low public profile both for himself and his movement. However, Modou Kara was to reenter the political domain in an even more explicit fashion during the Wade years.

Throughout the 1990s, then, the heretofore virtually unassailable dominance of the established Sufi model came into question, challenged both by Islamist alternatives and by new movements from within the orders that borrowed from the themes and the organizational techniques of the Islamist movements in competing with them for a primarily youthful and urban clientele. At the universities there were some efforts at responding intellectually in the name of secularism, and politicians occasional flirted cautiously with exploiting these trends. But among much of the intellectual and state elite one found primarily a rather alarmist fear of the potential for rising Islamist challenges in Senegal. The religious domain was thus one of many factors that contributed to an extremely tense climate in the period leading to the 2000 presidential elections.

The New Terrain of *Alternance*: Islamic Issues in a Changing Landscape

Eight candidates ran in the 2000 elections, including incumbent president Abdou Diouf; Abdoulaye Wade, the longtime leader of the opposition PDS; and a couple of major politicians with significant followings who had broken with the ruling Parti Socialiste to found their own parties in the crisis years, Djibo Kâ and Moustapha Niasse. The field also included two candidates who ran on explicitly religious themes.

Following a national electoral campaign in an atmosphere of intense anticipation, the first round of elections in March failed to produce the required absolute majority for any of the candidates. Abdou Diouf was thus obliged to face Abdoulaye Wade in a second round run-off election in April. Most of the other candidates ultimately announced their support for Wade, and in a remarkable second round Diouf was defeated after twenty years in power, and his long-time rival was elected president of Senegal.[8]

The process of the elections, then graceful concession by Abdou Diouf, and the subsequent smooth transition of power were truly extraordinary political events. While a full discussion is beyond the scope of this chapter, for our purposes it is important to note that the religious candidates each received only negligible support, less than 1 percent of the vote, in the first round, and were of virtually no significance in the second. Neither was particularly credible, to be sure, nor ran a strong campaign, but nevertheless their abysmal showing was widely hailed by secular intellectuals as another element in what was described as a clear "victory of citizenship" against "anti-republican" threats (see, e.g., Diop et al. 2000; Mbow 2003).

The 2000 elections signaled a shift—but by no means a rupture—with the historic ties of political elites to the maraboutic leadership. In the context of the "pluralisation of the religious sphere" (Dahou and Foucher 2004), all of the candidates—including Wade—flirted with religious themes and openly courted the support of religious figures. And while the major caliphs all maintained their silence on the candidates themselves (as they had done throughout the 1990s), various other marabouts took public stances in favor of one candidate or another. This included the surprise (and ultimately ill-considered) last-minute announcement by Shaikh Tidiane Sy, father of Moustarchidine leader Moustapha Sy, in support of incumbent president Diouf. But in any case, *soppi* initially appeared to take the wind out of the sails of earlier discourses of contestation that were beginning to be formulated along Islamic lines.

In the euphoria of victory following the presidential elections, Wade was immediately confronted with a serious political dilemma: the old ruling Parti Socialiste remained in control of the National Assembly, with no constitutional mechanism for dissolving it. In a bold move, the new government opted to write a new constitution, submit it to popular approval, and then follow with new legislative elections under new rules. Within a year this had been accomplished, and in April 2001 elections gave Wade's PDS a significant majority in the legislature.

Within this extremely fluid and changing political landscape that followed the demise of the Parti Socialiste system, the arrival of Wade, and the initiation of significant changes in the political system, then, there were also shifts in the discourses and discussions on the role of Islam in the country. Given the overwhelmingly dominant figure of Wade himself in the new regime, it is not surprising that the initial lines of these new discussions were traced by the president himself.

Most publicly and significantly at first, Wade provoked what can only be described as a major uproar in Senegal by seeming to violate the implicit understanding of the PS years that no preferential treatment be accorded on confessional lines. The very day of his 2000 election, Wade traveled to the Mouride holy city of Touba, where he was photographed kneeling before the venerable figure of the aged and arthritic caliph, receiving his blessing. Copies of the photograph were plastered in the press and sold by the thousands in the streets of major cities.

The act provoked significant unease among many—including among Wade's own supporters—raising some doubts and fears to cast a shadow on the widespread euphoria at change. Wade did nothing to allay these fears initially, and indeed seemed to feed them with promises such as that of building an international airport in the Mouride holy city of Touba. Indeed, when the legislative elections were held a year later, Wade responded by immediately leading a delegation of all members of his newly elected government—regardless of their own religious affiliations—to Touba to be blessed by the caliph, further feeding the fears of secularists and others. One influential academic expressed the outrage of many in an article in the press entitled "La République couchée," bemoaning the submission of the secular "republic" to religious authorities (Kane 2001).

Wade's actions provoked real tensions between the orders and, most important, difficult relations between his government and the Tijani families, especially the Sy family of Tivaouane (see, e.g., *Nouvel Horizon,* May 24, 2002, and December 3–9, 2004). Wade, however, remained unapologetic about this stance. In an interview in 2001, he proudly insisted on his Mouridism as a personal rather than a political choice. He bears a heavy load as president, he argued, and it is only reasonable for him to seek spiritual help and blessings from his own spiritual guide (Wade, interview 2001). This, he argues, has no impact on his policies. In a variety of public statements, however, Wade has regularly echoed the fascination of many (including, it must be noted, Western academics) with the cohesion and dynamism of the Mouride order, and it is clear that he sees in their "work ethic" a potential instrument for development. Although very much a part of the secular and francophone elite himself. Wade had long held these views on the Mourides; in 1970 he published a work entitled *La Doctrine Economique du Mouridisme,* describing the orders' doctrine as a sort of Protestant work ethnic, particularly beneficial to development (see Cruise O'Brien 2003:39).

The controversy seemed to gradually diminish after 2001, in part at least because of Mouride ambivalence about Wade's subsequent actions; having raised expectations among at least some Mourides, Wade's policies have ultimately disappointed many. In the wake of September 11, the new Senegalese president may also have become hypersensitive to any perception that he was allowing Islamic sentiments to influence raison d'état: he was, after all, host of an "antiterrorism" summit that grouped fellow African leaders in Dakar just one month after the September 2001 attacks (Whiteman and Yates 2004:374).

Wade's actions vis-à-vis the Mourides has nevertheless had a lasting impact, and Mouride-Tijani tensions remained real, if latent. Thus in the political crisis that followed the 2004 falling out between Wade and his prime minister (and presumed heir), Idrissa Seck, who is a Tijani, and especially after Seck's arrest for alleged financial improprieties in July 2005, Senegalese did not hesitate to see this as another element feeding tensions between the orders.[9] The word *taalibe*, or disciple, has entered political discourse in a new form, one Senegalese observer remarked, as politicians appropriate the term, seeing in it a political advantage. Thus, for example, it was widely reported that the ambitious politician Landing Savané, a potential heir to Wade, had made the trip to Touba to make an act of submission (*jebbelu*) to the caliph and hence become his disciple. This is all the more remarkable given Savané's background as leader of a longtime radical leftist party, and with no religious background or credentials. In this context, one influential academic and political activist predicts, Senegal is likely to see the emergence for the first time of *un vote confrérique*—voting along Sufi confessional lines—in the next elections.

Perhaps even more significantly for the role of religion in politics, Wade also threw wide open the debate about the nature and type of political system in Senegal in the days and months following his victory. After a quarter century in opposition and as a vocal critic of the previous system, Wade entered office promising to redefine the entire political system and in numerous public debates expressed willingness to question all established patterns. In the end, Wade's regime resembles the PS system far more than it differs from it; the new constitution that he had touted with such fanfare, for example, shares in all essential outlines the main lines of the previous one. But in this process, issues that had long seen settled were reopened in new ways.

Most dramatically, the first published draft of the new Senegalese constitution proposed by Wade after his election omitted the term *état laïc*, the secular state. The omission produced an immediate and vociferous uproar in the press and among intellectuals, and in the final version the term was eventually restored. The controversy nevertheless reanimated a historical debate and seemed to open the door to a previously unimaginable change in the official character of the postcolonial state.[10]

This event was followed the next year by another controversy after Wade's government sponsored and passed a law to mandate religious instruction in the state schools. The implementation of this law remains unclear, but it was generally well received by all religious groups, including the small Christian minority, since it will give students the choice of Christian or Muslim instruction. The secular elite in Senegal strongly and vocally denounced it, however, since it seemed to further erode the foundation of the secular state.

There is certainly no reason to think that Wade has any sympathy for what might be called an "Islamist" line in any way—quite the contrary. It would seem, however, that he was willing to introduce such debates as experiments in distancing himself from the PS system he had so long criticized. In addition, as Tarik Dahou and Vincent Foucher (2004) have argued, as Wade's presidency has been caught up in infighting and scandal, most notably surrounding the falling out with his prime minister and presumed dauphin, Idrissa Seck, the regime has been faced with two "temptations" as strategies for survival: an authoritarian turn, or the religious card. Authoritarianism in the form of such efforts as press censorship, they argue, has failed in the face of resistance from Senegal's deeply liberal society and strong culture of democracy. Thus, "there remains the religious temptation, which seems to open the door to greater chances of success" (Dahou and Foucher 2004: 21).

Importantly, however, in the changed circumstances and following the shifts of the 1990s, the regime's flirtations with religion have also opened the door to new religious postures. Thus, despite the constitutional ban on political parties with an explicitly religious identity or ideology, various small parties have followed the lead of Moustapha Sy in founding PUR and positioned themselves as "defenders of Islam."

Reacting to this trend, in mid-2004 the weekly *Nouvel Horizon* magazine devoted its cover story to the theme "Political Parties: The Islamist Danger" (No. 430), and highlighted ten parties described as explicitly religious in orientation. Often similarly led by younger members of religious families, the most remarkable of these may be that founded by the once-discredited Modou Kara. Flamboyantly dressed in white suits and highly original turbans, carefully cultivating his public persona and keeping his image in the press (see *Nouvel Horizon*, June 24–30, 2005) Modou Kara succeeded in reviving his "Worldwide Movement for the Oneness of God" in the Wade years. Then in February 2004 he announced the founding of a political party, Le Parti de la Verité pour le Développement (PVD, "The Party of Truth for Development"), insisting that in so doing he was asserting his rights as a citizen and not acting as a marabout. Nevertheless, he declared, if his party were to come to power, he would undertake to change the constitution, leaving unspecified the precise modifications he envisaged.

While it is difficult to take Modou Kara as a serious contender for power—indeed to many in Senegal he seems a caricature of a religious charlatan—neither can the strength of his following be dismissed. He thus represents another sign of the increased scope of action for politicized movements based on the maraboutic model, but borrowing from and experimenting with other (including Islamist) rhetoric and tactics.

In this context there is also greater religious dynamism in addressing the political issues that have been raised in the Wade years, even beyond his ability to control them. Thus, for example, a new organization was founded in 2003 to reinvigorate an old debate; the Comité Islamique pour la Reforme du Code de la Famille au Sénégal (CIRCOFS) has launched a public campaign to push for reforms in the 1972 Family Code in order to bring it into line with Islamic law (Brossier 2004). Wade has categorically rejected the demand, and the francophone intellectuals were immediately up in arms to denounce it, but clearly the issue would have strong popular resonance in Senegal, and is thus unlikely to be abandoned soon.

Rethinking Sufism and Islamism in the New World of Muslim Identities

The CIRCOFS debate is significant in that it unites a broad range of Islamic tendencies in Senegal, including both the marabouts and Islamist groups. Such common cause is not completely new; indeed, unity has often been displayed before precisely on this issue—an indication that the academic distinction between Sufis and Islamists only imperfectly captures the more complex reality of identities (Sambe 2003).

But the revival of this older (and at one time seemingly settled) debate, with new vigor, is also an indication that in the context of significant internal debates about the country's future, shifts are taking place. These have, of course, also coincided with a global questioning of the relationship between Islamic faith and political action, not least within the Muslim world, including Senegal. Thus, in the weeks and months following the September 11, 2001, attacks on the United States, there was a real "soul-searching" to be noted in Senegal as Muslims attempted to understand the motivations behind these events. This was reflected, for example, by front-page articles in the press asking such questions as: "Are Muslims Ben [*sic*] Laden?" and "Our Islamists: Are They Dangerous?" (*Nouvel Horizon,* October 19, 2001, and November 29–December 5, 2002).

This dynamic intersected with, and was fed by, the angry reactions of various groups in Senegal as the United States launched a retaliatory war against the Taliban regime in Afghanistan. Led by the Ibadou Rahmane and other "Islamists," the issue found an echo among many others, notably in the new youthful movements from within the Sufi orders. At a demonstration in Dakar called by Islamist groups to protest US actions in Afghanistan, Moustapha Sy, leader of the Moustarchidines, and Atou Diagne, from the Hizb at-Tarqiyyah, joined in the speeches. Strikingly, Diagne's speech suggested a call for an Islamic state in Senegal, under Mouride control (*Nouvel Horizon*, November 9, 2001).

By early 2003, as popular anger grew in Senegal—as around most of the globe—concerning US preparations for a preemptive war in Iraq, the distinction between Sufis, Islamists, and other Muslims in Senegal was further blurred by the public exchanges and discussion among these different segments of Senegalese society. This was evident in a variety of discursive and symbolic shifts that signaled notable departures from past practice in Senegal. Three subtle but important trends might be identified: A willingness to reinterpret Sufi traditions in the new contexts, mutual borrowings between Sufis and Islamists, and a new respect for *arabisants* intellectuals—those with a religious and Arabic-language education rather than a francophone one. These evolving dynamics are visible in multiple ways and might best be illustrated anecdotally.[11]

Thus, in a June 2003 lecture on "Sufism and the state," Sidi Lamine Niasse, editor and founder of the important media group Wal Fadjri, made a distinction between three aspects of Sufism, illustrating his points with key historical figures of Senegalese Islam. Sufism, he began, has often been marked by an attitude of *dialogue and engagement* with political authorities. The founder of the Tijani maraboutic lineage at Tivaouane, El Hajj Malik Sy, he noted, might exemplify this stance in Senegal. Second, Sufi relations with political authority have at other times been marked by a stance of respectful *withdrawal* (*hijra* is the Arabic term)—maintaining a distance between the secular and the sacred. It is in this way that the founder of the Mouride order, Shaikh Amadou Bamba, based his cohabitation with colonial authorities, and the order has maintained such relations with the state since. To be sure, Niasse suggested, these two figures, and their respective attitudes of dialogue or withdrawal, have historically dominated the relations between Sufi Muslims and the state in Senegal. But, he insisted, it is important to remember that there is a third tradition within Sufism that may at times be relevant: the attitude typified in Senegal by El Hajj Umar Tall, the nineteenth-century jihadist leader who resisted the French conquest. This attitude of *militant resistance*, he suggested, is the appropriate Sufi one when confronted with political aggression, and every indication is that such is the nature of the times in which we are living.

While Niasse is himself from an important Tijani Sufi family, he began his career as an Islamist sympathizer of the Iranian revolution, and such a stance therefore echoes his well-known public persona and is hardly surprising in itself. What is striking, however, is his willingness to root a political posture that smacks of "Islamism" squarely in the Sufi tradition and in Senegalese history.

In the spirit of this type of reinterpretation, one can note a growing tolerance and respect, and a sense of mutuality of positions on many issues, between Sufis and Islamists. This is perhaps particularly marked at the universities and among intellectuals and demonstrated, for example, in a forum at the Université Gaston Berger in the northern city of St. Louis. Representatives of two student groups, one a Tijani association (*daaira*) and the other the campus chapter of the reformist Jamatou Ibadou Rahmane student association (MEEJIR), found themselves unexpectedly together in a panel discussion of religious attitudes on campus. Throughout the event, the representatives of each side insisted emphatically on their mutual respect for each other as fellow Muslims, refusing to be baited into publicly stating their differences. In the culture of public politeness and decorum that characterizes Senegal, especially in the presence of guests, this may not in itself be too revealing. But the sincerity of this stance was underlined by particularly striking symbolic elements, the most visible of which was the veiled head and "modest" Islamic dress of the young Tijani woman on the panel.

As noted above, such veiling of young women is of recent vintage in Senegal, only appearing in any noticeable numbers at the universities in the mid-1990s. As it grew to include perhaps some 5 percent of female students, the veil became the single most salient public mark of Islamist sympathies and thus represented an implicit critique and distancing from the Sufi majority. The surprising adoption of this "Islamic" dress by a young university woman serving as a public representative of a Sufi student association thus signals the degree to which, in a relatively brief time, Islamist critiques and behavior have influenced the thought and behavior of Tijani, Mouride, and other Sufi groups.

The statements and behavior of various intellectuals in Senegal illustrate the third salient trend: in the new contexts of Muslim identity, *arabisant* intellectuals in Senegal have been given a public standing in a way they had never before enjoyed. Educated in Arabic and frequently having studied in universities in the Arab world, these individuals have historically had very limited career opportunities in the official francophone setting of Senegalese education and government, and they have historically been given very little standing in intellectual circles. The depth of this is illustrated by the fact that even within the Arabic department of the Université Shaikh Anta Diop in Dakar, the *arabisant* students—who typically had a better mastery of Arabic but more limited French capabilities—were held in less esteem than those who had come up through the francophone state school system. It is thus especially striking that, for the first time in a country where a French-language education was the essential key to public recognition as an intellectual, the francophone elite is publicly acknowledging the legitimacy of other forms of knowledge and is indeed willing to critique its historical dismissal of those educated in Arabic education (Kane 2003a).

Clearly, there is a broad willingness in contemporary Senegal to reconsider Muslim identity and to ask specifically what this should entail in terms of individual behavior and public policy. More than ever before in the country, there is a willingness to think broadly and to borrow widely from a variety of Muslim opinions. Is this an indication of Islamism on the rise? Some definitions might describe it that way. I would suggest, however, that a more useful way to conceptualize the phenomenon is to note that Muslim thinking about the meaning of being Muslim in the modern world is in flux, and that in this context different societies find themselves engaged in examining their traditions and in reinterpreting, questioning, and at times reaffirming different elements of it (Villalón 2006).

And in thinking specifically about Senegal, it is crucial to note that a key element of that religious tradition, and one with a significant history of success, is of an open and tolerant society, largely at ease with its deeply religious currents but also well accommodated to the "republican" institutions of the Senghorian secular state inherited, with adaptations, from the French. In the give and take of Senegalese democratic politics there is today a lively and vigorous open debate about the extent to which politics and state institutions should be shaped by religion. This should be hardly surprising in the international context of politicized religion, and within a democratic political system, and indeed more or less the same dynamic might be said to mark the United States.

Religious groups take part in these debates, at times finding common ground and at other times disagreeing. And in the current contexts they often find sympathetic ears that in the past may have been less receptive. It would follow from this, I would suggest, that it is misleading and confusing to attempt to analyze such dynamics by distinguishing "Islamists" from "Sufis," or "radical" from "moderate" Muslims—in an exercise reminiscent of the colonial efforts to sort out the "good" from the "bad" Muslims. Rather, we should understand this as a period of flux and realignment of understandings of religion. Ultimately a deep and profound anger at the United States in particular—and at much of the West more generally—for the policies and actions in Iraq and elsewhere in the Muslim world would seem to be central factors giving voice to new interpretations of the role of religion in politics. And these same facts have created receptive audiences for opinions that might be labeled Islamist but that in fact are the product of an intense debate in difficult circumstances.

A telling, and indeed rather amazing, example of this national soul-searching and the extent to which there is a real public debate about religion taking place in Senegal is provided by an essay question that appeared on the national baccalaureate exam for 2005. Students taking the exam in history found themselves asked to write an essay on this question: "Is it justified to say that Islam is a religion of violence? Using precise arguments, justify your point of view."[12] In an article in the press observing that students were thus being "invited to judge Islam," students who had answered the question both positively and negatively were interviewed. Tellingly, one student who argued that Islam was indeed a religion of violence added that the international actions of the United States in the current context had served to exacerbate those violent aspects of Islam. Given the importance of the baccalaureate exam, it is fair to assume that this question, and the range of reported answers, reflect the preoccupations of at least a wide swath of Senegalese intellectuals.

A final point must be noted: the search for defining a Muslim identity in the new contexts also has an external, global component. In numerous settings and contexts, through the new technologies of communication and via the international connections developed in the increasingly important Senegalese diaspora communities across the world, Senegalese Muslims are entering into dialogue with Muslims from different traditions and different political contexts. In the first five years of the new millennium, it was clear that as never before the global Muslim community, while divided and highly diverse in its answers to core questions of the role of religion and politics, is also conscious of its common fate and engaged in what may be the most significant exchange of religious ideas in its history.

And in this exchange, Senegalese Sufis are both borrowing from abroad and staking their claim to the legitimacy of their own interpretations of Muslim modernity. The point is illustrated in the globalized world of the AfroPop music market. Departing musically from his famous style, Senegalese superstar Youssou Ndour released an album in 2003 entitled *Sant* (Praise) in Senegal and *Egypt* in its international release. The entire album is composed of religious songs, dedicated to a wide range of Senegalese maraboutic figures. Such songs are a common theme in Senegalese popular music, which frequently invokes Sufi figures and themes (McLaughlin 1997; McLaughlin 2000). But for the first time, Ndour is accompanied by an Egyptian orchestra, and his lyrics of praise to key figures of the Black African Sufi tradition are sung in Arabic rhythms rather than *mbalaax*, positioning the music squarely in the global Muslim context. Youssou Ndour thus simultaneously wraps himself in the broader Muslim identity but also reaffirms the validity of the specific Sufi Muslim heritage of his space on the western edge of the Dar al-Islam.

Notes

1. The terms and their precise definitions have varied in the literature, but scholars frequently posit a basic distinction between a more tolerant indigenous (African) religion and a more militant (Arab) one. For a noteworthy example, see Rosander and Westerlund 1997. At times scholars have additionally distinguished between "reformist" Islamic movements, referring to those whose primary goal is the correction of religious practice, and "Islamist" ones that have an overtly political agenda. In practice, however, the distinction is not always clear, and for purposes of this chapter the term *Islamist* will be used to refer to both.

2. There is a long intellectual pedigree to these distinctions, building on the work of such colonial administrators as the famous Paul Marty.

3. For a recent insightful analysis of the nature of that democracy, see Gellar 2005.

4. Approximately 5 percent of Senegalese are Christians, and by the late 1990s perhaps some 5 to 10 percent of Muslims would not claim affiliation with a Sufi order.

5. It should be noted that other scholars have a less benign interpretation of the Mourides—most notably, Jean Copans (1980), who described the order as "an infernal machine" in a Marxist analysis of the order's role in organizing peasant labor in the service of private and state elite interests.

6. For an elaboration of the argument in this section, see Villalón 1999.

7. This form of dress, initially signifying adherence to the Ibadou Rahmane movement, was virtually nonexistent in the early 1990s but was worn by some 5–10 percent of the women on university campuses by the end of the decade. An insightful study of the women's participation in the movement is provided by Augis 2005.

8. The exception was Djibo Kâ, who after considerable hesitation made the significant miscalculation of backing Abdou Diouf.

9. This and other observations in this paragraph are drawn from interviews carried out in Dakar in July 2005. Seck's arrest—officially for misusing public works funds as mayor of the city of Thiès—was certainly motivated in large part by the increasingly heated public political rivalry between him and the president.

10. The motivations for this entire event remain cloudy, and there are various interpretations as to both why the term was left out and how and why it was restored. A cynical view suggests that Wade used the debate as a tactic to divert attention from institutional issues of the constitution. One member of the constitutional commission appointed to write the draft insisted that the term was removed without the commission's knowledge and reinserted at the members' insistence (Gueye, interview 2001).

11. The following examples are drawn from a series of interviews, lectures, and discussions with academics, activists, and representatives of a number of different groups, which the author organized in Senegal as part of a summer institute for university faculty on Islam in Africa, sponsored by the West African Research Association, in June 2003.

12. "Est-il fondé de dire que l'Islam est une religion de violence? A partir d'arguments précis, justifiez votre point de vue." The baccalaureate question was discussed in an article in *Wal Fadjri*, No. 3990, July 5, 2005, entitled: "Baccalaureat 2005: Les candidats invités à faire le procès de l'Islam."

8

West Africa Transformed: The New Mosque-State Relationship

WILLIAM F. S. MILES

WEST AFRICAN ISLAM IS EVOLVING POLITICALLY, AND FAST: SO THESE RICH CASE studies on Niger, Nigeria, Mali, Mauritania, The Gambia, and Senegal assure us. How quaint now seems the early postcolonial notion that meaningful separation of mosque and state would remain a bedrock of the independent nation-state in a region of Africa marked by such a strong Muslim presence. Before September 11 recalibrated focus on Islam in West Africa, significant inroads into the superimposed European ideal of governance through secular institutions (without religious ones) had already been made. Partisan democratizing pressures in Nigeria and Senegal, Roman Loimeier and Leonardo Villalón show us, had put sharia and anti-Mouride reformism on the theopolitical table well before Osama bin Laden became a household name and (as noted by Robert Charlick) a Sahelian T-shirt logo. Similarly, the emergence of civil society associations in Niger and Mali (according to Charlick and Victor Le Vine) and Wahhabi proselytizing in The Gambia (according to Momodou Darboe), elevated Islamist movements there prior to the airborne suicide attacks on the Twin Towers and Pentagon. *After* September 11, the significance of political Islam in West Africa is of course inescapable: Cédric Jourde frames Mauritanian politics in terms of the war on terrorism, and Loimeier discusses a Taliban offshoot in Nigeria. It is crucial, however, that scholars of West African Islam not fall into the reductio ad Al-Qaidum trap of neophyte Africanist students and intelligence analysts.

For Islamism is not a specter haunting West Africa. Despite the politicization of Islam in the six countries under consideration (representative, in terms of religion, of West Africa writ large), the likelihood of a national theocratic state arising in any one of them is virtually nil. Nor are national integrity and identity existentially endangered by Islamist movements that have arisen. Not even in Mali, where Tuareg secessionism has been most violent, is secessionist splintering a likely imminent outcome. State-mosque relations have distinct outcomes in the different states, and no pan-Islamic revolution is going to dissolve West African states into a jihadist confederation.

Nevertheless, *there is in all of the cases under consideration a remarkable blurring of postcolonial lines between mosque and state*. Even if the specific forms thus taken differ from (often neighboring) country to country, the general encroachment of Islamic preoccupations into *res publica* needs to be taken into account. Six areas are worth singling out: political Islam in an era of democratization; the rise of "reformist" organizations; domestic splits between Islamic groups; anti-Westernization; women's issues as Islamist flashpoints; and external influences.

Political Islam and Democratization

Perhaps it is ironic, perhaps it is logical, but the resurgence of political Islam in West Africa has overlapped with restored norms of democratic governance. Negotiation between religion and politics in West Africa is thus critical. Le Vine demonstrates how Amadou Toumani Touré's prodemocratic coup in Mali "triggered an extraordinary explosion of . . . explicitly Muslim groups and organizations." Electoral power of Islamic groups was a factor (albeit not a decisive one) in the 2002 presidential elections. Ibrahim Keita did lose, but the mere mobilization of Muslim associations on his behalf energized this interest group. Malian democracy will certainly see more Islamic politicking.

In Niger, the return in the 1980s to electoral politics entailed, we have seen from Charlick, cultural associations with strong revivalist overtones. In its campaigning and public functions, leaders of the Convention Démocratique et Social party (both those appointed and elected) make a point of demonstrating their religiosity. President Mahamane Ousmane and the mayor of Maradi are prime examples. In rural Matameye, a region with which Charlick has had decades-long familiarity, villagers shared that their voting decisions are informed (at least in part) on their adherence to Islam.

Senegal has had a more continuous experience with formal democracy than either Mali or Niger. Here, the necessity of Islamic support for victorious candidates has been a constant. Yet even in Senegal it appears that the more open and democratic the electoral system becomes, the more significant is the "Islamic factor." Villalón focuses on the 2000 election, in which presidential challenger Abdoulaye Wade "flirted with the marabouts" and an important Muslim group leader openly endorsed the incumbent Abdou

Diouf. For sure, most major caliphs respected the habitual neutrality that they had exercised during the democratizing 1990s. Yet the public stances taken by other marabouts appear more likely a pattern in Senegalese electoralism than their discretion of yesteryear.

Nigeria's situation is complicated, of course, in that it is the most religiously pluralistic of the cases under consideration. Party leaders must be politically and constitutionally careful not to exclude or favor followers of either major faith. In the context of Nigeria, "democratization" is not a wave beginning in the 1990s with a national conference. There have been periodic waves (roughly corresponding with the respective Nigerian "republics"), between which democracy has lurched: the early 1960s, early 1980s, late 1990s. Loimeier shows how the character of Islamic politics has changed according to the nature of the Nigerian democratic wave. Lest it be overlooked within the endnotes, Loimeier invokes the fundamentalist Abubakar Gumi's famous (and extensively reinterpreted) newspaper quote in 1982 that made clear that "politics was more important than prayers." (The context was mobilization of Muslim women in the forthcoming elections.)

Were it not for the impending Gambia elections in 1996, it is unlikely that President Jammeh would have sent personal apologies to Gambissara to make amends for his impetuous vice president. (The latter had approved the building of a Wahhabi mosque in the village, overriding the will of the traditional elders.) Elections in 2001, in contrast, were preceded by tacit presidential approval of extremist Islamism elsewhere, as signaled by Jammeh's silence in response to sermons by the imam of the State House mosque that countenanced the attacks of September 11.

In Mauritania, it is too early to tell if leaders of the 2005 coup will reopen the door to a veritable democratization, as opposed to the ongoing neoauthoritarian facsimile. Jourde gives us enough hints that Islamist opposition groups would have sufficiently survived their intervening repression and sought the sunlight of electoral support.

Reformist Renaissance

Africanized Islam is defective. From Banjul to Maradi, this tendentious belief has been used to mobilize and invigorate new Islamist groups throughout the region. The famously syncretistic, tolerant, and assimilationist varieties of Islam (best described here by Darboe, Le Vine, and Villalón) are on the defensive. Reformist (or "orthodox") interpretations of Islam, whose legitimacy is derived outside of Africa, aim to supersede traditionalist ways of praying, believing, and networking.

These "reformist" groups enjoy varying degrees of connection with one another. Charlick and Loimeier focus on Izala, a northern Nigerian movement that, especially on account of mercantilist connections, has carried over into Niger. Differing national contexts have inflected the scope and importance of Izala in these two nations, however. A dismissive francophone elite in a much more homogeneously Muslim society (Niger) contains Izala in a manner without equivalent in Nigeria. Nigeria's polarization between (southern) Christian and (mostly northern) Muslim camps imparts to Izala an ethnically symbolic importance that it lacks in Niger. At the same time, northern Nigeria is host to an array of competing Islamist groups against which Izala in Niger need not contend in like measure. For sure, as Charlick informs us, there has been in Niger a significant proliferation of Islamic civil society associations. Yet they are not Islamist in even the largely inclusive way that we have been using the term.

On the geographical and theological fringes of both Mali and Mauritania are the Groupe Salafiste pour la Prédication et le Combat. Armed and insurrectionist, such GSPC groups are ignored by neither Africanist scholars (here, Le Vine and Jourde) nor counterinsurgency analysts. In between Izala and GSPC are such verbally subversive but (as yet) militarily unorganized fundamentalist movements as Dawa and Ummah. In Mali, according to Le Vine, Dawa has unsuccessfully attempted to restoke the flames of Tuareg rebellion; in Mauritania, shows Jourde, they are associated more with crackdown than uprising.

In his chapter, Villalón introduces us to the Moustarchidines, Ibadou Rahmane, Hizb, and MMUD, reformist groups that—like Izala in Nigeria and Niger—challenge traditional Muslim power hierarchies within Senegal. Organizationally, however, they are not linked to Izala. (Indeed, they are only loosely connected with each other.) If young successful merchants constitute the backbone of Islamic reformism in Niger, as do the marginalized and dispossessed in Nigeria, in Senegal several of the reformist movements are in contrast university-based and in any case youth-oriented. Reformist groups in our cases reflect different constituencies and varying aims.

Darboe does not identify specific reformist associations in The Gambia but rather invokes "orthodox Sunni Wahhabis" and their individual leaders. Imam Fatty is the most prominent of these. Unlike in Senegal, Niger, and Nigeria, in The Gambia the ruling regime under President Jammeh has deliberately, actively, and conspicuously promoted the reformists for its own ends. Thus did Jammeh appoint Fatty to be State House imam. Exceptional manipulation of Islamists for partisan purposes in The Gambia highlights the differential roles these groups have come to play in contrasting national contexts, even as they all share in the general phenomenon of reformist ascendancy.

Brotherhoods: Under Siege and Center Stage

Reformist groups share not only a positive agenda of "purification" of Islam but a negative policy of opposing entrenched Muslim networks and hierarchies. Tablighi in Mali inveighs against old order Sufis, themselves repositories of accommodation. In Mauritania, Sufism has an ethnic dimension, inasmuch as it is embraced by the sub-Saharan Futanke as much as the Moorish Islamists disdain it. In The Gambia, Imam Ratib Jobe represented the "old order" that orthodox Sunni Wahhabis opposed. (That Jobe was associated with the deposed Jawara régime stigmatized him in Jammeh's eyes, too.) In adjoining Senegal, traditional establishment Islam is represented by associational and family-based dynasties linked through the organizational-cum-ritualistic Sufi *daarias*: the Mourides are the most prominent of these orders and thus the most visible target of reformist critics, from within as well as from without. Likewise, in Nigeria (and, to a lesser extent, in Niger) it is the *tariqas*, the brotherhoods, that come under attack by reformist groups for their supposed deviation from strict quranic strictures. (In both Hausaland and Senegambia, Tijaniyya is the most widespread brotherhood; but it is the idea of religious brotherhoods, more than the specific type, that upsets reformists.)

Thus, in all six country cases Islamism, especially as it is represented through reformist organizations and associations, is internally divisive for Muslim communities. Theologically based disagreements over practicing the faith and structuring Islamic society inevitably entail political tension between, on the one hand, custodians and followers of religious tradition and, on the other, "orthodox," text-based purists. This is no less the case in the country with the greatest number and proportion of non-Muslim citizens: in Nigeria, Izala is reprobated by brotherhood coreligionists no less than by fundamentalist-fearful Christians.

Can the brotherhoods themselves be regarded as Islamist? For sure, they do mobilize, and can be mobilized for, political ends. In the West African polities more practiced in electoral democratic processes—among our sample, Nigeria, Mali, and Senegal—the electoral role of the brotherhoods has at times been key. Although Loimeier does not fully explore the Qadiriyya and Tijaniyya brotherhoods with respect to partisan competition leading up to and during the First Republic (1960–1966), one might identify a "*tariqa* factor" at play, with elements of the Tijaniyya siding with the more radical Northern Elements Progressive Union (NEPU) against the aristocratic, Sokoto-based, and Qadiriyya-friendly Northern People's Congress (NPC).

For Villalón, in the context of Senegal, Sufi orders did not initially, despite their occasional mobilization to affect political outcomes on Islamic issues, play an "Islamist" role during the rule of Léopold Senghor and the first decade of his successor Abdou Diouf. Although both Senghor and Diouf cultivated maraboutic authorities as rhetorical transmission belts with the populace at large, religious leaders accepted the overall secular character of the Senegalese state, as put forth by the Parti Socialiste. Islamist, non-Islamist? Definitional issues aside, Villalón relates the more straightforward politicization/Islamization of the Sufi brotherhoods in recent times.

With *soppi* (régime change by ballot) in the 1990s, mainstream Islamic intervention into *la politique* has become more prevalent: maraboutic endorsement of candidates is one unprecedented example. Accession to the presidency by Abdoulaye Wade seems to have sanctioned this slippage, given his postelection actions (public blessing by the caliph of Touba, waffling on the constitutional status of secularism, promotion of religious instruction in public schools). Theopolitical, Islamist evolution *within* the Mouride brotherhood is no less significant.

Where the brotherhoods have not been as historically developed (i.e., Niger) and where there is hardly a veneer of democracy (i.e., Mauritania, The Gambia), their potential as voting banks and regime props has been proportionately weaker. This must be why Charlick, Jourde, and Darboe touch on the brotherhoods less than do Loimeier, Le Vine, and Villalón. Here is a hypothesis worth exploring for a broader number of cases in the region: the combination of established brotherhoods and electoral politics simultaneously provides (1) reformist groups with expedient foils against which to promote themselves, and (2) wooable constituencies for competitive political parties and consolidation-seeking regimes. Regimes view the brotherhoods as bulwarks against reformist subversives as well as bases of popular support. The extent to which electoral dependence on traditional brotherhoods tempers or stimulates Islamization of the polity depends on a variety of factors, not least of which is the relative influence of reformist upstarts.

Yet we must also beware blithe dichotomizing of the reformist groups and the brotherhoods. In Senegal Villalón has discerned an important corollary to the major thread unifying the cases under review (i.e., a progressive blurring of mosque-state lines). For there, Villalón notes, "forms and manifestations [of Sufism] are adapting in ways that have blurred, if not completely erased, the distinction between 'traditional' Sufi and Islamist groups." Younger, contestatory Sufis have begun to challenge older authorities and their decisionmaking patterns on Islamist grounds. Might the center of brotherhood gravity eventually tip in an Islamist direction elsewhere in West Africa as it has begun to in Senegal? One overarching issue could unite brotherhoods and reformists: anti-Westernization.

Islamist Anti-Westernization

While all six contributors highlight the anti-Westernization plank of West African Islamism, Charlick, writing on Niger, makes it the centerpiece of his analysis. In The Gambia, Wahhabis may cast the West "as the enemy of Islam" (Darboe); in Senegal, university-based Sufi movements may take "a strong anti-Westernization stance" (Villalón); and in Nigeria, sharia may challenge "decolonization of the legal system," as inherited from Great Britain (Loimeier). For Niger, Charlick goes further. He deconstructs Islamism (at least in its most prominent organizational form, Izala) as an anti-Western form of capitalist modernization. By disaggregating capitalism from Westernization, he provides an economic explanation for the attraction of Islamism.

For sure, Islamism articulates a dissatisfaction with globalization and modernization, but there is modernization and then there is Western modernization. For Charlick and other sophisticated expositors of Izala, the West does not hold a monopoly on capitalist norms and incentives. Entrepreneurial rights may be advanced just as assuredly by West African merchants in *boubous* as by white (and blue-) collar Euro-Americans.

Izala also reflects dissatisfaction with "the basic norms and structure of 'traditional Hausa society'" (a situation echoing the reformist opposition to brotherhoods summarized in the previous section). In this sense, Islamism can be understood as a theologically framed resistance to both local and international forms of socioeconomic oppression.

Westernization can also mean little more than political sympathy or alliance making with the United States. It is in this sense that we may understand Islamist opposition in Mauritania to collaboration for the war on terrorism.

As long as the more vehemently lambasted adversary is distant and Western rather than proximate and coreligionist, Islamism can unite the otherwise antagonistic reformist and traditionalist camps. It makes little difference here whether the "traditionalist camps" take the form of specific dynastic brotherhoods or Charlick's more generalized "older social and normative constructs." Even if most brotherhoods and other traditionalist Islamic groups decline to join in the anti-Westernization reformist rhetoric, it is unlikely that they will become defenders of or platforms for pro-Western discourse. If only by default, then, West African framing of the Western world may devolve to the (hostile) reformists.

From Anti-Westernization to Antifeminism

Part and parcel of anti-Western theopolitics in Muslim West Africa is antifeminist Islamism. Charlick would argue that entrepreneurial rights *à la* Izala really refers to *male* entrepreneurial rights. (Indeed, even in the countryside women's economic freedom is supposedly being restricted.) Niger provides other examples of Islamist-led campaigns inimical to women's interests: demonstrations against the government's condom promotion campaign; against Nigérien ratification of the United Nations Convention on Ending All Forms of Discrimination Against Women; against the holding of fashion festivals; and stymieing of a more liberal Family Code.

Niger is not unique with respect to the centrality of women's issues for Islamist contestation. Darboe cites as a critical example of Islamist confrontation with state (and mission school) authorities the showdown—reminiscent of France's headscarf controversy—with radical clerics over schoolgirls' right to wear veils. In this case the government reversed its initial course and prohibited the veils in school. Yet the issue escalated to the point where the head of state was threatened with excommunication.

According to Villalón, the veiling of female Muslim students is a significant issue in Senegal, too. Here, however, the phenomenon occurs at the university level and, presumably, is both voluntary and uncontested. Its symbolism, however, is not to be underestimated, underscoring "the degree to which, in a relatively brief time, Islamist critique and behavior have influenced the thought and behavior of . . . Sufi groups." Calls by an "Islamic Committee" for a revisiting of the nation's Family Code also implicitly signals a non-Western trend with respect to Muslim women's rights.

It is in Nigeria, however, that Western and Islamist norms of women's rights have most noticeably clashed. Full sharia has led to death sentences—by stoning, no less—being meted out to convicted Muslim adulteresses. No such punishment has actually been carried out; but even if no woman is so executed, there remains a clash of judicial civilizations. "Almost all the convicted are poor and often female," writes Loimeier, "with little knowledge of legal procedures in general and sharia penal laws in particular."

Gender issues are key to Islamist initiatives in West Africa. There is of course a wide berth between females' susceptibility to capital punishment for marital infidelity in northern Nigeria and their threatened exclusion from school for wearing veils in greater Banjul. Still, our cases clearly show that one cannot examine Islamism apart from the role of women in West African society. Local disagreements over feminism elide easily into anti-Westernization arguments.

Le Vine, we have seen, raises the seeming paradox of Islamist silence in the face of human trafficking of women in Mali. Is there merely a time lag between this issue of global human rights being incorporated into Islamist discourse in West Africa? Or is there a hypocritical silence? Le Vine illuminates other paths that consideration of women and West African Islamism can take.

External Influences

Negative Western attention to West Africa and anti-Western Islamist polemics are only part of the "external influence" picture. From an indigenous perspective, more important are the influences, touched on by all six country specialists, of Muslim nations from outside the region.

Would Mauritania have reestablished diplomatic relations with Israel had Jordan and Egypt not already done so? The arrests in Mauritania of citizens with business and family ties to Afghanistan and Palestine is illustrative of such global Muslim politics.

For Muslim West Africa, globalization entails above all facilitated pilgrimage-driven transportation and communication links with Saudi Arabia. As a result, contemporary Wahhabi interpretations of Islam have been taking a transformative theological stance in opposition to hitherto indigenous and syncretistic varieties of African Islam. On a doctrinal level, Loimeier and Charlick elaborate on this phenomenon with respect to Izala in Nigeria and Niger. Darboe and Villalón, for their part, delineate the Wahhabi connection in terms of recognizable new actors: bearded Gambian graduates of Saudi schools by the former; "*arabisant*" intellectuals by the latter. (Villalón himself does not use the term *Wahhabi*.)

But West Africans do not only come to Muhammad's mountain; thanks to a mountain of Saudi money, Arabian-style mosques devoted to the Prophet's teachings are sprouting throughout West Africa. Saudi influence in Muslim Nigeria, Niger, The Gambia, and Senegal is not architectural alone. Further research into Saudi–West African relations is needed, particularly with respect to international Islamist activity.

If Saudi involvement in West Africa is ascending if discreet, Libya's has been waning if sobering. Mu'ammar Qaddafi abetted a coup to oust the first Gambian president on account of beer brewing. Motivations for the Libyan leader's periodic interventions in Niger have been mixed, but to some extent have included spreading his idiosyncratic blend of socialism and Islam. Further research into West African Islamism will need to take into account this internationalist dimension even more. Villalón's concluding musical reference points to a much wider and broader space of Islamic influence than that suggested by the Wahhabist connection alone.

West Africa and the Broader Muslim World

Despite centuries of Islamization, the existence of faithful, organized, vibrant Muslim communities in West Africa has been basically ignored by the wider public. That "wider public" extends to the broader Muslim world. Black Africa, East and West, has been viewed as peripheral to Islam, a bias as real in Tehran as it is in Washington. It is unfortunate that only violent events that can be dubbed "Islamist" draw wider attention to a region that, nineteenth-century jihadist antecedents notwithstanding, has cultivated a form of Islam whose adherents by and large practice the peace that their leaders preach. This is not to gainsay the radical strands of African Islam that have indeed adopted confrontational and intolerant stances vis-à-vis other religions and Muslim denominations. But the composition of West African states and society militates against overall Islamist ascendance, especially when compared with the rest of the Muslim world.

One major reason is diversity. West African Islam overlays an ethnic multiplicity the likes of which are rarely found elsewhere in the Muslim world. Yes, the Middle and Near East includes Arab, Berber, Kurdish, Pashtun, Persian, and Turkic Muslims, among others. Southeast and South Asia is much more diverse than the listing of ethnic Indic, Javanese, Kashmiri, and Malay Muslims suggests. But these areas are vast, encompassing many more countries and much larger populations. The sixteen West African states are home to twenty-six ethnic groups, eight of whom are almost entirely Muslim (Kanuri, Moor, Nupe, Songhay, Susu, Tuareg, Tukolor, Wolof), four of whom are significantly Muslim (Fulani, Hausa, Serer, Soninke), and one of whom—the Yoruba—are about half Muslim by percentage but number in the tens of millions. The Manding, about 40 percent Muslim, are spread out over ten separate West African nations (Weekes 1978). The Muslim world is indeed diverse: West Africa epitomizes ethnic diversity within Islam.

For all its real diversity, in terms of political Islam writ large, the Muslim world is currently perceived as binary: Sunni versus Shi'ite. This polarity, however real or ephemeral, has little currency within West African Islam. For sure, the older competition between Tijaniyya and Qadiriyya brotherhoods is being replaced by that between Reformist and Sufi strands; but neither pair of movements is wracking West African Muslim communities the way Shi'ite-Sunni tensions are destroying Iraq, or stoke tensions between Iran and Saudi Arabia.

If West African society is characterized by diversity, statehood throughout Muslim-majority West Africa, compared with the wider Muslim world, is typified by lesser experience (all achieved independence after 1958) and relative inefficacy. All six countries we have examined fall within the low human development category of the United Nations Development Report; only two non-African Muslim nations (Pakistan and Yemen) do. For sure, poverty and state inefficacy can beget Islamist militancy; but where this has happened (Algeria, Egypt, Iran, Lebanon, Palestine) there have been deeper-rooted expectations of good governance according to Islamic principles. Given the artificiality, recency, and secularism of the inheritor states to West African colonialism, such religiously grounded expectations from government have been relatively nonexistent. State and society in West Africa's Muslim nations are historically and systemically distinct from those of the wider Muslim world. That their mutual transformation should take different contours or rhythms should not be surprising.

For Islam is not an independent variable in West African politics. Its power depends on how well the postcolonial state manages to salvage its legitimacy in the wake of economic decline and urban insecurity. Inasmuch as religion provides an alternative legitimizing structure to crisis in Banjul and Bamako, Nouakchott and Niamey, Abuja and Dakar, it can play a critical role in West Africa's political future. Will the form of Islam that reasserts itself be oppositional, or accommodationist, to the state? Will the state struggle to repress, or co-opt, the mosque? What balance may it strike in trying to do both? What will state attitudes toward intrareligious conflict be?

Just as the forms that Islamism has already taken within the societies of the six countries under consideration have been different, so will state responses likely differ. But it is certain that the broader world, Muslim and non-Muslim alike, will be increasingly forced to confront the overarching, growing phenomenon of political Islam in West Africa.

Bibliography

Abdoulaye, Galilou. 2003. "L'Islam au Benin: acteurs, courants et stratégies d'ancrage dans les arènes musulmanes." PhD diss., University of Mainz, Germany.

Abun-Nasr, Jamil M. 1965. *The Tijaniyya*. London: Oxford University Press.

ACSS (Africa Center for Strategic Studies). 2003. *North and West Africa Counter-Terrorism: Topical Seminar, Program Highlights*. Bamako, Mali: National Defense University.

Adama, Hamadou. 2004. Historian. Nijmegen, Nigeria. Interview with R. Loimeier, September 12.

Adamu, Muhammad Uba. 1968. "Some Notes on the Influence of North African Traders in Kano." *Kano Studies* 1:43–49.

Agence France Presse. 2002. "Les religieux s'invitent dans la campagne électorale." April 26. http://www.africatime.com.

Ahmad, Mirza Ghulam of Qadian. 1992. "The Philosophy of the Teachings of Islam." Surrey, UK: Islam International.

Ahmed, Asif Folarin. 1986. "The Qadiriyyah and Its Impact in Nigeria." PhD diss., University of Ibadan.

Al-Jamiat, Newsletter of Jamiatul Ulama. 1996. Council of Muslim Scholars, Durban, South Africa. August 26.

Amselle, Jean-Loup. 1998. *Mestizo Logics: Anthropology of Identity in Africa and Elsewhere*. Stanford, CA: Stanford University Press.

An-Naqar, Umar. 1972. *The Pilgrimage Tradition in West Africa*. Khartoum: Khartoum University Press.

Audrain, Xavier. 2004. "Du 'ndigël avorté' au Parti de la Verité: Evolution du rapport religion/politique à travers le parcours de Cheikh Modou Kara (1999–2004)." *Politique Africaine* 96:99–118.

Augis, Erin. 2005. "Dakar's Sunnite Women: The Politics of Person." In Muriel Gomez-Perez, ed., *L'Islam politique au sud du Sahara: Identités, discours, et enjeux*. Paris: Karthala.

Babou, Cheikh Anta Mbacké. 2002. *Amadu Bamba and the Founding of the Muridiyya: The History of a Muslim Brotherhood in Senegal (1853–1913).* PhD thesis, Michigan State University.

Badji, Alieu K. Alhaji. 2005. Banjul mosque elder and founding member, former Bathurst Young Muslim Society. The Gambia. Interview with M. N. Darboe, June.

Baduel, Robert. 1992. "Chronique mauritanienne 1990–1991: de la répression à l'esquissė d'une transition démocratique ou des capacités d'adaptation d'un régime autoritaire." *Annuaire de l'Afrique du Nord* 30:887–932.

Bari, Sarki Bello. 1997. *Taurarin Kadiriyya: Littafi na farko (1).* Kano: Gwadabe Zakari Kurạwa.

Barnett, Michael. 1998. *Dialogues in Arab Politics.* New York: Columbia University Press.

Bathily, Abdoulaye, Mamadou Diouf, and Mohamed Mbodj. 1995. "The Senegalese Student Movement from Its Inception to 1989." In Mahmood Mamdani, ed., *African Studies in Social Movements and Democracy.* Dakar: CODESRIA.

Bayart, Jean-François. 1993. "Fin de partie au sud du Sahara? La politique africaine de la France." In Serge Michailof, ed., *La France et l'Afrique: Vade-Mecum pour un nouveau voyage.* Paris: Karthala.

Ben Amara, Ramzi. 2005. "Die Entwicklung der Scharia-Frage in Nigeria seit den 1990er Jahren." Master's thesis, University of Bayreuth.

Bensouda, Amie. 2005. Solicitor, Amie Bensouda and Co., Legal Practitioners. The Gambia. Interview with M. N. Darboe, June.

Bierschenk, Thomas, and Georg Stauth. 2003. "Introduction: Islam and Contemporary Social Change in Africa." In Thomas Bierschenk and Georg Stauth, eds., *Islam in Africa: Yearbook of the Sociology of Islam,* Vol. 4. Münster: Lit Verlag.

Bojang, Momodou Major. 2005. Former Minister of Interior and Commissioner of Central River Division, 1994–2001. The Gambia. Interview with M. N. Darboe, March.

Bojang, S. (n.d.) "Interview—Alhaji Banding Drammeh, President, Supreme Islamic Council." *The Observer.*

Boni, Nazi. 1971. *Histoire synthétique de l'Afrique résistante.* Paris: Présence Africaine.

Boubrik, Rahal. 1998. "Pouvoir et hommes de religion en Mauritanie." *Politique africaine* 70:135–143.

Boyd, Jean. 1989. "Sultan Abubakar III of Sokoto (1903–1988)." *Islam et Sociétés au Sud du Sahara* 3:119–127.

Brenner, Louis. 1988. "Concepts of Tariqa in West Africa: The Case of the Qadiriya." In D. B. Cruise O'Brien and Christian Coulon, eds., *Charisma and Brotherhood in African Islam.* Oxford: Oxford University Press.

———. 1993a. "Constructing Muslim Identity in Mali." In Louis Brenner, ed., *Muslim Identity and Social Change in Sub-Saharan Africa.* Bloomington: Indiana University Press.

———. 1993b. *Muslim Identity and Social Change in Sub-Saharan Africa.* Bloomington: Indiana University Press.

———. 2001. *Controlling Knowledge: Religion, Power, and Schooling in a West African Muslim Society.* Bloomington: Indiana University Press.

Brigaglia, Andrea. 2004a. "Testo, Traditizione e Conflitto Esegetico: Gli 'Ulama' Contemporanei e gli Sviluppi dell Esegesi Coranica nella Società Nord-Nigeriana (Kano e Kaduna, 1960–2002)." PhD diss., University of Naples.

———. 2004b. Researcher. Bayreuth. Interview with R. Loimeier, June 30.

———. 2005a. "Two Published Hausa Translations of the Qur'an and Their Doctrinal Background." *Journal of Religion in Africa* 34:424–449.

———. 2005b. "Sacred Words and Learned Men in the Media: The Radio Kaduna qur'ânic exegesis in Nigeria (1978–1992)." Paper presented to the AEGIS conference, London.

Brossier, Marie. 2004. "Les Débats sur le droit de la famille au Sénégal: Une mise en question des fondements de l'autorité légitime?" *Politique Africaine* 96:78–98.

Brownlee, Jason. 2002. " . . . And Yet They Persist: Explaining Survival and Transition in Neopatrimonial Regimes." *Studies in Comparative International Development* 37:35–63.

Bunza, Mukhtar Umar. 2004. "Muslims and the Modern State in Nigeria: A Study of the Impact of Foreign Religious Literature, 1980s–1990s." *Islam et Sociétés au Sud du Sahara* 17–18:49–66.

———. 2005. "The Iranian Model of Political Islamic Movement in Nigeria." In Muriel Gomez-Perez, ed., *L'Islam politique au sud du Sahara: Identités, discours et enjeux*. Paris: Karthala.

Butterworth, Charles E., and I. William Zartman. 1992. "Preface." *The Annals of the American Academy of Political and Social Science* 524 (special issue on Political Islam).

CARE. 1997. "Mali Case Study: The Operating Environment for Civil Society." Bamako.

"Le cinquième sommet de l'UMA." 1992. *Marchés Tropicaux* 2455 (November 27):3129.

Carothers, Thomas. 2002. "The End of the Transition Paradigm." *Journal of Democracy* 13:5–21.

Ceesay, Faramang. 2006. Member, the Tabligh Jama'at (Ma'shala) Center, The Gambia. Interview with M. N. Darboe, July

Charlick, Robert. 1974. "Power and Participation in the Modernization of Rural Hausa Communities." PhD diss., University of California–Los Angeles.

———. 1991. *Niger. Personal Rule and Survival in the Sahel.* Boulder: Westview.

———. 1994. "The Political Economy of Niger's Foreign Policy." In Tim Shaw and Julius Okolo, eds., *The Political Economy of the Foreign Policy in ECOWAS.* Cambridge: Cambridge University Press.

———, Leslie Fox, Sheldon Gellar, Pearl Robinson, and Tina West. 1994. *Improving Democratic Governance for Sustainable Development: An Assessment of Change and Continuity in Niger*. Washington, DC: Associates in Rural Development and Management Systems International.

Charlick, Robert, and Abdoulrazack Hima. 2006. "Fundamentalist Islam and Aspirations of an Emerging Merchant Class." Unpublished manuscript.

CIA (Central Intelligence Agency). 2004. *World Factbook.* Washington, DC: CIA.

Clark, Andrew Francis. 1999. "Imperialism, Independence, and Islam in Senegal and Mali." *Africa Today* 46:148–167.

Clarke, Peter B. 1987. "Islam, Development and African Identity: The Case of West Africa." In Kirsten Holst Petersen, ed., *Religion, Development and African Identity*. Uppsala: Scandinavian Institute of African Studies.

Clausen, Ursel. 1994. "Mauritanie: Chronique intérieure 1992–1994." *Annuaire de l'Afrique du Nord* 33:641–674.

———. 1999. "Mauritanie: Chronique politique." *Annuaire de l'Afrique du Nord* 38:281–305.

Cleary, Michael. 2005. Bishop of The Gambia Catholic Mission. Interview with M. N. Darboe, June.

Cheruiyot, Faith. 2006. "Women's Rights: A Tale of Two National Assemblies in Africa." http://www.Pambazuka.org.

Cooper, Barbara. 1995. "The Politics of Difference and Women's Associations in Niger: Of 'Prostitution,' the Public, and Politics." *Signs* (Summer): 851–882.

Copans, Jean. 1980. *Les Marabouts de l'arachide: La confrérie Mouride et les paysans du Sénégal.* Paris: Le Sycomore.

Coulon, Christian. 1983. "Le réseau islamique." *Politique africaine* 9:63–83.

———. 1993. "Les nouveaux oulémas et le renouveau islamique au Nord-Nigeria." In Réné Otayek, ed., *Le radicalisme islamique au sud du Sahara.* Paris: Karthala.

Counselor (Conseiller, Informations). 2005. Embassy of Mali. Washington, DC. Interview with V. T. Le Vine, June 7.

CRIDEM (Convergence républicaine pour l'instauration de la démocratie). 2005. "Impasse politique et réflexes sécuritaires en Mauritanie: Comment fabriquer du terrorisme utile." http://www.cridem.org/Photos/Memorandum-rim.pdf.

Crowder, Michael. 1968. *West Africa Under Colonial Rule*. Evanston, IL: Northwestern University Press.

———. 1969. "The Administration of French West Africa." *Tarikh* 2:59–71.

———, ed. 1971. *West African Resistance: The Military Response to Colonial Occupation.* London: Hutchinson.

Cruise O'Brien, Donal B. 1988. "Introduction." In Donal B. Cruise O'Brien and Christian Coulon, eds., *Charisma and Brotherhood in African Islam.* Oxford: Clarendon.

———. 2003. *Symbolic Confrontations: Muslims Imagining the State in Africa.* London: Palgrave Macmillan.

Da Costa, Peter. 1994. "Senegal: Shades of Algeria?" *Africa Report* (May-June): 58–61.

Dahou, Tarik, and Vincent Foucher. 2004. "Le Sénégal entre changement politique et révolution passive." *Politique Africaine* 96:5–21.

Danfulani, Umar H.D. 2005. *The Sharia Issue and Christian-Muslim Relations in Contemporary Nigeria.* Stockholm: Almquist and Wiksell International.

Darboe, M. N. 1982. "The Interaction of Western and African Traditional Systems of Justice: The Problem of Integration (A Case Study of the Gambia)." PhD diss., University of Pennsylvania.

Darboe, Momodou. 2004. "Islamism in West Africa: Gambia." *African Studies Review* 47:73–82.

Darboe, Ousainou A. N. 2005. Solicitor and barrister-at-law. The Gambia. Interview with M. N. Darboe, June.

Darling, Dan. 2005. "ICG Report on the Sahel Region." April 11. http://www.WindsofChange.net/archives/006649.php#niger.

Davis, Shelby Collum. 1934/1970. *Reservoirs of Men: A History of the Black Troops of French West Africa.* Westport, CT: Negro Universities Press/Greenwood.

Delafosse, Maurice. 1912. *Haut-Sénégal-Niger.* Paris: Leroux.

Delavignette, Robert. 1950. *Freedom and Authority in French West Africa.* London: International African Institute and Oxford University Press. Originally published in 1946 as *Service Africain.* Paris: Gallimard.

Derrick, Jonathan. 1975. *Africa's Slaves Today.* New York: Shocken.

Deutsche Presse-Agentur. 1994. "Mauritania Announces Amnesty for Islamic Activists." October 12.

Diarrah, Cheikh Oumar. 1986. *Le Mali de Modibo Keita.* Paris: L' Harmattan.

Diop, Momar Coumba, Mamadou Diouf, and Aminata Diaw. 2000. "Le Baobab a été déraciné: L'alternance au Sénégal." *Politique Africaine* 78:157–179.

Docking, Timothy W. 1998. "The Roots of Democracy's 'Success' in Mali." *L'Afrique Politique 1997.* Paris: Karthala.

Drammeh, Alhaji Banding. 2005. President, Supreme Islamic Council. The Gambia. Interview with M. N. Darboe, June.

Echenberg, Myron. 1991. *Colonial Conscripts: The Tirailleurs Senegalais in French West Africa, 1857–1960.* Portsmouth, NH: Heinemann.

Eickelman, Dale F., and James P. Piscatori. 1996. *Muslim Politics.* Princeton, NJ: Princeton University Press.

Ellis, Stephen. 2005. "How to Rebuild Africa." *Foreign Affairs* 84:135–148.

Esposito, John L. 1997. *Political Islam: Revolution, Radicalism, or Reform?* Boulder: Lynne Rienner.

———. 1998. *Islam: The Straight Path.* New York: Oxford University Press.

———. 1999. *The Islamic Threat: Myth or Reality?* New York: Oxford University Press.

———. 2002. *Unholy War: Terror in the Name of Islam.* New York: Oxford University Press.

Fall, Mar. 1993. "Les arabisants au Sénégal: Contre-élite ou courtiers?" In Réné Otayek, ed., *Le Radicalisme islamique au sud du Sahara: Da'wa, arabisation, et critique de l'occident.* Paris: Karthala.

Fall, Mohamed. 1991. "L'Umma ou l'embryon de l'islamisme en Mauritanie." *Éveil-Hebdo* 15 (December 2): 4.

Fatty, Alhaji Abdoulie. 2005. State House imam. The Gambia. Interview with M. N. Darboe, June.

Faulkingham, Ralph. 1974. *Succession and Political Support for a Hausa Chief: A Case Approach.* Unpublished manuscript.

Fisher, Humphrey J. 1993. "Love for Three Oranges, or, the Askiya's Dilemma: The Askia, al-Maghili, and Timbuktu, c. 1500 AD." *Journal of African History* 34:65–91.

Fleischman, Janet. 1994. *Mauritania's Campaign of Terror: State-Sponsored Repression of Black Africans.* New York: Human Rights Watch/Africa.

Friedman, Thomas L. 1999. *The Lexus and the Olive Tree.* New York: Farrar, Straus, and Giroux.

Foltz, William J. 1965. *From French West Africa to the Mali Federation*. New Haven, CT: Yale University Press.

Gailey, H. A. 1965. *A History of the Gambia*. New York: Praeger.

Gambia Supreme Islamic Council. 1998. "A Report on Fact Finding Mission in Kiang Keneba," October.

Gellar, Sheldon. 2005. *Democracy in Senegal: Tocquevillian Analytics in Africa*. New York: Palgrave Macmillan.

Glew, Robert. 1996. "Islamic Associations in Niger." *Islam et Sociétés au Sud du Sahara* 10:187–204.

———. 2001. "A Discourse-Centered Approach Toward Understanding Muslim Identities in Zinder." *Islam et Sociétés au Sud du Sahara* 14, no. 5:99–122.

Glickman, Harvey. 2003. "Africa in the War on Terrorism." *Journal of Asian and African Studies* 38:162–174.

Gomez-Perez, Muriel. 1991. "Les associations islamiques à Dakar." *Islam et Sociétés au Sud du Sahara* 5:5–19.

———. 2005. *l'Islam politique au sud du Sahara–Identiées, discourse et enjeux*. Paris: Karthala.

Gray, Christopher. 1988. "The Rise of the Niassene Tijaniyya, 1875 to the Present." *Islam et Sociétés au Sud du Sahara* 2:34–60.

Gray, J. M. 1966. *A History of the Gambia*. London: Frank Cass.

Grégoire, Emmanuel. 1986. *Les Alhazai de Maradi (Niger): Histoire d'un groupe des riches marchands sahéliens*. Paris: ORSTOM.

———. 1992. *The Alhazai of Maradi: Traditional Hausa Merchants in a Changing Sahelian City*. Boulder, CO: Lynne Rienner.

———. 1993. "Islam and the Identity of Merchants in Maradi (Niger)." In Louis Brenner, ed., *Muslim Identity and Social Change in Sub-Saharan Africa*. Bloomington: Indiana University Press.

Grey-Johnson, Nana. 2005. Public Diplomacy desk officer, United States Embassy. The Gambia. Interview with M. N. Darboe, June.

Grundy, Kenneth W. 1964. "Mali: The Prospects of 'Planned Socialism.'" In William H. Friedland and Carl G. Rosberg, Jr., eds., *African Socialism*. Stanford, CA: Hoover Institution.

Gueye, Babacar. 2001. Professor of public law and member of the Constitutional Commission of 2001. Dakar, Senegal. Interview with L. A. Villalón, April 23.

Haarmann, Ulrich. 1998. "The Dead Ostrich. Life and Trade in Ghadames (Libya) in the Nineteenth Century." *Die Welt des Islams* 38:9–94.

Hamès, Constant. 1994. "Le rôle de l'Islam dans la société mauritanienne contemporaine." *Politique africaine* 50:46–51.

Hassane, Sulay. 2002. "Islam, élites et pouvoirs au Niger 1990–2002." Paper presented to the conference, L'Islam politique en Afrique subsaharienne d'hier à aujourd'hui: discours, trajéctoires et réseaux.

Haynes, J. 1998. *Religion in Global Politics*. London: Pearson Longman.

Hazard, John H. 1969. "Marxian Socialism in Africa: The Case of Mali." *Comparative Politics* 2:1–15.

Hiskett, Mervyn. 1980. "The 'Community of Grace' and Its Opponents, the 'Rejecters': A Debate About Theology and Mysticism in Muslim West Africa with Special Reference to Its Hausa Expression." *African Language Studies* 17:99–140.

———. 1984. *The Development of Islam in West Africa.* London: Longman.

———. 1994. *The Course of Islam in Africa.* Edinburgh: Edinburgh University Press.

Hock, Klaus. 1992. "How Religious Are Religious Riots: A Case Study from Bauchi State, Nigeria." *Afrika Spectrum* 1:43–58.

———. 1996. *Der Islam-Komplex. Zur christlichen Wahrnehmung des Islams und der christlich-islamischen Beziehungen in Nordnigeria während der Militärherrschaft Babangidas.* Münster: LIT.

Hodgson, Marshall G.S. 1974. *The Venture of Islam. Conscience and History in a World Civilization.* Chicago: University of Chicago Press.

Hodgkin, Elizabeth. 1990. "Islamism and Islamic Research in Africa." *Islam et sociétés au sud du Sahara* 4:73–130.

Hogben, S. J., and A. H. M. Kirk-Greene. 1966. *The Emirates of Northern Nigeria.* London: Oxford University Press.

Holzbauer, Christine. 2002. "La nebuleuse Ben Laden: Les inquiétants émirs du Sahel." *L'Express* (Paris), November 28.

Hopkins, Nicholas S. 1972. *Popular Government in an African Town.* Chicago: University of Chicago Press.

Horowitz, Michael, ed. 1983. *Niger: A Social and Institutional Profile.* Binghamton, NY: Institute for Development Anthropology.

Hughes, Arnold, and David Perfect. 2005. *The Political History of the Gambia, 1816–1994.* Unpublished manuscript.

Human Rights Watch. 2004. *Political Sharia? Human Rights and Islamic Law in Northern Nigeria.* New York: Human Rights Watch.

Huntington, Samuel P. 1984. "Will More Countries Become Democratic?" *Political Science Quarterly* 99:193–218.

———. 1996. *The Clash of Civilizations and the Remaking of the World Order.* New York: Simon and Schuster.

Hunwick, John O. 1965. "Islam in West Africa, AD 1000–1800." In J. F. Ade Ajayi and Ian Espie, eds., *A Thousand Years of West African History.* London: Ibadan University Press and Thomas Nelson.

———. 1997. "Sub-Saharan Africa and the Wider World of Islam." In Eva Evers Rosander and David Westerlund, eds., *African Islam and Islam in Africa: Encounters Between Sufis and Islamists.* Athens: Ohio University Press.

Ibrahim, Jibrin. 1991. "Religion and Political Turbulence in Nigeria." *Journal of Modern African Studies* 29:115–136.

Idrissa, Abdourahmane. 2003. "Defining the Polity: Cultural Dynamism, Islam, and the State in Niger." Paper presented to the conference Islam, Society, and the State in West Africa, Rutgers University, March 28–29.

———. 2005. "Modèle islamique et modèle occidental: le conflit des élites au Niger." In Muriel Perez-Gomez, ed., *L'Islam politique au sud du Sahara: Identités, discours, et enjeux.* Paris: Karthala.

Imam. 2005. The Tabligh Jama'at (Ma'shala) Center. The Gambia. Interview with M. N. Darboe, June.

Imperato, Pascal James. 1986. *Historical Dictionary of Mali,* 2nd ed. Metuchen, NJ: Scarecrow.

———. 1989. *Mali: A Search for Direction.* Boulder, CO: Westview.

ICG (International Crisis Group). 2004. *Islamism, Violence, and Reform in Algeria: Turning the Page.* Middle East Report, No. 29, July 30.

———. 2005a. *Islamist Terrorism in the Sahel: Fact or Fiction?* Africa Report, No. 92, March 31.

———. 2005b. *L'Islamisme en Afrique du Nord IV: Contestation Islamique en Mauritanie: Menace or Bouc Émissaire?* Rapport Moyen-Orient/Afrique du Nord Report, No. 41, May 11.

———. 2006. "La transition politique en Mauritanie: bilan et perspectives." Rapport Moyen-Orient/Afrique du Nord Report, No. 53, April 24.

Jah, Alhaji Ousman. 2005. Imam of Pipeline Mosque and chairman of the Fact Finding Mission in Kiang Keneba. The Gambia. Interview with M. N. Darboe, June.

Janson, Marloes. 2004. "Appropriating Islam: The Tensions Between 'Traditionalists' and 'Modernists' in the Gambia." Paper presented at the African Studies conference in New Orleans, November.

———. 2006. "The Prophet's Path: Tabligh Jama'at in the Gambia." *ISIM Review* 17 (Spring): 44–45.

Jeppie, Shamil. 2004. Historian and professor of religious studies. Nijmegen, Nigeria. Interview with R. Loimeier, September 12.

Jourde, Cédric. 2004. "Rivalités inter-(intra) ethniques et luttes symboliques dans la vallée du fleuve Sénégal avant l'indépendance." In Zekeria Ould Ahmed Salem, ed., *Les trajectoires d'un État-frontière: espaces, évolution politique et transformations sociales en Mauritanie.* Dakar: CODESRIA.

———. Forthcoming. "The International Relations of Small Neoauthoritarian States: Islamism, Warlordism, and the Framing of Stability." *International Studies Quarterly.*

Jouve, Edmond. 1974. *La République du Mali.* Paris: Berger-Levrault.

Kaba, Lansiné. 1974. "The Wahhabiyya: Islamic Reform and Politics in French West Africa." Evanston, IL: Northwestern University Press.

———. 2000. *Islam in West Africa: Radicalism and the New Ethic of Disagreement, 1960–1990.* In Nehemia Levtzion and Randall L. Pouwels, eds., *The History of Islam in Africa.* Athens: Ohio University Press.

Kabara, Shehu Usman. 1981. *Shakhsiyat ash-Sheikh Muhammad an-Nasir Kabara wa-adabuhu.* Master's thesis, University of Khartoum.

———. 1988. Professor; nephew of Nasiru Kabara. Kano, Nigeria. Interview with R. Loimeier, March 9.

Kabir, Muhamed. 2006. Member, Tabligh Jama'at (Ma'shala) Center. The Gambia. Interview with M. N. Darboe, July.

Kane, Mouhamad Moustapha. 1997. "La vie et l'œuvre d'Al-Hajj Mahmoud Ba Diowol (1905–1978). Du pâtre au patron de la 'Révolution Al-Falah.'" In David Robinson and Jean-Louis Triaud, eds., *Le temps des marabouts: Itinéraires et stratégies islamiques en Afrique occidentale française v. 1880–1960.* Paris: Karthala.

Kane, Ousmane. 1994. "Izala: The Rise of Muslim Reformism in Northern Nigeria." In Martin Marty and R. Scott Appleby, eds., *Accounting for Fundamentalism: The Dynamics of Change*. Chicago: University of Chicago Press.

———. 2000. "Muhammad Niasse (1881–1956) et sa réplique contre le pamphlet anti-tijânî de Ibn Mayaba." In Jean-Louis Triaud and David Robinson, eds., *La Tijâniyya: Une confrérie musulmane à la conquête de l'Afrique*. Paris: Karthala.

———. 2003a. *Intellectuels non europhones*. Dakar: Codesria.

———. 2003b. *Muslim Modernity in Postcolonial Nigeria: A Study of the Society for the Removal of Innovation and Reinstatement of Tradition*. Leiden: E. J. Brill.

———, and Leonardo A.Villalón. 1995. "Entre Confrérisme, Réformisme et Islamisme: Les Mustarchidine du Sénégal. Analyse et Traduction Commentée du Discours Electoral de Moustapha Sy, et Réponse de Abdou Aziz Sy, Junior." *Islam et Sociétés au Sud du Sahara* 9:119–201.

———, and Jean-Louis Triaud. 1998. *Islam et islamismes au sud du Sahara*. Paris: Karthala.

Kane,Ousseynou. 2001. "La République Couchée." *Wal Fadjri* 2744 (May 8).

Kanya-Forstner, A. S. 1971. "Mali-Tukolor." In Michael Crowder, ed., *West African Resistance: The Military Response to Colonial Occupation*. London: Hutchinson.

Keenan, Jeremy. 2006. "Security and Insecurity in North Africa." *Review of African Political Economy* 108:269–296.

Keita, Kalifa. 1998. *Conflict and Conflict Resolution in the Sahel: The Tuareg Insurgency in Mali*. Carlisle, PA: US Army War College, Strategic Studies Institute.

Keita, Modibo. 1962. *Le Mali en Marche*. Bamako: Edition du Secretariat d'Etat à l'Information.

Kepel, Gilles. 2004. *Fitna: guerre au coeur de l'Islam*. Paris: Gallimard.

Kirwin, Matthew. 2005. "The Political and Economic Effects of Nigerian Shari'a on Southern Niger." *Review of African Political Economy* 104/105 (Summer): 407–414.

Klein, Martin. 1998. *Slavery and Colonial Rule in French West Africa*. New York: Cambridge University Press.

Konaré, Adame Ba. 2000. "Perspectives on History and Culture: The Case of Mali." In R. James Bingen, ed., *Democracy and Development in Mali*. East Lansing: Michigan State University Press.

Kukah, Matthew Hassan. 1993. "An Assessment of the Intellectual Response of the Nigerian Ulama to the Shari'a Debate Since Independence." *Islam et Sociétés au Sud du Sahara* 7:35–55.

Kurawa, Ibrahim Ado. 1987. Civil servant. Kano, Nigeria. Interview with R. Loimeier, March 1.

Laremont, Ricardo, and Hrach Gregorian. 2006. "Political Islam in West Africa and the Sahel." *Military Review* 86:27–36.

Last, Murray. 2000. "La Charia Dans le Nord-Nigeria." *Politique Africaine* 79:141–152.

Leigh, Alhaji Baba. 2005. Imam Kanifing Mosque. The Gambia. Interview with M. N. Darboe, June.

Le Troquer, Yann. 1992. "Chronique internationale." *Annuaire de l'Afrique du Nord* 31:507–509.

Le Vine, Victor T. 2004. *Politics in Francophone Africa*. Boulder, CO: Lynne Rienner.

Les Populations des Territoires d'Outre-Mer. 1956. Paris: Documentation Française.

Levitsky, Steven, and Lucan A. Way. 2005. "International Linkage and Democratization." *Journal of Democracy* 16:20–34.

Levtzion, Nehemia. 1972. "The Early State of the Western Sudan to 1500." In J.F.A. Ajayi and Michael Crowder, eds., *History of West Africa*. New York: Columbia University Press.

———. 1979. "Islam in West African Politics: Accommodation and Tension Between the *'Ulama'* and the Political Authorities." *Cahiers d'Etudes Africaines* 18:333–345.

———. 2000. "Islam in the Bilad al-Sudan to 1800." In Nehemia Levtzion and Randall L. Pouwels, eds., *The History of Islam in Africa*. Athens: Ohio University Press.

———, and Randall L. Pouwels, eds. 2000. *The History of Islam in Africa*. Athens: Ohio University Press.

Lewis, Bernard. 2005. "Freedom and Justice in the Modern Middle East." *Foreign Affairs* 84:36–51.

Lewis, I. M., ed. 1966. *Islam in Tropical Africa*. London: Oxford University Press.

Loimeier, Roman. 1988. "Das 'Nigerian Pilgrimage Scheme': Zum Versuch, den hajj in Nigeria zu organisieren." *Afrika Spectrum* 2:201–214.

———. 1992. "Die Dynamik religiöser Unruhen in Nordnigeria." *Afrika Spectrum* 1:59–80.

———. 1996. "The Secular State and Islam in Senegal." In David Westerlund, ed., *Questioning the Secular State: The Worldwide Resurgence of Religion in Politics*. New York: St. Martin's Press.

———. 1997a. *Islamic Reform and Political Change in Northern Nigeria*. Evanston, IL: Northwestern University Press.

———. 1997b. "Die radikale islamische Opposition in Nordnigeria." *Afrika Spectrum* 32:5–23.

———. 2000. "L'Islam ne se vend plus: The Islamic Reform Movement and the State in Senegal." *Journal of Religion in Africa* 30:168–190.

———. 2001. *Säkularer Staat und Islamische Gesellschaft: Die Beziehungen zwischen Staat, Sufi-Bruderschaften und islamischer Reformbewegung in Senegal im 20 Jahrhundert*. Hamburg: LIT.

———. 2003. "Patterns and Peculiarities of Islamic Reform in Africa." *Journal of Religion in Africa* 22:237–262.

———. 2005. "Playing with Affiliations: Muslim in Northern Nigeria in the Twentieth Century." In André Mary and Réné Otayek, eds., *Réseaux transnationaux et nouveaux acteurs religieux en Afrique de l'Ouest*. Paris: Karthala.

———. 2006. "Sufis and Politics in Subsaharan Africa." In Paul Heck, ed., *Islam in Africa,* Princeton Papers, Special Issue.

———, and Stefan Reichmuth. 1993. "Bemühungen der Muslime um Einheit und politische Geltung." In Jamil M. Abun-Nasr, ed., *Muslime in Nigeria: Reli-*

gion und Gesellschaft im politischen Wandel seit den 50er Jahren. Hamburg: LIT.

Lovejoy, Paul. 2000. *Transformations in Slavery: A History of Slavery in Africa,* 2nd ed. New York: Cambridge University Press.

Lubeck, Paul M., Michael J. Watts, and Ronnie Lipschutz. 2007. "Convergent Interests: U.S. Energy Security and the 'Securing' of Nigerian Democracy." *International Policy Report.* Washington, DC: Center for International Policy.

Lund, Christian. 1998. *Law, Power, and Politics in Niger: Land Struggles and the Rural Code.* Hamburg: LIT Verlag.

———. 2001. "Precarious Democratization and Local Dynamics in Niger: Micro-Politics in Zinder." *Development and Change* 32:845–869.

Ly, Djibril. 1993. "L'Etat de droit dans la constitution mauritanienne du 20 juillet 1991." *Revue mauritanienne de droit et d'économie* 9:43–58.

Lyman, Princeton, and J. S. Morrison. 2004. "The Terrorist Threat in Africa." *Foreign Affairs* 83:75–86.

Mahmud Ahmad, Hadhrat Mirza Bashir-ud-Din Khalifatal Masih II. 2002. "Invitation to Ahmadiyyat." *Islam International Publication,* 4th ed.

Mahmud, Saidu Sakah. 2004. "Islamism in West Africa: Nigeria." *African Studies Review* 47:83–96.

Mamdani, Mahmood. 2002. "Good Muslim, Bad Muslim: A Political Perspective on Culture and Terrorism." In Eric Hershberg and Kevin Moore, eds., *Critical Views of September 11: Analyses from Around the World.* New York: New Press.

Marchesin, Philippe. 1990. "Juge moderne et droit musulman: le cas de la Mauritanie." *Afrique contemporaine* 156:261–266.

Markovitz, Irving Leonard. 1977. *Power and Class in Africa.* New York: Prentice Hall.

Marty, Paul. 1917. *Etudes sur l'Islam au Sénégal.* Paris: Leroux.

———. 1921. *Etudes sur l'Islam et les Tribus du Soudan.* Paris: Leroux.

Masquelier, Adeline. 1996. "Identity, Alterity, and Ambiguity in a Nigerien Community: Competing Definitions of 'True' Islam." In Richard Werber and Terrence Ranger, eds., *Postcolonial Identities in Africa.* Atlantic Heights, NJ: Zed.

———. 1999. "Debating Muslims, Disputed Practices: Struggles for the Realization of an Alternative Moral Order in Niger." In John L. and Jean Comaroff, eds., *Civil Society and the Political Imagination in Africa: A Critical Perspective.* Chicago: University of Chicago Press.

———. 2005a. "How Is a Girl to Marry Without a Bed? Weddings, Wealth, and Women's Value in an Islamic Town of Niger." In Wim van Binsbergen, Rijk van Dijk, and Jan-Bart Gewald, eds., *Situating Globality. African Agency in the Appropriation of Global Culture.* Leiden: Brill.

———. 2005b. "The Scorpion's Sting: Youth, Marriage, and the Struggle for Social Maturity in Niger." *Journal of the Royal Anthropological Institute* 11:59–83.

Mattes, Hanspeter. 1986. *Die innere und äußere Mission Libyens.* Mainz: Grünewald und Kaiser.

———. 1993. "La dawa libyenne entre le Coran et le Livre Vert." In Réné Otayek, ed., *Le radicalisme islamique au sud du Sahara.* Paris: Karthala.

"Mauritanie: Les Islamistes dans le collimateur du pouvoir." 2000. *Sud-Quotidien* 2258, October 12.

Mayer, Jean-François. 2002. "Mali: Le Facteur Islamique." *Religioscope,* April 27. http://www.religioscope.com.

Mazrui, Ali. 1988. "African Islam and Competitive Religion: Between Revivalism and Expansion." *Third World Quarterly* 10:499–518.

Mbow, Penda. 2003. "Civisme, Laïcité, République." Unpublished manuscript.

McCormack, David. 2005. "An African Vortex: Islamism in Sub-Saharan Africa." Occasional Paper Series, No. 4. Washington, DC: Center for Security Policy.

McLaughlin, Fiona. 1997. "Islam and Popular Music in Senegal: The Emergence of a 'New Tradition.'" *Africa* 67:560–581.

———. 2000. "'In the Name of God I Will Sing Again, Mawdo Malik the Good': Popular Music and the Senegalese Sufi Tariqas." *Journal of Religion in Africa* 30:191–207.

Meillassoux, Claude, ed. 1975. *L'Esclavage en Afrique précoloniale.* Paris: Francois Maspéro.

Meunier, Olivier. 1997. *Dynamique de l'enseignement islamique au Niger: Le cas de la ville de Maradi.* Paris: L'Harmattan.

———. 1998. *Les voies de l'islam au Niger dans le Katsina indépendant du XIXe au XXe siècle (Maradi, pays hawsa).* Paris: Museum de l'histoire naturelle.

Miles, William F. S. 1990. "Islam and Development in West Africa." In Julius Okolo and Stephen Wright, eds., *West African Regional Cooperation and Development.* Boulder, CO: Westview Press.

———. 1994. *Hausaland Divided: Colonialism and Independence in Nigeria and Niger.* Ithaca, NY: Cornell University Press.

———. 1996. "Political Para-Theology: Rethinking Religion, Politics, and Democracy." *Third World Quarterly* 17:525–535.

———. 2000. "Religious Pluralisms in Northern Nigeria." In Nehemia Levtzion and Randall L. Pouwels, eds., *The History of Islam in Africa.* Athens: Ohio University Press.

———. 2003. "Sharia as De-Africanization: Evidence from Hausaland." *Africa Today* 50:51–76.

———. 2004. "Islamism in West Africa: Introduction and Conclusions." *African Studies Review* 47:55–59, 109–116.

———, and David A. Rochefort. 1991. "Nationalism Versus Ethnic Identity in Sub-Saharan Africa." *American Political Science Review* 85:393–403.

Minteh, Alhaji Sadia. 2005. Imam of Kombo Police Station Mosque and one of the applicants in the Kiang Keneba case. The Gambia. Interview with M. N. Darboe, June.

Morier-Genoud, Eric. 2002. "L'Islam au Moçambique après l'indépendance." In *L'Afrique politique: Islams d'Afrique: Entre le local et le global.* Paris: Karthala.

Moumoni, Adamou. 2004. "Les Pouvoirs Locaux à Bana." *Etudes et Travaux* 21. Niamey: Observatoire de la décentralisation au Niger.

Muhammad, Yusuf Abdulrahman. 1992. *Memoirs of the Late al-Marhum al-Seyyid Omar bin Abdulla Ali Sheikh.* Zanzibar: n.p.

Napier Hewett, J. F. 1969 (reprint of 1862 edition). *European Settlements on the West Coast of Africa*. New York: Negro Universities Press.

Nasr, Sayyed Hossein. 2002. *The Heart of Islam: Enduring Values for Humanity*. San Francisco: Harper.

Nicolas, Guy. 1965. "Circulation des richesses et participation sociales dans une société haousa du Niger (Canton de Kantche)." Doctorat de Troisème Cycle, University of Bordeaux (France).

———. 1978. "L'enracinement ethnique de l'Islam au sud du Sahara." *Cahiers d'Etudes Africaines* 18:347–377.

———. 1979. "Detours d'une conversion collective: ouverture á l'Islam d'un bastion soudanais de résistence à une guerre sainte." *Archives de Sciences Sociales de Religions,* 48:83–105.

Niandou-Souley, Abdoulaye, and Gado Alzouma. 1996. "Islamic Renewal in Niger: From Monolith to Plurality." *Social Compass* 43:249–265.

Niane, D. T. 1965. *Sundiata: An Epic of Old Mali*. London: Longman.

Nyang, Sulayman S. 1979. "The Role of the Gambian Political Parties in National Integration." PhD diss., University of Virginia.

———. 1984. "Islam and Politics in West Africa." *Issue: A Journal of Africanist Opinion* 13:20–25.

———. 1988. "The Islamic Factors in Libya's Africa Policy." *Journal of Africa and the World* 1:13–23.

———. 1988. "West Africa." In Shireen Hunter, ed., *The Politics of Islamic Revivalism*. Bloomington: Indiana University Press.

Nzouankeu, Jacques Mariel. 1993. "The Role of the National Conference in the Transition to Democracy: The Cases of Benin and Mali." *Issue* (African Studies Association) 21:44–50.

O'Brien, Ria. 2005. Former Peace Corps volunteer, Mali. Interview with V. T. Le Vine, June 30, St. Louis, Missouri.

Oloruntimehin, B. Olatunji. 1971. "Senegambia-Mahmadou Lamine." In Michael Crowder, ed., *West African Resistance: The Military Response to Colonial Occupation*. London: Hutchinson.

Ostien, Philip. 2003. "An Opportunity Missed by Nigeria's Christians." Paper presented to the conference The Sharia Debate and the Shaping of Muslim and Christian Identities in Northern Nigeria, University of Bayreuth.

Otayek, Réné, ed. 1993. *Le radicalisme islamique au sud du Sahara*. Paris: Karthala.

Ottaway, Marina. 2003. *Democracy Challenged: The Rise of Semi-Authoritarianism*. Washington, DC: Carnegie Endowment for International Peace.

Ould Ahmed Salem, Zekeria. 1996. *Retour sur la politique par le bas: De quelques modes populaires d'énonciation du politiques en Mauritanie*. Université Lumière-Lyon 2, Institut d'Études Politiques, Thèse de Doctorat.

———. 2000. "De la fronde au consensus mou: l'opposition dans l'imaginaire mauritanien." *Le Calame* 278:8–9.

———. 2001. "Prêcher dans le désert: l'univers du Cheikh Sidi Yahya et l'évolution de l'islamisme mauritanien." *Islam et sociétés au sud du Sahara* 14/15:5–40.

Ould el-Bara, Yahya. 2004. "Mutations des formes de religiosité: sources et débats." In Zekeria Ould Ahmed Salem, ed., *Les trajectoires d'un État-frontière: espaces, évolution politique et transformations sociales en Mauritanie*. Dakar: CODESRIA.

Ould Bouboutt, Ahmed Salem. 1989. "L'évolution des institutions de la République islamique de Mauritanie." *La revue du monde musulman et de la méditerranée* 54:130–139.

Paden, John N. 1973. *Religion and Political Culture in Kano*. Berkeley: University of California Press.

———. 1986. *Ahmadu Bello, Sardauna of Sokoto*. Zaria: Hudahuda.

———. 2005. *Muslim Civic Cultures and Conflict Resolution: The Challenge of Democratic Federalism in Nigeria*. Washington, DC: Brookings Institution.

Peel, J.D.Y., and C. C. Stewart, eds. 1985. *"Popular Islam" South of the Sahara*. Manchester, UK: Manchester University Press.

Person, Yves. 1968. *Samori: Une Revolution Dyula*. Dakar: IFAN.

———. 1971. "Guinea-Samori." In Michael Crowder, ed., *West African Resistance: The Military Response to Colonial Occupation*. London: Hutchinson.

Peters, Ruud. 2003. *Islamic Criminal Law in Nigeria*. Ibadan: Spectrum.

Philipps, John E. 1985. "The Islamization of Kano Before the Jihad." *Kano Studies* 2:32–52.

Piga, Adriana. 2002. "Neo-Traditionalist Islamic Associations and the Islamist Press in Contemporary Senegal." In Thomas Bierschenk and Georg Stauth, eds., *Islam in Africa*. Münster: LIT Verlag.

Piscatori, James P. 1983. *Islam in the Political Process*. New York: Cambridge University Press.

———. 1986. *Islam in a World of Nation-States*. New York: Cambridge University Press.

Quinn, Charlotte A. 1972. *Mandingo Kingdoms in the Senegambia: Traditionalism, Islam, and European Expansion*. Evanston, IL: Northwestern University Press.

———, and Frederick Quinn. 2003. *Pride, Faith, and Fear. Islam in Sub-Saharan Africa*. Oxford: Oxford University Press.

Rabasa, Angel, et al. 2004. *The Muslim World After 9/11*. Santa Monica, CA: Rand.

Radio Africa. 1994. "Islàmic Group Dissolved; Mosque Speeches Banned." Transcription in *FBIS* (October 21): 22–23.

Radio-Mauritanie. 1994a. "Radio gives details of plans and policies of the Islamic Movement in Mauritania; Members of 'extremist jihad group' arrested; 'confessions' broadcast." Transcription in *BBC Summary of World Program*, October 13.

———. 1994b. "Members of Jihad Group Arrested, Confess Crimes." Transcription in *FBIS* (October 11): 25–26.

Radu, Michael. 1992. "Islam and Politics in Black Africa: The Growing Impact of Politicized Religion." *Dissent* (Summer): 408–413.

Rashid, Ismail. 2004. "West Africa's Post–Cold War Security Challenges." In Adekeye Adebago and Ismail Rashid, eds., *West Africa's Security Challenges: Building Peace in a Troubled Region*. Boulder: Lynne Rienner.

Reese, Scott. 2004. *The Transmission of Learning in Islamic Africa.* Leiden: Brill.

Robinson, David. 2000. *Paths of Accommodation: Muslim Societies and French Colonial Authorities in Senegal and Mauritania, 1880–1920.* Athens: Ohio University Press.

Robinson, Pearl. 1991. "Niger: Anatomy of a Neotraditional Corporatist State." *Comparative Politics* 24:1–20.

———. 2005. "Research Note: September 2005: Islam and Female Empowerment Among the Tijaniyya in Niger." Unpublished manuscript.

Rosander, Eva Evers, and David Westerlund, eds. 1997. *African Islam and Islam in Africa: Encounters Between Sufis and Islamists.* Athens: Ohio University Press.

Ross, Eric S. 2002. "Marabout Republics Then and Now: Configuring Muslim Towns in Senegal." *Islam et Sociétés au Sud du Sahara* 16:35–65.

Roy, Olivier. 1994. *The Failure of Political Islam.* Cambridge, MA: Harvard University Press.

———. 2004a. *Globalized Islam: The Search for a New Ummah.* New York: Columbia University Press.

———. 2004b. *L'islamisme mondialisé.* Paris: Éditions du Seuil.

Ryan, Patrick. 1987. "Islam and Politics in West Africa: Minority and Majority Models." *Muslim World* 77:1–15.

Sall, Ibrahima Abou. 1999. "Crise identitaire ou stratégie de positionnement politique en Mauritanie: le cas des *Fulbe Aynaabe.*" In André Bourgeot, ed., *Horizons nomades en Afrique sahélienne.* Paris: Karthala.

———. 2000. "La diffusion de la Tijâniyya au Fuuta Toor (Mauritanie-Sénégal)." In Jean-Louis Triaud and David Robinson, eds., *La Tijâniyya: Une confrérie musulmane à la conquête de l'Afrique.* Paris: Karthala.

Salifou, André. 1993. *La question touarègue au Niger.* Paris: Karthala.

———. 2002. "La résolution du conflict touareg au Mali et au Niger." *Note de recherché No. 10.* Montréal: Chaire Raoul-Dandurand, Groupe de recherches sur les interventions de paix dans les conflicts inter-etatiques.

Salih, Ibrahim. 1988. Tijaniyya leader. Maiduguri, Nigeria. Interview with R. Loimeier, March 27.

Salih, M. A. Mohamed. 2002. "Islamic NGOs in Africa: The Promise and Peril of Islamic Voluntarism," rev. ed. Occasional Paper, Centre of African Studies, University of Copenhagen.

Sambe, Bakary. 2003. "Nouveau visage du militantisme islamique sénégalais depuis les années 80: l'opposition confréries/associations est-elle encore pertinente?" Paper presented at an international conference on Political Islam South of the Sahara, Université Paris VII, September 2002.

Sanneh, Lamin. 1997. *The Crown and the Turban: Muslims and West African Pluralism.* Boulder, CO: Westview.

Sène, Ibra. 2003. "Islam as a Site of Agency, Mediation, and Resistance: Hizbut Tarqiyya (Senegal), 1975–2002." Paper presented at the annual meeting of the African Studies Association, Washington, DC, October 30.

Schatzberg, Michael. 1998. "Hijacking Change: Zaire's 'Transition' in Comparative Perspective." In Marina Ottaway, ed., *Democracy in Africa: The Hard Road Ahead.* Boulder, CO: Lynne Rienner.

Schmitt, Eric. 2005. "As Africans Join Iraqi Insurgency, US Counters with Military Training in Their Lands." *New York Times*, June 10: A10.

Schmitz, Jean. 2000. "L'Islam en Afrique de l'Ouest: les méridiens et les parallèles." *Autrepart* 16:117–137.

Schulze, Reinhard. 1990. *Islamischer Internationalismus im 20 Jahrhundert*. Leiden: Brill.

———. 1993. "La dawa saoudienne en Afrique de l'Ouest." In Réné Otayek, ed., *Le radicalisme islamique au sud du Sahara*. Paris: Karthala.

Seely, Jennifer C. 2001. "A Political Analysis of Decentralization: Coopting the Tuareg Threat in Mali." *Journal of Modern African Studies* 39:499–524.

Seesemann, Rüdiger. 2004. *Nach der 'Flut': Ibrahim Niasse (1900–1975), Sufik und Gesellschaft in Westafrika*. Bayreuth: University of Bayreuth Habilitationsschrift.

Senghor, J. C. 1979. "Politics and the Functional Strategy to International Integration: Gambia in Senegambia Integration, 1958–1974." PhD diss., Yale University.

Sheikh, M. Amadou. 2005. Malian official. Bamako. Interview with V. T. Le Vine.

Smith, Zeric Kay. 1966. "Civil Society and Political Learning: The Case of the Malian Association of Students and Pupils." Paper presented at the meeting of the American Political Science Association.

Sounaye, Abdoulaye. 2001. "Structuring Islam in a Context of Democratization: A Case Study of Niger." Paper presented to the conference on Islam and Africa: Global, Cultural, and Historical Perspectives, Binghamton, NY, April.

———. 2005. "Les Politiques de l'Islam au Niger dans l'ère de la démocratisation de 1991 à 2002." In Muriel Perez-Gomez, ed., *L'Islam politique au sud du Sahara: Identités, discours, et enjeux*. Paris: Karthala.

Stone, Diana. 1994. "Aspects du paysage religieux: marabouts et confréries." *Politique africaine* 55:52–56.

Sulaiman, Ibrahim. 1987. Political scientist. Zaria, Nigeria. Interview with R. Loimeier, September 9.

Ṣulaiman, Muhammad Dahiru. 1993. "Shiaism and the Islamic Movement in Nigeria, 1979–1991." *Islam et Sociétés au Sud du Sahara* 7:5–16.

Sy, Yusufu. 1965. Malian official. Interview with V. T. Le Vine.

Tahir, Ibrahim. 1975. "Scholars, Sufis, Saints, and Capitalists in Kano, 1904–1974." PhD diss., Cambridge University.

Taine-Cheikh, Catherine. 1994. "Les langues comme enjeux identitaires." *Politique africaine* 55:57–65.

Takaya, Bala J., and S. G. Tyoden. 1987. *The Kaduna Mafia: A Study of the Rise, Development, and Consolidation of a Nigerian Power Elite*. Jos: Jos University Press.

Tarawale, Baba. 2005. Amir of the Gambian Ahmadiyya Jamat. Interview with M. N. Darboe, June.

Touray, Karamo Imam. 2005. Imam of the Brikama Central Mosque. The Gambia. Interview with M. N. Darboe, March.

Triaud, Jean-Louis, and David Robinson, eds. 1997. *Le temps des marabouts*. Paris: Karthala.

Trimingham, J. Spencer. 1962. *A History of Islam in West Africa*. London: Oxford University Press.

———. 1968. *Influence of Islam upon Africa*. London: Longman.

———. 1980. "The Phases of Islamic Expansion and Islamic Culture Zones in Africa." In I. M. Lewis, ed., *Islam in Tropical Africa,* 2nd ed. Bloomington: IAI and Indiana University Press.

Tsiga, Ismaila A. 1992. *Sheikh Abubakar Gumi: Where I Stand*. Ibadan: Spectrum.

Umar, Muhammad Sani. 1988. "Sufism and Anti-Sufism in Nigeria." Bachelor's thesis, University of Kano, Nigeria.

———. 2000. "The Tijaniyya and British Colonial Authorities in Northern Nigeria." In Jean-Louis Triaud and David Robinson, eds., *La Tijaniyya: Une confrérie musulmane à la conquête de l'Afrique*. Paris: Karthala.

———. 2002. "Islamic Arguments for Western Education in Northern Nigeria: Mu'azu Hadejia's Hausa Poem *Ilmin Zamin*." *Islam et Sociétés au Sud du Sahara* 16:85–106.

———. 2004. "Islamic Education and Emergence of Female Ulama in Northern Nigeria: Background, Trends, and Consequences." In S. Reese, ed., *The Transmission of Islamic Learning in Africa*. Leiden: Brill.

US Department of State. 1996. *Country Reports on Human Rights Practices for 1995: The Gambia*. Washington, DC: Government Printing Office.

———. 2002. *The Protection Project*. Mali country report. Washington, DC: Government Printing Office.

———. 2005. *Trafficking in Persons Report*. Washington, DC: Government Printing Office.

Vandervort, Bruce. 1998. *Wars of Imperial Conquest in Africa, 1830–1914*. Bloomington: Indiana University Press.

van Binsbergen, Wim, Rijk van Dijk, and Jan-Bart Gewald. 2003. "Introduction." In Wim van Binsbergen, Rijk van Dijk, and Jan-Bart Gewald, eds., *Situating Globality: African Agency in the Appropriation of Global Culture*. Leiden: Brill.

Vengroff, Richard. 1993. "Governance and the Transition to Democracy: Political Parties and the Party System in Mali." *Journal of Modern African Studies* 31:541–562.

———. 2005. "Elections in Mali." http://www.electionworld.org.

Vikør, Kurt. 2000. "Sufi Brotherhoods in Africa." In Nehemia Levtzion and Randall L. Pouwels, eds., *The History of Islam in Africa*. Athens: Ohio University Press.

Villalón, Leonardo A. 1994a. "Sufi Rituals as Rallies: Religious Ceremonies in the Politics of Senegalese State-Society Relations." *Comparative Politics* 26:415–437.

———. 1994b. "Democratizing a (Quasi)Democracy: The 1993 Senegalese Elections." *African Affairs* 93:163–193.

———. 1995. *Islamic Society and State Power in Senegal: Disciples and Citizens in Fatick*. Cambridge: Cambridge University Press.

———, and Ousmane Kane. 1998. "Senegal: The Crisis of Democracy and the Emergence of an Islamic Opposition." In Leonardo A. Villalón and Phillip A.

Huxtable, eds., *The African State at a Critical Juncture: Between Disintegration and Reconfiguration.* Boulder, CO: Lynne Rienner.

———. 1999. "Generational Changes, Political Stagnations, and the Evolving Dynamics of Religion and Politics in Senegal." *Africa Today* 46:129–147.

———. 2000. "The Moustarchidine of Senegal: The Family Politics of a Contemporary Tijan Movement." In Jean-Louis Triaud and David Robinson, eds., *La Tijaniyya: Une confrérie musulmane à la conquête de l'Afrique*. Paris: Karthala.

———. 2003. "The Moral and the Political in African Democratization: The *Code de La Famille* in Niger's Troubled Transition." *Democratization* 3:41–68.

———. 2004. "Islamism in West Africa: Senegal." *African Studies Review* 47: 61–71.

———. 2006. "Sufi Modernities in Contemporary Senegal: Between the Local and the Global." In Martin Van Bruinessen and Julia Howell, eds., *Sufism and the Modern in Islam*. London: I. B. Tauris.

Voll, John. 1992a. "Conservative and Traditional Brotherhoods." *Annals of the American Academy of Political and Social Science* 524:66–78.

———. 1992b. "Religion and Politics in Islamic Africa." In Matthew Moen and Lowell Gustafson, eds., *The Religious Challenge to the State*. Philadelphia: Temple University Press.

Wade, Abdoulaye. 2001. President of the Republic. Dakar, Senegal. Interview with L. A. Villalón, April 19.

Warms, Richard L. 1992. "Merchants, Muslims, and Wahhabiya: The Elaboration of Islamic Identity in Sissako." *Canadian Journal of African Studies* 26:485–507.

Weekes, R. 1978. *Muslim Peoples: A World Ethnographic Survey*. Westport, CT: Greenwood.

Westerlund, David. 1997. "Reaction and Action. Accounting for the Rise of Islamism." In Eva Evers Rosander and David Westerlund, eds., *African Islam and Islam in Africa: Encounters Between Sufis and Islamists*. Athens: Ohio University Press.

Whiteman, Kaye, and Douglas Yates. 2004. "France, Britain, and the United States." In Adekeye Adebago and Ismail Rashid, eds., *West Africa's Security Challenges: Building Peace in a Troubled Region*. Boulder: Lynne Rienner.

Zakari, Maikorema. 1998. "La Tijaniyyah au Niger." *Revue de l'Institut de Recherches en Sciences Humaines* (Université Abdou Moumouni) 9:33–45.

The Contributors

Robert B. Charlick is professor emeritus of political science and international relations at Cleveland State University. He is a graduate of the Fletcher School of Law and Diplomacy (MA) and UCLA (PhD) with a certificate from Ecole National des Sciences Politiques in Paris. He has done extensive research and consulting in West Africa and was the senior governance adviser to the Africa Bureau of USAID from 1991 to 1994. He is the author of a number of articles on Niger and the book *Niger: Personal Rule and Survival in the Sahel* (1991). Recently he has been focusing on issues of security threats and failed states in the Sahara and Sahelian regime and has conducted several studies of Islamic fundamentalism among the young merchant class in Niger.

Momodou N. Darboe is professor and chair, Department of Sociology and Geography, Shepherd University, Shepherdstown, West Virginia.

Cédric Jourde is assistant professor at the School of Political Studies, University of Ottawa. His research concentrates on the development of neoauthoritarian regimes in West Africa, the various trajectories of political Islam in the Sahel, and the interaction between cultural practices and political domination. He has published articles in several journals as well as in edited volumes, including *Hegemony or Empire? The Redefinition of US Power under George Bush,* and *Countries at the Crossroads 2005: A Survey of Democratic Governance.*

Victor Le Vine is professor emeritus of political science at Washington University in St. Louis, Missouri. A scholar of Africa since 1958, he has traveled widely on the continent, taught at the Universities of Ghana and

Yaounde, and lectured in a dozen African states. The results of his research in Africa have been published in nine books, including the *Cameroon Federal Republic* (1971), *Political Leadership in Africa* (1967), and, with Timothy Luke, *The Arab-African Connection* (1969), and in more than sixty articles. His most recent book is *Politics in Francophone Africa* (Lynne Rienner, 2004). Le Vine has also published on ethnic conflict, conflict resolution, corruption, and international law. He is currently working on a book on nonformal politics, consulting to the US State Department and USAID, and assisting the immigration bar on asylum cases.

Roman Loimeier is presently working as a research fellow at the Centre of Modern Oriental Studies in Berlin on the project "Multiple Concepts of Time in (Trans-)Local Contexts," which has a focus on East Africa. He has done research in northern Nigeria, Senegal, and East Africa and has published widely on Islam in Africa. His works include *Islamic Reform and Political Change in Northern Nigeria* (1997) and *The Global Worlds of the Swahili: Interfaces of Islam, Identity, and Space in 19th- and 20th-Century East Africa* (coedited with Ruediger Seesemann, 2006).

William F. S. Miles is professor of political science at Northeastern University in Boston. As a Fulbright scholar in Nigeria (1983–1984, 1986), Miles was a research associate with the Department of Sociology at Bayero University, Kano. Previously he had served as a Peace Corps volunteer in Niger (1977–1979) and State Department intern in Kaduna, Nigeria (1980). In 1988 he published *Elections in Nigeria: A Grassroots Perspective* (Lynne Rienner). His *Hausaland Divided: Colonialism and Independence in Nigeria and Niger* (1994) was selected by *Choice* magazine as an "Outstanding Academic Book" and cited in the *Encyclopedia Brittanica Book of the Year* for having made a "significant contribution to learning." Miles has consulted for the State Department, USAID, USDOL, and the Marine Corps.

Leonardo A. Villalón is director of the Title VI Center for African Studies and associate professor of political science at the University of Florida. He is author of *Islamic Society and State Power in Senegal* (1995) and coeditor of *The African State at a Critical Juncture: Between Disintegration and Reconfiguration* (Lynne Rienner, 1998) and *The Fate of Africa's Democratic Experiments: Elites and Institutions* (2005), as well as of numerous articles and book chapters on politics and religion, and on democratization, in West Africa. He taught for two years as a Fulbright senior scholar at the Université Cheikh Anta Diop in Dakar, Senegal. He has also taught at the Université Gaston Berger in St. Louis, Senegal, and has lectured and directed seminars and workshops throughout West Africa.

Index

About the Book

Long before the September 11 attacks galvanized Western attention on what has variously been called political Islam, Islamic fundamentalism, and Islamism, African nations with sizeable Muslim populations were experiencing significant transformations in the relationship between religion and state. *Political Islam in West Africa* explores those ongoing transformations in key countries of the Sahel region.

Each country chapter provides both historical context and an examination of the changing nature of domestic politics and foreign policy in the post–September 11 world. Introductory and concluding chapters provide additional context and highlight overarching themes. A notable feature of the book is a comprehensive bibliography of Islamism in West Africa.

William F. S. Miles is professor of political science at Northeastern University. His numerous publications on Africa include *Hausaland Divided: Colonialism and Independence in Nigeria and Niger* and *Elections in Nigeria: A Grassroots Perspective.*